The 10 Best-Ever Depression
Management Techniques

THE 10 BEST-EVER DEPRESSION MANAGEMENT TECHNIQUES

Understanding How Your Brain Makes You Depressed

& What You Can Do to Change It

MARGARET WEHRENBERG

W. W. NORTON & COMPANY

New York • London

For information about permission to reproduce selections from this book, write to
Permissions, W. W. Norton & Company, Inc., 500 Fifth Avenue, New York, NY 10110

For information about special discounts for bulk purchases, please contact
W. W. Norton Special Sales at specialsales@wwnorton.com or 800-233-4830

Manufacturing by Quad Graphics, Fairfield
Book design by Bytheway Publishing Services
Production manager: Leeann Graham

Library of Congress Cataloging-in-Publication Data

Wehrenberg, Margaret.
   The 10 best-ever depression management techniques : understanding how your brain
makes you depressed & what you can do to change it / Margaret Wehrenberg. — 1st ed.
        p.   cm.
Includes bibliographical references and index.
ISBN 978-0-393-70629-1 (pbk.)
1. Depression, Mental—Popular works.   2. Depression, Mental—Prevention.
I. Title.   II. Title: Ten best-ever depression management techniques.
RC437.W335 2010
616.85'27—dc22   2010004803

ISBN: 978-0-393-70629-1 (pbk.)

W. W. Norton & Company, Inc., 500 Fifth Avenue, New York, N.Y. 10110
www.wwnorton.com
W. W. Norton & Company Ltd., Castle House, 75/76 Wells Street, London W1T 3QT

1 2 3 4 5 6 7 8 9 0

To Ellie and Hal.
With you in my life it is easy to be happy.

Contents

Acknowledgments

If I could start a list of all the people who helped me with this book, I would have to start with my clients over the years of doing therapy. Their hard work, their honesty, and their openness have contributed to my education as a therapist. I thank them, one and all, for working with me.

I want to thank people who talked me through parts of the writing of this book, especially Dr. Shannon M. Burns and Drs. Syed and Fatima Ali.

My editors also deserve appreciation. Andrea Costella was a guide through the concept and development of each stage of this process. Her wisdom and patience make it easy to hear her feedback. And she is always right!

A very special "thank you!" to Casey Ruble, my copyeditor. She seems to have a sixth sense about how to "hear" what I am saying and make it come out right. Her ideas about organization and her reflections on the content were invaluable in shaping this material.

And as always, I thank the crowd of my family for the support and encouragement they always give: Marge Polzin (and Dad in absentia), Pat & Myron Schumacher, Mark & Jeanne Polzin, Mary Polzin, Jerry & Sue Lohr, Tom & Linda Polzin, Janet Crowder, Bill & Su Polzin, and Katy & Dick Deitte. I must also mention Wes Proffer, my brand-new grandson Max, and all my wonderful nieces, nephews, and their little ones who bring me so much comfort and joy. *You are my lifelines.* Thanks.

The 10 Best-Ever Depression Management Techniques

Introduction:

What You Can Do About

Your Depressed Brain

Although depression is a common mental-health complaint and a leading cause of disability over the course of a lifetime, it is hard to understand what causes it and how to treat it. That is not surprising when you look at how many varied symptoms constitute this one category of mental illness. Listing the symptoms a depressed person might have, the *Diagnostic and Statistical Manual, Fourth Edition, Text Revision* (DSM-IV-TR; American Psychiatric Association, 2000) includes, among others, such diverse symptoms as:

- Loss of interest or pleasure in things that might have otherwise been interesting
- Loss of concentration (low mental energy)
- Vegetative symptoms such as loss of appetite, trouble sleeping, or loss of libido
- Negative mood (feelings of hopelessness and helplessness)
- Rumination
- Suicidal ideation

In addition, therapists diagnose the course of the disorder from mild to severe, recurrent or single-episode, with or without psychosis—the options are many. And these symptoms do not include the effects of bipolar disorder, which is a form of depression that includes cycling between depressed and manic moods.

Depression also affects a large number of people, exacting a great cost in disability and suffering throughout the lifespan. Information from the National Institute of Mental Health (NIMH; 2008) about the numbers of people affected includes:

- About 20.9 million American adults (9.5% of the population) suffer from some sort of depression.
- Major depressive disorder is a recurring and chronic illness, frequently returning for two or more episodes, with episodes that often last 2 years or more.
- Major depressive disorder is the leading cause of disability in the U.S. for people ages 15 to 44.
- Depression is currently the fourth-most disabling illness worldwide, and according to the World Health Organization, it will be the second leading cause of disability by the year 2020.
- About 10% of men and up to 25% of women will experience depression in their lifetime.
- Dysthymic disorder (a type of low-grade depression that is more like persistent negative mood) affects approximately 1.5% of the U.S. population age 18 and older in a given year. This figure translates to about 3.3 million American adults.

The cost of the disorder is nothing short of phenomenal: an estimated $83 billion in the U.S. in the year 2000, including $26 billion in treatment costs and $57 billion in losses such as absenteeism, reduced productivity at work, and the value of lifetime earnings lost due to suicide-related deaths. According to the NIMH, "people with depression fare even more poorly at work, socially, and with their families than do people with a variety of general medical conditions" (NIMH, 2006, para. 2).

Yet depression is often regarded as something of a generic mental-health disorder in that most clinicians, regardless of their specialties, are expected to know how to treat it. With such a variety of symptoms and causes, therapists face a Herculean challenge in knowing which methods to try and where to start to help their clients manage depression. The goal of this book is to offer insight into how the inner workings of the brain contribute to depression, and, in doing so, shed light on how to more effectively control its symptoms. By presenting what I believe are the 10 best depression-fighting techniques, I demonstrate how to manage the physical, cognitive, and behavioral ramifications of depression, as well as change the brain to think in a healthy way.

TYPES OF DEPRESSION AND DEPRESSION SYMPTOMS

The possible reasons that a person may become depressed are varied. Scientific studies on the neurobiology of depression increasingly recognize that "depressive disorders represent a family of related but distinct conditions" (Shelton, 2007, p. 1). Depression may occur due to genetic vulnerability to the disorder or as the outcome of abuse or neglect in childhood that has disrupted brain function and altered the individual's ability to handle life's challenges. It may be the outcome of trauma or even long-term, nontraumatic chronic stress. Each of these causes of depression affects the appearance, severity, and course of the illness as well as the treatment choice for recovery.

Working in the therapy office, I have noted distinctive differences between clients complaining of depression, based on the underlying history of the illness.

- When depression developed subsequent to a serious loss, especially early life adversity, clients show an intensity of symptoms, especially plunging into despair and hopelessness.
- Depression that emerged subsequent to a period of chronic stress requires changing the stressor in order to improve the

depression. I often see these clients suffering exhaustion and isolating themselves to try to replenish themselves.

- People who describe feeling depression most of their lives without a history of trauma or neglect (endogenous depression) seem to have the most difficulty with motivation for recovery, feeling limited reward and pleasure in life.
- Depression consequent to traumatic stress requires resolving traumatic memory, but in the immediate recovery, thoughts of helplessness and rumination on the trauma need attention.

Each of these causes of depression shows up in physical, mental, and behavioral symptoms that can be treated with the techniques in this book. The techniques are intended to raise physical and mental energy, to alter mental negativity, and to bolster behavior that will enhance energy and positivity. The symptoms of depression and the techniques used to treat them include:

- *Low mental and physical energy.* One hallmark of depression is lethargy. People with depression feel lack of energy physically. They feel little reward from the physical activities that energize others. They suffer from aches and pains more than others. These symptoms can be helped with the techniques "Start Where You Already Are" and "Mobilize Your Energy."
- *Depressed behavior.* Chronic stress can result in burnout, and the depressed person who is burned out will show signs of compulsive activity coupled with exhaustion and isolation from others. Some with depression that stems from early life adversity behave in self-injurious ways when overwhelmed with despair. The "Cool Down Burnout" and "Prevent Destructive Behavior" techniques are useful in these circumstances.
- *The thinking of depression.* Rumination, rigidity, and negativity go hand in hand in the thinking of the depressed person.

People need to not only interrupt the negativity but also de-velop strong brain circuits for positive thinking and flexible problem-solving. Techniques that help with this include "Broaden Your Perspective," "Increase Flexibility," and "Learn to Live Fully."

Symptoms in these arenas are the outcome of activity in different parts of the brain. When something is not working efficiently in the brain, the result shows in the way a person feels, thinks, and acts. All of the physical, mental, and behavioral depression symptoms can be controlled by techniques that use the brain to change the brain. The reason the methods in this book are the "best-ever" is because they are known by therapists to be effective for interrupting the negatives of depression and increasing balancing, positive emotions. Now scientific research has shown *why* they work. Since the advent of brain-imaging research, we have learned more and more about how *consistent* application of depression management techniques energizes and elevates the mood of a depressed brain. You can achieve a positive, flexible brain when you know which methods to try and how to make them really work.

Working Alone or With a Therapist

These techniques are straightforward, proven ways to alleviate depression and are intended for symptom management. They can be done by anyone. They are not, however, meant to replace psychotherapy if depression is severe or recurrent. They will not relieve depression that is the result of trauma unless the trauma is resolved, nor will they take the place of long-term treatment for complicated mental-health disorders.

When a person has the low energy of depression, self-help may be an overwhelming prospect. Working with an involved therapist who is a good personality match with you may predict a good outcome (Hardy, Cahill, Shapiro, Barkham, Rees, & Macaskill, 2001). Initially, your treatment will focus on finding motivation that you can hang onto, and it will progress no faster than your mental energy can allow. The close observation and continuing assessment of the therapist can promote that motivation.

Using the support, encouragement, and guidance of therapy to help you discern how to apply these techniques may give you the external boost you need to stick with practicing these techniques until they work. For these many reasons, getting an evaluation and support from a psychotherapist who knows how to treat depression is, for most people, the wisest course of action.

WHAT YOU WILL GET FROM THE 10 BEST-EVER DEPRESSION MANAGEMENT TECHNIQUES

The sad news is that less than half of people with major depression are recognized as being depressed, and only half of those who are diagnosed with depression receive treatment. Of those treated, only about a third achieve remission from all symptoms (Nemeroff, 2004). Men in particular avoid treatment because admitting to the pain of depression is tantamount to admitting to weakness (Real, 1997). They do not acknowledge the suffering they feel until it is far too serious and has wreaked unnecessary havoc in their lives.

Further, the symptoms of the disorder themselves can block response to treatment. Lethargy, hopelessness, pessimism, bad thinking habits, lifestyles that reinforce the depression, and refractory negative mood all interfere with useful interventions: "I know I would feel better if I exercised but I am too tired to do it." "If my family would just appreciate how hard I work for them, I would be nicer to be around. How can I feel good when no one helps me?" "I want my life to have some purpose, but I cannot imagine anything I do could be useful to other people." Depressed clients expressing these ideas will benefit if therapy can shift their behavior, attitude, or thinking in the right direction. Therapy for symptom management requires moving clients out of lethargy and into action, taking charge of cognitive habits, instilling hope, changing lifestyle, and reducing negative mood. Those are hard to accomplish on one's own.

The range of treatment options is both wonderful and confusing. As any quick Internet search will reveal, medication is considered a first-line approach to treatment, yet cognitive-behavioral therapy (CBT) methods are more helpful in the long run. Studies that look at the combination of medication and CBT suggest that people get a faster start, feeling better after 12 weeks or so on medication plus CBT, but that in the long run, many people do well utilizing CBT methods without any medication (Perlis, et al., 2002). There is growing evidence that building positive brain circuitry will balance and offset the brain circuits for ruminative, negative thinking, so techniques that enhance feeling centered, spirituality, and positive emotion will be of great value. There is no strict protocol for applying the techniques in this book, and therapists vary in their style, but all of these ideas will be useful during the course of your recovery, so the order in which you apply them may simply depend on what symptom you want to remove first.

Both individuals who suffer from depression and therapists working with depressed clients can use the materials in this book. I have tried to write without professional jargon, so that any person can benefit from the techniques. I begin this book by discussing how the brain works and how medications affect it in Chapters 1 and 2. Chapter 1, How Your Brain Makes You Depressed, describes brain basics. Knowing what is going on in your depressed brain will help you understand why the methods presented in this book are going to work to change the physical, behavioral, and mental signs of depression.

Chapter 2, Managing the Depressed Brain With Medication, discusses psychotropic drugs used in treating depression. Medications can be very useful and even necessary under certain circumstances. They can relieve sluggishness or diminish agitation, and they can increase the sense of reward from everyday activities that you should enjoy.

Chapter 3, Identify Triggers, Plan New Responses, describes four different causes of depression and how they can create triggers. By responding differently to those triggers, you stop the patterns that are based in your life history.

Chapters 4, 5, and 6 describe techniques specifically aimed at energizing the lethargic, unmotivated body and mind of depression. When a person feels sluggish and disinterested in daily life, starting treatments that can be used even in the face of low motivation and low energy is necessary. "Start Where You Already Are" and "Mobilize Your Energy" are techniques that can help even people whose depression is severe. You may be surprised to discover how just very small changes can start to improve the flow of energy and increase your ability to do even more of the techniques. "Cool Down Burnout" is geared more toward people who remain active during depression but are beginning to see signs that their overwork is contributing to the physical, mental, and emotional exhaustion of burnout.

When people have lost sight of what is valuable to them—connection to others, living a balanced life in accord with their values, or being connected to something greater than themselves—they become separated from those who can support and encourage them, and they can feel bereft. In an attempt to deal with the pain or emptiness, they may resort to behaviors that are destructive toward themselves or others. Techniques that balance the downward, negative pull of depression, that encourage connectedness with others and with something greater than oneself, diminish those symptoms that keep people isolated from resources they need. These techniques—"End Isolation," "Balance Your Life," and "Prevent Destructive Behavior"—are covered in Chapters 7, 8, and 9.

People with depression become rigid in their thinking and behavior and feel trapped in their narrow, negative point of view. The techniques "Broaden Your Perspective" and "Increase Flexibility," covered in Chapters 10 and 11, offer ways to break out of these harmful patterns and broaden one's thinking and behavior. They highlight many strategies to start drawing on joy, delight, and other positive emotions. Building positive emotions changes your brain, making it more capable of generating flexible, creative, and optimistic solutions to life's problems.

The final chapter discusses the technique "Learn to Live Fully." True recovery from depression is about more than just "fighting off" symptoms—it is about making fundamental changes in your way of being in the world. This chapter addresses how people can learn to embrace life—with all its ups and downs—rather than reacting out of fear, defensiveness, or negativity.

These 10 techniques each include many different methods to achieve your desired goal. The "real life" examples in this book are all based on the experiences of real people, but they are composites and do not represent any individual person I have treated. The examples demonstrate the effectiveness of the technique and the unique ways people can apply them. Although most readers will want to take advantage of all the techniques, they should start with those that work for the worst aspect of their symptoms and go on from there. There is no ideal order in which to learn the 10 "best-ever" techniques for depression management. Select the technique and the method that works best for you.

ONE

How Your Brain Makes You Depressed

There is more to know about how the brain works than we will learn in our lifetimes. But what we know so far is that every function in your body—every thought you have, every emotion you feel—is the result of activity in your brain. As an organ in the body, the brain continuously interacts with every aspect of physical functioning.

The brain is different from the *mind*. The mind is a brain-body exchange—a flow of information and energy that goes beyond physical processes alone (Siegel, 2007). However, this chapter will discuss the brain as if its parts were separately causing the physical, emotional, and behavioral effects that we call depression. Although it is a huge oversimplification, as you are getting to know the brain, it can be easier to think of parts as having separate functions. Then we will look at how problems in those functions contribute to the symptoms of depression.

To understand the experience of depression, you will want to remember that your mind is the unique outcome of your physiology and the accumulation of your life experiences, which together shape your awareness, interpretation, and integration of new experiences. For example, information flows into the brain from the heart, the gut, and the vast organ of the skin, carrying vital information about what is happening and whether it is positive, urgent, or challenging. In smooth integration with past experience (stored as conscious and unconscious memory), the brain shapes a response. That flow is a process—the mind, continuously in the moment, integrates and responds to new stimulation. For example, imagine you are walking down a street and smell a strong, acrid odor. If you have never smelled such an odor before, you may be curious or cautious, recognizing that nothing good would smell like that. You would appraise the environment for signals of whether you are at risk. But if you had been in a fire—no matter how long ago—within the blink of an eye your heart might race, your respiration might pick up, and your body would be poised to *run, now!* Why? Because the previous experience shapes your interpretation of that smell as immediate danger.

DEPRESSION AS NEUROBIOLOGICAL

How do you see what the activity of your brain is? You see it in your thoughts, feelings, and actions. People may try to see causes of depression simply as biological or, alternately, the result of things we have lived through. But depression is always biological and biology is always affected by life experience. Life experiences are felt, reacted to, and remembered because of brain activity. Brain and body and experience are continuously interacting in interdependent exchanges between all our parts.

It is possible, though, to describe how brain structures and functions contribute to being depressed, and this knowledge has made a difference in the psychotherapy of depression. The techniques we have used for years are effective, and now we know why they work so well. And we know better when and how to apply those techniques so that you can use your brain to change your brain. We also know that you can get some relief from depression symptoms even before you complete psychotherapy for the underlying cause of the depression or for other mental-health conditions.

The 10 best-ever depression management techniques are designed to help you diminish or eliminate the most common problems of depression: physical and mental lethargy, rumination, hopeless/helpless thinking, and self-injurious or stress-maintaining behaviors. They take advantage of what we know about how those symptoms are caused by problems in brain functioning and what we know about encouraging healthy brain function. You can successfully apply these techniques even if you don't understand how they work, so you needn't feel bad for skipping this chapter and moving on to those that cover the techniques. For those of you who *do* want to know a bit more about how you are creating change, read on.

NEURONS, NEUROTRANSMITTERS, AND COMMUNICATION IN YOUR BRAIN

Your brain is a complicated network of brain cells called "neurons." You have 10 billion neurons, and each of them can connect with 10,000 or so other neurons. The possibilities for how those cells connect and network are virtually endless. Those communication networks control everything that goes on in your body. If your brain is dead, nothing will work, even with healthy organs. And just like you do not feel your best if you have an organ in your body that is malfunctioning, your thoughts and emotions can be troubled if parts of your brain are not working well.

How Does Your Brain Communicate?

All of those 10 billion neurons have to communicate with each other to create your thoughts, behaviors, and emotions (among other many tasks that we won't discuss here). So how do they do it? Neurons communicate by sending messengers back and forth in the space between brain cells, called the "synapse." These messengers of the brain are called "neurotransmitters." Different messages are carried by different neurotransmitters. I will describe those shortly.

Every message needs to be received. How a message is interpreted and how it affects brain function depends on where the message is received. The meaning of a message is determined by what part of the brain is reading it. Consider the metaphor of email. Let's say you get an email sent to your work team from your boss, who demands overtime to finish a project. If you forward the message to a coworker and add comments about your frustration with your boss, you may get a comforting response. If you mistakenly hit "reply" instead of "forward" and your boss reads your message, you may feel stressed about what the response will be. If you hit the "reply all" and send the message to your whole team, you will get varied responses, some of which may be confused or unwelcome. Or, if you put your email into the "send later" box, nothing much happens. Same message, different results, depending on the receiver.

In a way, that happens with neurotransmitters. Take dopamine, for example. Dopamine is a neurotransmitter that is received in one part of your brain as "I feel good!" If it is received in the thinking part of your brain, it works to help you pay attention. In yet another part of your brain, it helps you to have smooth motor functioning. (People with Parkinson's disease are losing dopamine.) If you do not have *enough* dopamine, you feel disinterested, are low on motivation, and find it hard to pay attention. So, as you can see, dopamine produces different results depending on how much goes out and where in the brain it is received.

Take a look at Figure 1.1 for a visual on how neurotransmitters cross the synapse from one cell (called the "presynaptic neuron") to another (called the "postsynaptic neuron"). When a neuron releases a neurotransmitter into the synapse, three things can happen:

- The neurotransmitter can be received by another cell on a part of the cell called the "receptor site." Those sites are ready to receive specific neurotransmitters.
- The neurotransmitter can be "cleaned up" out of the space so that new transmissions can occur.
- The neurotransmitter can be taken up again by the cell that released it. "Reuptake" is the function that the most common antidepressant medications affect. ("SSRI" stands for "selective serotonin reuptake inhibitor.") By blocking reuptake, SSRI antidepressants cause the cells to increase production of the neurotransmitter.

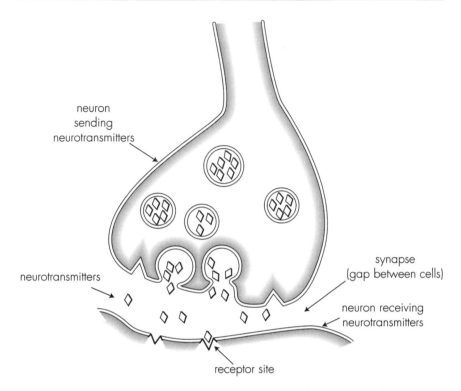

neuron
sending
neurotransmitters

synapse
(gap between cells)

neurotransmitters

neuron receiving
neurotransmitters

receptor site

Figure 1.1 Neurotransmitters, represented as diamonds, are released from a neuron into the synapse to be received by another neuron. From Wehrenberg (2008).

Problems in transmission of neurotransmitters occur when there is:

- Too little communication, with not enough of the neurotransmitter to make a good effect.
- Too much communication, swamping your brain with activity. For example, in excessive stress, a flood of neurotransmitters may be released, making everything feel like it is overwhelming. Over time, the brain's supply of neurotransmitters is exhausted.
- Out-of-balance neurotransmitter release, which may be caused by one neurotransmitter being low on supply. For example,

one theory of depression is that when supplies of serotonin are insufficient, norepinephrine boosts to stimulate production. Then you have agitation and impact on mood as well as other symptoms.

Receiving Messages

Even if the number of neurotransmitters and their transmission are fine, depression can occur if there are problems on the receiving end of the transmission. Just like a radio needs to be tuned to receive the signal, neurons need to be primed and ready to receive a neurotransmitter. Problems in reception can happen as the result of health issues, such as hormonal problems like thyroid malfunction, low testosterone, or fluctuating estrogen and progesterone. In particular, the impact of chronic stress can sensitize parts of your brain so that you overrespond to messages and feel more stress than a situation might otherwise call for.

You know that there are radio waves and cell-phone signals in the air all around you, but you need to have your equipment tuned in to make sense of the message. Once the signal is received, your equipment has to interpret and send information along. When we switched from analog to digital signals for TV in the U.S., people who wanted to watch TV had to have the right receiver for the signal or there would be no sound or picture on their screen. Your brain also has to be ready to receive and tuned to the right channel to get accurate messages from your neurotransmitters.

Different parts of the brain receive, send, interpret, and create responses to the signals they receive. They receive and relay information, coordinate and interpret signals that help to form a coherent picture of information, and create new responses to information as it comes in. Different parts of the brain have different functions, but just like completing a call on a wireless phone requires the phone to receive a signal, interpret it, and then reverse that to transmit back what you say, the parts of your brain all need to function smoothly for messages to be clearly received and sent.

Neural Networking

The concept of neurons networking is a vital one in the consideration of depression symptoms and the recovery from depression. There is a well-known maxim "neurons that fire together, wire together" (based on the work of Donald Hebb), meaning that emotion, thought, and physical sensations are all recorded together in the memory of an experience. The whole of that memory—thoughts, emotions, physical sensations— can be evoked by recalling any one aspect of it. It is quite useful that all aspects of an experience can be brought together for the next time we use the memory.

Not only do neurons network, but experiences that we have also stimulate brain growth. When brain cells fire, the activity of firing causes growth of supportive cells and blood vessels in the affected parts of the brain, so there are new cells and new connections between them (Siegel, 2007). One big cause of depression is the ways that *prior* experiences organize understanding of *new* experience. Prior experience is like a filter. A new experience may immediately evoke an old memory, making us see what is happening now through the lens of that memory. This efficient aspect of brain function and neural networking can create depression by coloring new experience with the shades of disappointment, sadness, or helplessness we felt in a previous experience. Even getting into a bad mood can elicit memories of other similar bad moods and the situations that surrounded them (Williams, Teasdale, Segal, & Kabat-Zinn, 2007). Think of how easy it is, when you are already upset at your partner or child, to recall how many other times that person irritated you. That is what neural networks do for you!

Balance Is Important

The brain likes everything to be in balance. It monitors everything that is going on in your body, trying to keep your body in balance. Think about what happens when you exercise. You increase the demand for oxygen, and when you start to run out of it, your respiration increases and your heart rate picks up to send it around. You can control your breath on purpose, too. You can direct your breathing as you might when practicing martial arts or weight-lifting or singing, but even without your conscious control, your brain makes sure you are getting the right amount of oxygen.

Similarly, your brain keeps neurotransmitters in balance via feedback loops that indicate how they are functioning. Just like insufficient oxygen shows up as shortness of breath or dizziness, insufficient or excessive amounts of neurotransmitters show up as problems in mood, behavior, or thought. If an imbalance occurs, the brain then initiates activity to achieve balance—a process called "homeostasis."

The techniques presented in this book can help the brain to achieve balance. When balance cannot be achieved because you are sick, not eating right, not sleeping, are too stressed out, or have a physical illness, you will probably have to make changes to your eating, sleeping, or lifestyle—or get some medical help.

Specific Neurotransmitters and Their Activities

The neurotransmitters that are of most interest in understanding depression are:

- Glutamate
- GABA (gamma aminobutyric acid)
- Serotonin
- Norepinephrine
- Dopamine

Briefly, the function of each neurotransmitter is as follows:

- *Glutamate.* Think of glutamate as the brain's "go!" signal. Glutamate signals (excites) neurons to fire—that is, to send out their neurotransmitters. It is distributed throughout the brain, because all the neurons need signals to fire. Glutamate

17

fires a lot when you are under stress, and one idea about why chronic stress causes depression is that the overexcitation of brain cells eventually damages them. Glutamate functions in balance with GABA.

- *GABA.* Every "go" signal needs a "stop" signal. GABA is the stop signal. It slows and stops the firing of neurons. GABA is also found throughout the brain. If GABA is not being received efficiently, or if there is too much glutamate so the balance is off, agitation and rumination (repetitive negative thinking) may occur—two big problems in depression.

- *Serotonin.* Although serotonin neurons are few in number compared to GABA and glutamate, they deposit their neurotransmitters throughout the brain and in that way they have many different effects. Serotonin affects your mood, appetite, sleep, libido, and mental functioning like impulse control, sensory reception, stress response, pain response, perception, and memory. Serotonin helps you recognize satisfaction, too. You can see why, if serotonin is depleted or not received well, you could have a lot of different problems with depression.

- *Norepinephrine.* If your brain had an Energizer bunny, norepinephrine would be it. Norepinephrine keeps you mentally and physically alert and energetic. It keeps your blood pressure balanced, and when you are under stress it helps mobilize your energy. When you are low on norepinephrine you may feel sluggish and have a hard time finding the mental energy to fight off negative thoughts.

- *Dopamine.* Dopamine's message depends a lot on what part of the brain is receiving it. In one part of your brain dopamine is the equivalent of "mm-mmm good" whereas in the thinking part of your brain it helps you pay attention. Dopamine is significant if you are depressed because without the "I feel good" message you will not have motivation to do things— even things you used to be interested in. Poor concentration may be a feature of insufficient norepinephrine or dopamine or both.

Two Other Factors: BDNF and NO

Two substances released by the brain do not neatly fall into the category of neurotransmitters but still affect your brain health. The first is BDNF (or "brain-derived neurotrophic factor"). Your brain can release BDNF to stimulate new brain cells to grow. It is possible that when you are depressed, your brain doesn't grow and change fast enough to help you adapt to new circumstances, so you feel more stressed or have trouble solving your problems.

NO (nitric oxide) is a gas that is released throughout the body and also in the brain. Its functions are many and still being understood, but it plays a specific role that is of interest in understanding depression. NO gets neurons together. Apparently, the cell that has to receive a message will release NO to help the neurotransmitter lock onto it (Nikonenko, Boda, Steen, Knott, Welker, & Muller, 2008). If you want to be more creative and a better problem-solver, anything you can do to encourage NO release will boost that kind of new activity in the brain (see Benson & Proctor, 2003).

THE STRUCTURES OF THE BRAIN AND DEPRESSION

The many symptoms of depression can be explained by the action of neurotransmitters as they are received in different parts of the brain. Your brain has many different structures within it, and some them work together in systems or circuits to get a task done. Keeping it simple, let's look first at some parts of these systems and then at how they work together in ways that can contribute to depression symptoms.

- The *nervous system* has nerves that get you going and nerves that calm you down again.

- The *stress response system* gets hormones such as adrenalin pumping.
- The *limbic system* is the center of emotion and memory.
- The *basal ganglia* is the center of motivation, reward, and movement.
- The *cortex* is where you think, make decisions, and control the rest of your brain.

The Nervous System

The central nervous system is your brain plus all the nerves that run throughout your body and connect to the spinal cord on up to the brain. Nerves tell your muscles to move and carry signals to your brain about how your body is doing. Nerves carry messages to and from the organs of your body. The arousal and calming of your nervous system (Figure 1.2) is related to depression. Two parts of the nervous system are:

The parasympathetic nervous system (PSNS). When the PSNS goes into action, it *slows* or calms agitation and restores balance to the brain and body. Many therapy methods promote a calmer physiology by helping the PSNS to go to work decreasing stress symptoms. When you meditate or relax, you are initiating activity here.

The sympathetic nervous system (SNS). This is the system that tells organs in your body to get busy and respond to a demand for action. If you walk up a steep flight of stairs, the SNS will demand a little extra heart activity and respiration so that your muscles can get more oxygen while they work harder. Even if you just think about something that scares you, your SNS will speed up your heart and respiration. And when you are stressed out, this system works overtime.

The Stress Response System

In order for your body to have the energy it needs when the sympathetic nervous system cranks up the organs of your body, you need some energy-boosting hormone action. The hypothalamus (explained in the

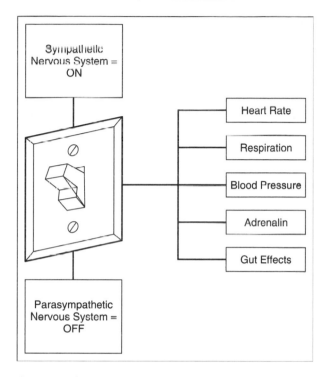

Figure 1.2 The sympathetic nervous system for arousal and the parasympathetic nervous system for calming. From Wehrenberg (2008).

next section) starts it off by sending a message to your adrenal glands to release adrenalin and cortisol, two of the hormones needed for energy. They race through your bloodstream to mobilize your body and brain to handle the demand for action to fight off the stress. This is the stress response system: a system to get you energy when you need it.

Stress is perhaps the most important contributor to the physiology of depression. When stress is ongoing, those stress hormones keep flowing, and their impact on your brain becomes negative. The overexcitation of chronic stress can damage the brain, making it more susceptible to depression (Nemeroff, 2004). Figure 1.3 shows a diagram of this process.

A dysregulated stress response may be the leading cause of depression. In some people, an overactive stress response makes small stresses seem very large. Overreaction may be the outcome of trauma or it may

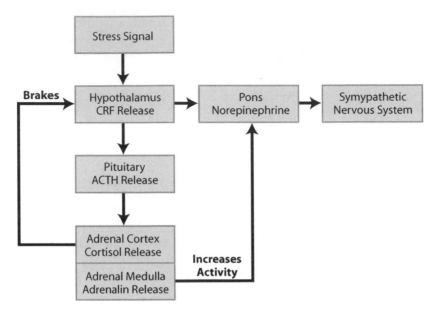

Figure 1.3 The stress response system. From Wehrenberg (2008).

be just be the way a person's brain works due to genetics. In any case, it sets people up to respond with too much stress in normal situations and it prevents them from developing positive coping skills (Goodyer, 2008).

Ongoing stress also depletes stores of neurochemicals like serotonin, dopamine, and norepinephrine, making you feel the symptoms of depression. Even more, stress can make you sick. It can turn on the "sickness response"—loss of appetite, fatigue, loss of interest in activity—all the things you feel when you get the flu, and a lot like depression in the absence of symptoms of an infection (Maier, 2001).

The Limbic System

The emotional work of the brain is the coordinated result of activity in several structures referred to as the "limbic system." The term *limbic* comes from a word that means "ring" and refers to the location in the center of the brain where these various structures are grouped. They work together to form emotion and memory. The names of the parts are:

- Thalamus
- Hypothalamus
- Hippocampus
- Amygdala

Each part plays a role in the creation of emotional responses, and each is connected to other parts of the brain and the nervous system so that some of their work can be done without thinking. For example, if you are faced with an emergency, like a child running into traffic, you don't want to take time to think about whether you need energy. Your body gives it to you without intentional thought. How these parts function together is relevant to understanding the negativity and mood of depression.

Thalamus. The thalamus has many important functions, but among the most important is its role in receiving information from the outside world through the senses and sending that information where it needs to go. It might be considered the "quarterback" for sensory information from the external environment. That is, it receives information and relays it onward for another part of the brain to take action on it. The "ball" of sensory information, hiked to your thalamus, is passed on to the amygdala for immediate action. Among the other jobs the thalamus does is passing that information on to the thinking brain, your cortex.

Hypothalamus. Located below the thalamus, the hypothalamus is like the quarterback for your internal team, gathering information from your blood about the functioning of your organs. It receives and relays signals from and to the organs of your body. The hypothalamus is directly responsible for starting your stress response by handing off the "ball" of information that you are under stress. It passes that information to your adrenal glands so they can run with the information and get you the energy you need.

Hippocampus. The hippocampus is the part of the limbic system that remembers details and helps you put incoming information into context. When you ask yourself, "Where have I seen this before?" the hippocampus is one part of the brain that helps you to figure that out. It is without emotions, registering and storing details of events, functioning like your memory's "Joe Friday." ("Just the facts, ma'am.") It records details—data and facts—and sends them up to your cortex, which will think about them and combine them with emotional information from the amygdala. If you need short-term or long-term memory to be made from the details the hippocampus is recording, other parts of the brain get involved to make that happen.

Amygdala. The amygdala could be called the brain's "early warning system" and is a major cause in generating depressed moods and negative thinking. It reacts immediately to the signals it gets from the thalamus and the hypothalamus. But it does not think. It reacts to incoming information with alarms like "Danger!" "Unpleasant!" "Failure!" The amygdala is an importance meter, registering tone and intensity and notifying your brain instantly if it should prepare for problems. The amygdala can set off the hypothalamus to get a stress response and can immediately get norepinephrine (the "energizer" neurotransmitter) pumping to prepare for fight or flight. All that excitement occurs faster than your brain can start thinking about what just happened.

The amygdala registers the tone of all incoming signals—not just negative ones, but it prefers noticing trouble first. An angry face gets first attention over smiling faces. Although that is a good thing in general— you need a fast response to threats to safety—once you have had a bad experience, the amygdala reacts later to any reminder of the situation: the other person involved, a tone of voice, or even to your own mood triggering a reminder of the mood in that bad experience. Changing that emotional tone requires a manual override on mood to purposely shift the automatic function from negative to positive.

The Basal Ganglia (BG)

A "ganglia" is a concentrated grouping of neurons forming a nuclei. The basal ganglia (BG) are several ganglia that work together to induce motivation, create energy to meet goals, and even coordinate physical movement with emotion. The BG are located under the cortex (covering) of the brain, where you do your thinking, and over the limbic system. One part of the BG, the nucleus accumbens, is specialized to interpret pleasure when it receives the messenger dopamine. When you do something that stimulates dopamine and its message is received in this part of the brain, you feel good. This makes you want to repeat whatever you were doing that made you feel so good.

The BG and its reception of dopamine strongly affect your motivation and energy, two features that are deficient in people who are depressed. Physical lethargy and lack of interest in life's activities are determined partly in this area. The BG have a direct role in coordinating physical movement with emotion. Feeling pleasure and energy when you do an activity will make you want to do it more. Without that kind of reward for doing an activity, you lose interest, even if you enjoyed it at one time. No wonder the activity in the BG has an impact on your mood, too!

The Cortex

The structures of the limbic system work together to send messages to the thinking parts of the brain—the cortex. *Cortex* means "bark" or "covering," and in human beings that covering over the limbic brain is thick in comparison to animal brains. We use that extra brain for the vast and complex social information we process and store. Our ability to think about thinking and about emotions, and our ability to think about what others are thinking and feeling, are possible because of the activities of the cortex. To understand the varied symptoms of depression, it is useful to look at activity in these parts of the cortex:

- Anterior cingulate gyrus
- Orbitofrontal cortex
- Insula
- Prefrontal cortex

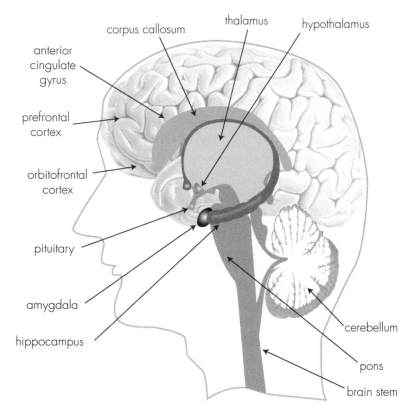

Figure 1.4 Interior view of the left half of the brain. From Wehrenberg (2008).

Look at the drawing of the brain in Figure 1.4.

Anterior cingulate gyrus (ACG). This area of the cortex helps to organize information. Located between the limbic system and the prefrontal cortex, it is like the vice-president in charge of forming context and preparing reports for CEO of the brain—the left prefrontal cortex (LPFC). It also sends the CEO's recommendations back out to the lower structures of the brain. It takes details from the hippocampus and emotional tone from the amygdala. It also works with the insula to incorporate the body's sense of what is being experienced, and it gets those all together so they can be analyzed by the LPFC. Imaging studies have shown the ACG to be sluggish in people with depression. That makes it hard to suppress negative thoughts or stop thinking about them over and over. It is hard to be a good problem-solver when you are swamped with emotion or stuck on old thoughts.

Orbitofrontal cortex (OFC). This area of the cortex is like the vice-president in charge of brainstorming. It commands the process called "working memory," which holds pieces of information just long enough to use them to complete tasks of everyday mental functioning. Also, working memory—or short-term storage—allows the OFC to compare information with other memories of similar situations. The work is necessary to generate several possible, reasonable responses to problems and then send the data forward to the prefrontal cortex for analysis and decision-making.

When this part of the cortex is functioning correctly, people have good impulse control; they don't jump the gun on "half-baked" ideas. Rather, they make decisions based on information. When neurotransmitters are in balance in the OFC, your mood is optimistic and it seems things can be explained or solved and are not hopeless. When neurotransmitters are deficient in amount or transmission, the depressed person may give in to impulses to eat or drink too much, to self-medicate with alcohol or drugs, or even to become self-destructive with a suicide attempt. One particularly important feature of depression—the sudden plunge into despair—occurs when there is poor control in the OFC over memories reminiscent of earlier, profound loss, such as early life neglect.

Insula. The insula collects data from your body about how you are feeling. It is located between the side of the cortex and the limbic brain. The functions of the insula give you a sense of self and of body awareness, and even play a role in your perception of pain. If a person is responding to a "gut feeling," it is likely that information from the insula is being utilized. One finding regarding people who experience both panic and depression noted decreased function of the neurotransmitter GABA in this area, indicating that the insula is overactive in this disorder (Cameron et al., 2007).

The insula connects the emotional (limbic) brain and the thinking

(LPFC) brain, and is where you have empathy or "feeling with" others. In depression, the sense of empathy can be disturbed: You may overreact to the pain (emotional or physical) of others as well as to your own pain. When you have healthy functioning here you have a sense of who you are and you know what you are able to do—what you can control and what you can't. People who meditate appear to develop more volume in this part of the brain—they enhance their sense of empathy and compassion for others in that way.

Prefrontal cortex. The prefrontal cortex (PFC) is the CEO of the brain. This is where all the information from your entire body and all the other parts of your brain is ultimately received and where decisions are made about how to respond to it. The buck stops here. When the PFC gets good data from the rest of the brain, it has what it needs to analyze whether a situation is actually disturbing or not. It decides whether the data should be put into long-term memory storage or dismissed as unnecessary. It creates new solutions to problems and plans how to carry them out. The PFC needs clarity and energy to do this.

You may have heard about differences between right-brain and left-brain activity and wonder if this is important to depression. The short answer is yes. All the parts of the brain just described have two sides, right and left. Your brain is efficient. It does not double up on activity— so the right and left sides, called "hemispheres," in effect have subspecialties with their individual functions. Look first at the differences between the right and left PFC.

Left prefrontal cortex (LPFC). This side of the brain is where verbal work occurs. It is the side where a person creates and understands the meaning of experiences. The left hemisphere categorizes, solves problems, and analyzes new information. It is sometimes referred to as the "optimistic brain" because it can form helpful conclusions about negative information, such as "this is not so bad," or "you have lived through harder things," or "there is a bright side to this problem." This function is critical to the control of and recovery from depression.

The left brain helps a person to comprehend time, both for putting events in sequential order and for knowing when in time they happened.

Timing for sequential (step-by-step) information helps people remember that certain tasks must be performed in a specific order. Time frames also help people know that an event is over and done, as well as help people create an autobiography, remembering when in the course of their lives an event occurred. Often in depression, past difficult experiences are relived as fresh and still influential, so learning to note and emphasize the here-and-now versus then-and-over, as in mindfulness, is a valuable technique.

Right prefrontal cortex. The right prefrontal cortex (RPFC) is like the COO of the brain, making major decisions but in the nonverbal realm. You may think of it as your creative brain, figuring out problems of space and time and emotion. When you are depressed and overly negative in mood and interpretation, the RPFC is analyzing all that negativity. Then it can dominate the left cortex in situations where negative mood, low expectations, or prior negative emotions in similar situations are grabbing its attention (Johnstone, van Reekum, Urry, Kalin, & Davidson, 2007). When you are depressed for whatever brain-based reason, the LPFC depends too much on the right hemisphere for problem-solving, paying too much attention to your mood and emotions when it is analyzing or making decisions. Your thought process is unbalanced in favor of the negatives, so you fall into hopeless and helpless thinking (Bajwa, Bermpohl, Rigonatti, Pascual-Leone, Boggio, & Fregni, 2008).

Orbitofrontal cortex, insula, and anterior cingulate gyrus. The orbitofrontal cortex, insula, and anterior cingulate gyrus (all described earlier) are parts of the cortex that are closer to the lower (or subcortical) parts of the brain, and they are especially important in impulse control, problem-solving, the generation of options in facing problems, and mood management. They register the visceral response to incoming stimuli, appraise the limbic reaction, and deliver coordinated information to the PFC as well as send responses downward from the PFC to the brain and body. These parts of the cortex are therefore essential in processing incoming information and transferring information back and forth between the command center (PFC) and the emotional (limbic) part of the brain. The impact of these areas is seen in many aspects of depression, and it is possible that a decreased volume in gray matter in these areas contributes to the apathetic symptoms of depression (Lavretsky, Ballmaier, Pham, Toga, & Kumar, 2007).

HOW THE PARTS OF THE BRAIN WORK TOGETHER TO CREATE DEPRESSION

The impact of neurotransmitters in different parts of the brain affect what kind of depression symptoms trouble you the most. Let's look briefly at why you may not have enough neurotransmitters and then I will chart how symptoms of depression might be generated by the activity of neurotransmitters in different parts of the brain.

A person may not have enough neurotransmitters for any number of reasons. You might have simply been born without a plentiful supply. This is often true for people who have been depressed all their lives. (This is referred to as "endogenous depression"—caused by the conditions in your body/brain.) Life circumstances can also make a low supply into a deficient supply. Trauma or illness can deplete the supplies of some neurotransmitters, like serotonin, or intensify levels of norepinephrine and therefore intensify the impact of the trauma or illness. If left untreated, that unbalanced state can go on for years. Chronic stress uses up extra supplies of neurotransmitters and creates a deficit while preventing the opportunity to rebuild your supply. Poor sleep and poor nutrition also diminish neurotransmitter supplies. So, depending on your circumstances, there could be one or many reasons your neurotransmitters get out of balance.

Take a look at the neurotransmitters, one at a time, to see how they interact with the parts of the brain to cause depression.

Serotonin. The neurotransmitter with the most wide-ranging impact in creating depression symptoms is serotonin (SE). When SE is low, it wreaks havoc in most of the brain systems (Table 1.1). If serotonin's main function is to regulate, then losing regulation has predictable de-

Table 1.1 How Brain Structures Are Affected When Serotonin Is Too Low

Brain Structure	→	Depression Symptom
limbic system (amygdala)	→	negativity, worry, sensitivity to threat
prefrontal cortex (PFC)	→	poor planning, unable to push negativity away or find a positive frame, loss of emotional control or affect regulation, inability to feel satisfied
orbitofrontal cortex (OFC)	→	poor impulse control, irrational responses to problems
anterior cingulate gyrus (ACG)	→	ruminating worry, inflexible attitude

pression results: difficulty feeling satisfied, poor pain regulation, bad mood, and poor control over pessimistic thinking, to name a few.

Norepinephrine. The next neurotransmitter with powerful influence is norepinephrine (NE). It affects depression symptoms in several ways. Norepinephrine is responsible for being awake and alert. The brain needs to be alert to register incoming information. Norepinephrine exists in a complicated balance with other neurotransmitters. One theory of depression is that when serotonin is too low, NE fires to stimulate production of it. This means that if the depression is caused by low levels of serotonin, it is possible that NE can become too high (and possibly then also start to become depleted). Thus, depression symptoms can include feelings of agitation or vigilance. However, there are other hypotheses. See the impact of NE on brain structures in Table 1.2.

- For a person with an overactive stress response or who suffers chronic stress, the overrelease of NE may produce the jittery, agitated feeling of being "stressed out."
- When NE is too high, it creates sensations of hyperarousal. When it is constantly too high, it leads to hypervigilance, an aspect of posttraumatic stress disorder that also includes depression symptoms (Rothschild, 2000; Yehuda, 1997).

Table 1.2 How Brain Structures Are Affected by Problems
With Norepinephrine

Brain Structure		Depression Symptom
throughout the brain		
high NE	→	general overarousal, inner jitteriness, physical and mental tension
low NE	→	physical and mental lethargy
prefrontal cortex		
high NE	→	hypervigilance
low NE	→	mental sluggishness
basal ganglia		
high NE	→	restlessness, high drive toward perfectionism and workaholism, which can result in depression
sympathetic nervous system		
high NE	→	chronic stress and attempts to relieve it

- Norepinephrine affects the basal ganglia (BG) and the prefrontal cortex (PFC). In some people with too much NE, the person may start out with high drive but develop perfectionism or workaholism that typically leads to depression.
- When NE is too low, low mental and physical energy results, making you feel mentally dull and physically sluggish.

Dopamine. Dopamine (DA) is an interesting neurotransmitter because, like NE, it can contribute to depression if it is either too high or too low, depending on the part of the brain and the circumstances that dysregulated it. High levels of DA occur during trauma, causing overfocus on the details of the trauma and intensifying memory of the details. This intensity increases the likelihood that the amygdala will signal trouble whenever a current situation carries a small reminder of the trauma. Such overreaction to reminders (cues of the trauma) will certainly increase stress for a person with a history that includes trauma.

Low DA, however, is a bigger problem in depression, making it difficult for people to gain pleasure even from things they once enjoyed. It is necessary to have enough DA to feel drive to meet goals and feel pleasure in accomplishment. Feeling low pleasure in accomplishment creates sadness or dysphoria and discourages people from doing, trying, experimenting, and exploring in both mental and behavioral ways.

When you don't have enough DA in the PFC, you experience loss of concentration—a hallmark of the cognitive symptoms of depression. Table 1.3 outlines how brain structures are affected by problems with DA.

GABA and glutamate. The balance between GABA and glutamate, two ubiquitous neurotransmitters, has a role in the physiology of depression in several ways, depending on where in the brain GABA is working (Table 1.4). Remember that GABA quiets activity, so when GABA is not working as it needs to in the basal ganglia (BG), it can result in increased overactivity in this region. The consequence is muscle tension that exacerbates the physical pain and aches that are not suppressed due to insufficient SE and NE modulation. Also, when individuals are under chronic, serious stress, the chronic triggering of glutamate release may overstimulate brain cells and result in damage, primarily by decreasing

Table 1.3 How Brain Structures Are Affected by Problems With Dopamine

Brain Structure		Depression Symptom
basal ganglia		
low DA	→	loss of interest or pleasure, low motivation, low energy
high DA	→	high drive toward perfectionism and workaholism, which can result in depression
prefrontal cortex		
low DA	→	lack of concentration
high DA, as in trauma	→	overfocus on details, with too much stress response to subsequent memory
chronically high DA	→	psychosis or delusional states

Table 1.4 How Brain Structures Are Affected by GABA and Glutamate Imbalance

Brain Structure		Depression Symptom
throughout the brain	→	agitation that exacerbates other problems, such as pain perception, and possibly increases risk of alcoholism
hippocampus (excess glutamate)	→	impaired memory
amygdala (excess glutamate)	→	oversensitivity, excess negativity

the volume of neurons in the hippocampus and enlarging the volume of neurons in the amygdala. The outcome creates depression symptoms, because the overstimulation in the amygdala contributes to excessive negativity and the loss of hippocampal volume creates difficulty with memory.

Brain regions and systems are involved in creating depression—and they are involved in *eliminating* depression. People can use their brains to change their brains when they know what is going wrong and what to target. The best news is that the 10 best-ever depression management techniques work on the brain whether you know what is happening in your brain or not. They work if you use them. Your brain does the rest of it for you.

TWO

Managing the Depressed Brain
With Medication

Typically, people get medication for depression before they receive any prescription for psychotherapy. Understandably, when people consult a physician, whose role is to medicate, they will receive a prescription. Medication does work, and that is what physicians are for. In fact, many of the signs of depression are somatic: pain, fatigue, feeling stressed, insomnia. All are understandable reasons to seek medical attention. Medical interventions for depression are strongly promoted by people involved in healthcare. However, as noted earlier, research indicates that people without severe depression can do as well with psychotherapy over the long haul, and that in the short run, medication and therapy together seem to offer the fastest start to recovery from depression. There are good reasons for medication and good reasons for psychotherapy. In this chapter, I review some of the good reasons for medication, look at which medications are often prescribed, and describe what the medications are intended to help with. Whether to use medication and how to integrate it into a recovery program is always going to be an individual, case-by-case decision, in consultation with your physician.

HOW DO YOU KNOW IF YOU NEED MEDICATION?

Competent psychotherapy can help you eliminate symptoms without medication, but using medication in combination with therapy can calm your brain so therapy techniques work faster and more effectively. Your physician may need to perform some medical tests to rule out physical causes of your symptoms before diagnosing the cause as depression. Once depression is determined to be the culprit, the physician may prescribe one of several medications for relieving depression. Medication can help you start feeling better faster than psychotherapy alone, but it is the psychotherapy that will change your thoughts and behaviors and give you strategies you can use anywhere for the rest of your life without side effects (Blackburn & Moore, 1997; Clark, Ehlers, & McManus, 2003; Fava, Rafanelli, & Grandi, 1998; Frank, 1991; Gould, Otto, & Pollack, 1995; Kroenke, 2007).

How do you know if you should be using medication? Talk with your doctor, of course. It is typically best to consult a psychiatrist rather than your primary-care physician because doctors with this specialty best understand the complex choices of medications for the diverse symptoms of depression. Based on my years of working with depressed people and reading research results, I offer the following questions to help you assess whether medication might be a good option to pursue in addition to therapy.

- Are you having intensely ruminating, negative thoughts? Are these thoughts hard to shake off? Do you feel, as some of my clients so aptly describe, that your thoughts are like the ball in a pinball machine, bouncing around without much control?
- Are you able to push aside ruminating worry when you have something important to concentrate on, only to find yourself worrying again the minute you have nothing to focus on?
- Do you feel very fatigued and wish you could stay in bed or feel like you want to go back to bed or lie on the couch even after you have had enough time in bed?
- Do you have difficulty with concentration? Does even the effort of considering therapy seem like it is overwhelming?
- Are you having trouble remembering things that you should

know and trouble remembering new things that should not be that hard to learn?

- Are you feeling very agitated but unable focus your efforts on anything?
- Do you feel achy, sore, or in pain and know that this is worse than it ought to be?

If You Are Already on Medication Before Starting Therapy

Often people enter psychotherapy with prescriptions for medications that they have begun trying out to manage the impact of depression. This is a time to continue on your doctor's orders. Whether you are trying the techniques in this book on your own or working with a therapist, it is *never* a good idea to stop taking medication abruptly. Many medications have withdrawal effects. And if you are getting benefit from your medication, it just means that you will have a head start on feeling better.

The major downside to using medication while practicing depression control techniques is that it is harder to know what it is like to feel and control depression without the effects of the medication in your system. Be aware that you will feel different when you stop taking the medication, even if you gradually wean off it according to your doctor's orders, so reviewing therapy techniques or going back for a few "booster sessions" of psychotherapy is a good idea when you are ready to stop.

WHAT DO MEDICATIONS DO FOR YOUR BRAIN?

Medications are used to change specific brain or neurotransmitter functions. There are several mechanisms by which they work to control depression. This section describes the different kinds of medications that may be prescribed.

SSRIs. Selective serotonin reuptake inhibitors (SSRIs) are intended to make the neurotransmitter serotonin more available in your brain.

When serotonin levels are not sufficient, people can lack concentration and attention, be negative, worry excessively, and have trouble suppressing that worry or negative thinking. They may have trouble sleeping, feel very hopeless about the possibilities for change, or have trouble seeing good solutions to their problems. The limbic system becomes overactive in producing negative, worrying thoughts and the cortex lacks energy to suppress the negativity. The anterior cingulate gyrus gets stuck on worry thoughts and does not efficiently transfer information between the limbic system and the cortex for decreasing the focus on negativity. The orbitofrontal cortex can be inefficient in its work to evaluate and compare new situations with old ones, and this contributes to negative appraisals of new situations and trouble making new, creative solutions to problems.

Improving serotonin levels or action in the brain promotes regulation of thoughts and mood, making the brain work more effectively so that pychotherapy techniques that might alter depression can be learned and so that the depressed person will have the mental energy to comply with therapy suggestions.

SSRIs are not mood-altering, in that a person will not immediately feel relief from depression when taking them. Therefore they are not addictive. These medications help your brain increase its production of serotonin by blocking the return ("reuptake") of serotonin molecules into the cell that released them (Figure 2.1). When the cell that releases serotonin does not pick any back up from the synapse (gap) between cells, it gets a message that there is not enough serotonin, so the brain goes to work to make more serotonin neurotransmitters in the cells. SSRIs also contribute to the production of new brain cells that will produce serotonin. For reasons that are not entirely clear, they stimulate a substance called BDNF (discussed in Chapter 1), which encourages the growth of new brain cells.

Even though SSRIs have a very small impact on serotonin availability right away, it usually takes weeks for the brain to start producing enough additional serotonin neurotransmitters to change depression. It takes *months* for the brain to maintain that level of production without

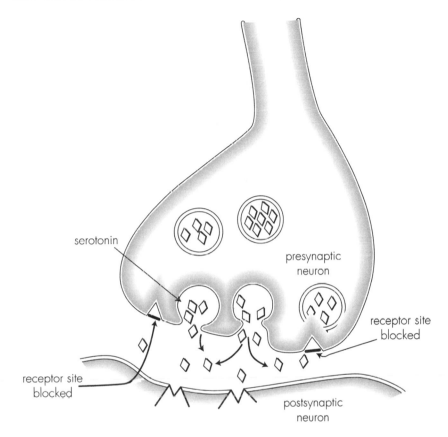

serotonin

presynaptic neuron

receptor site blocked

receptor site blocked

postsynaptic neuron

Figure 2.1 SSRIs function to block return of serotonin into the cell.

the medication, and it requires nutrients to build new cells and adequate sleep during that time to produce the serotonin. People taking SSRIs should expect to be on these medications for some time, typically for a year or more. The medications should only be discontinued under the supervision of your doctor.

If a physician prescribed an SSRI before a person started therapy, it is usually best to continue using it until it has had enough time to work. That will probably be many months, not weeks, on the drug. If the drug is discontinued too soon it is possible that the symptoms will come right back. In fact, reemerging symptoms indicate that the SSRI was doing a good job. A person can continue learning therapy techniques while getting help from the medication. When your symptoms are sufficiently improved, your physician may suggest that it is time to stop using medication. He or she will come up with a plan to withdraw from the medication slowly in order to prevent feeling sick from discontinuing too quickly. During the discontinuation of medication, it is wise to also work with a therapist, who can help you use techniques without medication to make sure the transition is smooth.

The commonly prescribed SSRIs are included in the following list. The brand name for each is followed by the generic name in parentheses.

Prozac (fluoxetine)
Zoloft (sertraline)
Paxil (paroxetine)
Luvox (fluvoxamine)
Celexa (citalopram)
Lexapro (escitalopram)

Drugs that affect both the serotonin neurotransmitter and also the norepinephrine neurotransmitter are called "SNRIs." They include:

Effexor (venlafaxine)
Cymbalta (duloxetine)
Pristiq (desvenlafaxine)

Tricyclic Antidepressants. These medications are older drugs and have been largely replaced as the first choice for antidepressant treatment, but they work similarly to the SSRIs and SNRIs, blocking reuptake of serotonin, norepinephrine, and dopamine. They are less selective in their targeting, so they tend to have more side effects than newer medications and are more risky in potential for overdose. They are effective, though, and may be prescribed by your psychiatrist in specific situations. The tricyclic antidepressants include:

Elavil, Endep (amitriptyline)
Asendin (amoxapine)
Anafranil (clomipramine)
Norpramin (desipramine)
Sinequan (doxepin)
Tofranil (imipramine)
Ludiomil (maprotiline)
Pamelor, Aventyl (nortriptyline)
Vivactil (protriptyline)
Surmontil (trimipramine)

MAOIs. Monoamine oxidase inhibitors (MAOIs) are medications that slow down the action of the enzyme that clears neurotransmitters from the synapses. Thus there is more opportunity for the necessary neurotransmitters to be received after they are released. Because these medications have potential for dangerous side effects when taken in combination with foods that contain tyramine, dietary precautions must be followed carefully. That is one significant reason why these medications are less frequently prescribed. These medications include:

Nardil (phenelzine)
Parnate (tranylcypromine)
Marplan (isocarboxazid)
Ensam (selegiline; available as a transdermal patch)

Benzodiazepines. These medications are only likely to be prescribed if a person has serious anxiety along with the depression. They are potentially addictive, but this should not be viewed as a reason not to use them, except for people with alcohol addiction or perhaps in the very young or the elderly, because these groups may experience problems related to use of benzodiazepines. Whenever drugs pose complications, the best person to help decide about the risks and the benefits is your physician.

Benzodiazepines work best to decrease the high degree of physical arousal that goes with intense feelings of stress or agitation, and typically

41

they are prescribed in tandem with an SSRI for the first few weeks on that medication. They should not be discontinued abruptly but rather weaned off to avoid potentially unpleasant or serious effects of discontinuation, depending on the length of time they have been used.

The benzodiazepines work on GABA, a neurotransmitter that makes firing between brain cells slow down. It may be necessary to help that system when a person is under considerable stress—a serious problem in some forms of depression. The calming effects of benzodiazepines work within 30 to 60 minutes and last for several hours, depending on the type of drug prescribed. That is why they are considered mood-altering. They are helping GABA to do its job, but only while they are active in your system. Typically your doctor will prescribe this drug for a brief period of time—weeks, not months.

The most commonly prescribed benzodiazepines include:

Xanax (alprazolam)
Ativan (lorazepam)
Klonopin (clonazepam)

BuSpar (buspirone). BuSpar is an atypical anti-anxiety drug in the class of medications called "azapirones." These work on the serotonin system differently than the SSRIs, causing neurons to release more serotonin neurotransmitters whenever they fire. Thus, a little more serotonin is available to affect all the systems where it is active. BuSpar has some impact on the dopamine system, and it is more likely to "take the edge off" the kind of anxiety that besets those with depression and agitation together. It does not work immediately, but rather takes a few weeks. This is a medication that someone with generalized anxiety and depression might benefit from using for a period of months.

Wellbutrin (bupropion). This medication selectively raises levels of dopamine in the brain. It is particularly helpful to boost energy and help people feel more interest in life, as dopamine affects attention and reward feelings. It is very helpful for people who are lethargic or disinterested. This same drug is used for people who are quitting smoking to help with the lack of focus and the urge to smoke.

Antipsychotics. When people have serious trouble with thinking, as may occur in major depression, drugs called "antipsychotics" may be helpful. These medications affect the way dopamine and norepinephrine bind to the receptor sites, making the brain less agitated. Not all the drugs in this class are used for depression, but aripiprazole and quetiapine are two that have been approved by the FDA for depression treatment.

Abilify (aripiprazole)
Seroquel (quetiapine)
Geodon (ziprasidone)
Clozaril (Clozapine)
Zyprexa (Olanzapine)
Risperdal (risperidone)

Complicated Situations

A person with depression may have other problems that complicate treatment with medication. When more than one condition is present, this is referred to as a "comorbid" condition. In these cases, psychiatrists are best equipped to identify and prescribe the combination of medications that will stabilize all the aspects of the depression with its comorbid conditions. The American Medical Association has guidelines for this process. This section discusses some of the problems that may coexist with depression.

Insomnia. It is typical for a person with depression to have trouble sleeping, and usually antidepressants will resolve that problem over time as long as the person practices good sleep hygiene. However, there are many causes of insomnia, including some medical conditions such as sleep apnea, that require appropriate diagnosis and medical treatment. In depression, debilitating insomnia may require a short-term use of sleep medication, with the type of insomnia affecting the choice of medication. Sleep medications vary widely in the way they affect the onset and quality of sleep.

Age-related concerns. The age of the person with depression is an important consideration in medication. Although many people are reluctant to medicate children, when the depression is severe it has an impact on the child's development, making medication the better option. Prozac (fluoxetine) and Lexapro (escitalopram) are two SSRI medications that have been approved by the FDA for use in children. Another age-related concern is the possibility of attention deficit disorder (ADD). Especially into adolescence and young adulthood, if ADD has not been correctly diagnosed or treated, the condition can contribute to depression as the low self-esteem, mistakes, social errors, and failure to achieve commensurate with ability can be very discouraging, and those deficits accrue over time. Treating the ADD will improve any comorbid depression.

In geriatric patients, comorbid physical conditions (or the medications to treat them) can produce depression. A diagnostic concern when a geriatric patient presents with mental distraction or confusion is to differentiate dementia and depression. Treating with an antidepressant medication alone may not be enough.

Other issues. People with depression may suffer from any number of other comorbid problems, including panic disorder, generalized anxiety, posttraumatic stress disorder, and obsessive-compulsive disorder, or have bi-polar depression. In these kinds of situations, other types of drugs may augment antidepressant treatment to improve thought clarity and mood stability, decrease anxiety, and so on. For example, a person with bipolar disorder will require medications that stabilize the mood or that control both depression and mania. Finding the right medication is a process that involves careful appraisal of the rapidity of the bipolar cycle, the severity of the symptoms, and the person's response to the medication.

Trial and Error

There is no medical test that can predict whether you will respond well to one type of SSRI but not to another. Thus, finding the medication that is right for you is not always possible on the first try—you may have to try a few different medications before you find one that gives you good relief from your symptoms and doesn't have too many side effects. This trial-and-error process can be frustrating—you might think, "These drugs are just a waste of time!" or "I will never find the right medication!"—but working with your prescribing physician ultimately will usually bring you to the right medication. Finding the right dose level of the drug can also be an issue. Usually physicians start by prescribing a low dose and then gradually raise the dose until you find the right level for you—a process that requires good communication with your physician. And, at times, adding a medication to your regimen ("augmenting") can make a world of difference.

Because changes in medication take time to take effect, the process can be slow and discouraging. However, if you need medication, patient pursuit of the right type, dose, and combination of medications can greatly improve the outcome of your treatment.

Because there many complex individual situations, the best suggestion for anyone with complicated symptoms is to see a psychiatrist, who is the medical specialist for mental health. Psychiatrists have specialized training to know:

- How psychotropic medications affect people at different ages
- How psychotropic medications affect people with different symptom expressions
- What medications work best for people with complicated depression or who have other additional mental-health conditions
- New options for medication or augmenting medication that can improve your regimen

It is well worth a visit to get medication right.

HERBAL AND SUPPLEMENTAL OPTIONS FOR BRAIN HEALTH

There is abundant evidence that you can improve your mood, create a healthier brain and body, and revitalize your health by what you eat, what kinds of supplements you add into your diet, and how you deliberately employ physical exercise. If you are interested in how your brain uses nutrients to manufacture neurotransmitters and how you can provide a better balance of those nutrients, the information is readily available. The "nutrition and supplements" section of the Recommended Reading and Resources list at the end of this book includes some excellent resources, such as *How to Use Herbs, Nutrients, and Yoga in Mental Health Care* (Brown, Gerbarg, & Muskin, 2009) and *Potatoes, Not Prozac* (DesMaisons, 2008).

Medication is a first-line treatment according to insurance companies and medical protocols for all kinds of depression. Medication never can teach you the techniques that will help you to use your brain to change your brain, but they *can* enable your brain to learn and effectively use depression management techniques. The best use of medication occurs when a psychotherapist and a physician work together as a team with you. Together you can formulate an effective plan of medication and depression management techniques that will help you diminish or eliminate depression symptoms altogether.

THREE

Technique #1: Identify Triggers, Plan New Responses

The more we know about depression, the clearer it becomes: Depression has not one cause but many. The varied symptoms of depression suggest that there are several types of the disorder, and scientific studies on the neurobiology of depression increasingly recognize that "depressive disorders represent a family of related but distinct conditions" (Shelton, 2007, p. 1). Studies of dysfunction in brain systems and neurotransmitter functions point to different origins of neuropathology—in other words, different symptoms of mood or behavior have different causes. It may be that "points of vulnerability" in the brain—due to genetics or disease or injury or developmental insult—predispose a person to depression. If you have the genetic setup for it, you may develop depression when life brings challenges. And different causes also result in different clusters of symptoms. According to Shelton, for example, "it is likely that the core pathophysiology of depression associated with early life adversity is different from non-trauma related disorders" (p. 2). Shelton went on to comment that understanding the causes may lead to more targeted treatments. His work to unravel the neurobiological bases of depression gives substance to clinical observations I have made over the years regarding the physical, cognitive, and behavioral manifestations of depression in my clients.

DIFFERENT DEPRESSIONS

Working in the therapy office, I have noted distinctive differences be-tween clients complaining of depression. For example, when I saw peo-ple whose depression developed after they experienced a serious loss, the intensity of symptoms seemed more severe in those who had an early life history of loss or adversity versus those who did not suffer troubles in their early life. Depression that emerged subsequent to a period of chronic stress seemed different than that in people who described feeling depres-sion most of their lives. As I studied neurobiology to understand how treatments work, I developed ideas about how depression symptoms fall into clusters based on the possible etiology of the depression. This think-ing has given shape to distinctions I automatically make between clients to help me spot triggers for their depressive moods and episodes. It also has helped me choose effective early interventions for them based on what is known about their histories.

How Do We Identify Clusters of Symptoms in a Useful Way?

The following broad groupings of depression are based on my clinical observations of clients I have seen throughout years as a therapist and are founded in what I know about neurobiology. Differentiating types of depression according to clusters of symptoms and their possible causes can help people identify triggers for the mood, thinking, and behavior that typify their depression. Everyone who has suffered depression knows there are times when it seems more severe—times when it seems to roll in like a fog, shrouding mood and thinking, and times when it feels as if even small things can push you off the cliff into a chasm of depression. Those times may be prompted by various triggers or may reflect the un-derlying nature of your depression. Many techniques in this book address what to do about the symptoms, but you can diminish depression by starting to pay attention to what happens to trigger depression symp-toms. Identifying triggers and responding differently to them can avert symptoms when depression threatens.

48

An important side note regarding depression in people with bipolar disorder: I am not looking at triggers in bipolar depression in this chapter, because the cycling of bipolar I and bipolar II are both biologically determined. However, a person with bipolar disorder may still benefit from considering whether there are discernable triggers for shifts in mood. For example, even a brief but serious environmental stress, such as a person's child being ill, can shift that person into a manic state.

This chapter focuses on the causes of and triggers for noncycling depression. The ideas presented should serve as general guidelines more than as "gospel" about depression and its causes. The following list outlines what I see as the different types of depression:

- *Endogenous depression*. This type of depression is genetic and neurobiological—the kind of depression that people are "born to have."
- *Depression as a consequence of attachment problems or abuse*. This type of depression may look similar to endogenous depression in the length of time symptoms have been around, but these symptoms are consequent to an early life loss or adversity, or failure of parents to provide a secure base and safe haven for the developing child.
- *Situational or stress-induced depression*. Serious stress, often chronic, can deplete the brain of critical neurotransmitters and thus oversensitize it to stress—the outcome of which may be a hard-to-shake depression.
- *Posttraumatic stress depression*. I see this as the outcome of traumatic-stress experiences occurring later than childhood— for example, depression emerging after accident, injury, natural disaster, medical trauma, or combat-related trauma.

NEURAL NETWORKING

Before describing the possible causes of the types of depression just listed, it would be helpful to discuss a particularly relevant feature of neural networking, which is a factor in feeling depressed no matter what other underlying causes are leading to the depression. This feature is relevant because of the way human beings store and retrieve memories. When something triggers one memory, a network of similar memories is automatically activated. Aspects of the memory—the emotion and the details—connect to similar experiences. For example, hosting your child's birthday party may bring back memories of birthday parties you had at that age, along with many small details about those events that you thought you'd forgotten.

This is an efficient way to recall information. However, in depression, it accounts for the tendency to recall every similar *negative* experience once a person starts to think about one negative experience. To use the example of the birthday party again, if you are suffering from depression, and the cake you made for the party accidentally gets burned, you may react to that by remembering all the other times you've "failed" as a parent and fall into a downward spiral of self-reproach.

This is true of moods as well. Once a person gets into a bad mood, the whole network of "previous bad moods" may light up, causing the person to reenter the memories of negative thoughts, negative expectations, memories of negative outcomes and disappointments, and even negative behavior patterns that reinforce the mood.

An overarching goal of therapy is learning to interrupt negative networking and deliberately shift into a positive network. The ability to make that shift is a natural outcome of many of the techniques in this book. When a person learns how neural networking shows up—for example, in the negative-thinking tendency of depression—the knowledge boosts the energy needed for persistence in applying these techniques to interrupt the self-reinforcing neural networking.

ENDOGENOUS DEPRESSION

People who complain of low cognitive energy ("I just can't think about that now," or "I just can't decide what I should do," or "I just sit and look at the work")—who have persistently negative mood, irritability, and limited pleasure or interest in daily life, without any particular trauma or stress they identify as causing their lethargy—are probably suffering from endogenous depression. They have a tendency to be passive and hard to motivate; their attitude toward therapy can be summed up as "What's the use?"

What Might Underlie Endogenous Depression?

One hypothesis suggests that the cause of this set of symptoms is a genetically determined inadequate supply of the neurotransmitters serotonin, norepinephrine, and dopamine, which affect mood and energy.

- Low levels of serotonin result in negativity, a tendency to ruminate, and less mental energy. Serotonin is also a contributor to the sense of satisfaction when effort is exerted to achieve something, so an inadequate supply of this neurotransmitter can prevent people from feeling rewarded by their accomplishments, making it difficult for them to get motivated to exert effort in the first place.
- In the right amounts, norepinephrine gives the overall state of arousal necessary to feel both physical and mental energy. A lack of it leads to feelings of lethargy.
- Dopamine is necessary to feel focused and also to feel rewards. It directly helps people to learn that what they just experienced was pleasurable and thus provides the motivation to "do that again!" Low dopamine levels can lead to lack of motivation.

Without sufficient supplies of these neurochemicals, people can feel negative and have little energy or motivation to try to feel better. This can cause you to overlook what is right about your life.

Another hypothesis of endogenous depression has to do with the neurotransmitter glutamate. Some people may have a genetically determined, neurobiological overresponse to stress. Excessive stress produces high levels of cortisol and glutamate, both of which atrophy brain cells. In fact, it is surmised that the excitatory neurotransmitter glutamate is more at fault for brain-cell atrophy than cortisol itself (Yehuda, Bierer, Schmeidler, Aferiat, Breslau, & Dolan, 2000). The brain likes balance, so if there are genetic alterations in brain function, these imbalances can increase the likelihood of dysregulated stress response and thus increase vulnerability to depression (Shelton, 2007). This means that people with genetically determined overresponse to stress may be especially sensitive to environmental situations that trigger the depression.

What Can Help?

According to some researchers, endogenous depression may be best treated through pharmacological approaches. But making cognitive and behavioral changes can also help—either in tandem with antidepressant drugs or, in some cases, without them.

Although neurotransmitter imbalances underlie all types of depression, in endogenous depression, those imbalances themselves are the trigger (rather than, say, a traumatic event that triggers neurochemical imbalances and thus triggers depression). Therefore, the way of responding differently to this trigger is to consciously override that biochemically determined low energy by entering into positive neural networks on purpose. In other words, neural networking can be a culprit, keeping you stuck in negative patterns of thought, but it also can be a way out of the problem if you deliberately override your brain's negative default setting. Doing this allows you to enter into and strengthen neural networks of positive experience. You can enter into positive networks by purposefully thinking positive, optimistic thoughts that will boost your motivation to do something different.

In depression, the pull is to *not* do rather than do. It is to avoid rather than approach. It is to stop rather than go. It is to have negative feelings, whether they are physical or emotional. At some point you must deliberately choose to believe that it is possible to change the lethargy and disinterest in life that you have in endogenous depression. One way to begin doing that is to look at your level of satisfaction in life and consciously work toward improving it.

Improve Satisfaction

Satisfaction is a state of being, not a transient mood. Whereas cheerful emotions come and go, satisfaction is an appraisal that reflects the sum total of an experience more than a specific point in the experience. For example, you might comment after finishing a project, "Although I was not happy that it took so long, I am satisfied with the way it turned out and would do it again."

The first step to improving satisfaction is rating your current level of satisfaction with life. Edward Diener at the University of Illinois has researched what makes people satisfied. He developed his scale for measuring satisfaction in 1980 and has been researching with it since then (Diener, Emmons, Larsen, & Griffen, 1985; Diener & Biswas-Diener, 2008). It is a surprisingly accurate list of five simple questions (Figure 3.1). If you are feeling depressed you can quickly measure where you fall on the satisfaction scale and direct interventions to improve depression based on how you answered.

Knowing where you stand can be helpful if you are feeling depressed. It can give you an objective measure and a place to rate your progress.

Once you have assessed your level of satisfaction, you can begin improving it in several ways. But a significant component of *how* you rate is *what* you rate. According to learning theory, people learn new things based on primacy and recency—you remember best what came first and what came last. This applies to satisfaction as well. Daniel Kahneman, a Nobel laureate, has researched what makes people feel satisfied and observed that when you are rating an experience, you tend to focus your rating on the high points, the low points, and the endings (Coady, Cray, & Park, 2005). Knowing that, you can shape your memories to be more positive. Get into the habit of reviewing *what went right* in any situation—observe what worked out fine despite the stumbling blocks along the way. For people with endogenous depression, this may take some practice! You are probably accustomed to instead focusing on what went wrong. But ignoring what satisfies you can be a trigger to depressed mood.

Figure 3.1 Satisfaction With Life Scale. Used with permission of Dr. Edward Diener.

Below are five statements that you may agree or disagree with. Using the 1–7 scale below, indicate your agreement with each item by placing the appropriate number on the line preceding that item. Please be open and honest in your responding.

7 - Strongly agree
6 - Agree
5 - Slightly agree
4 - Neither agree nor disagree
3 - Slightly disagree
2 - Disagree
1 - Strongly disagree

_____ In most ways my life is close to my ideal.
_____ The conditions of my life are excellent.
_____ I am satisfied with my life.
_____ So far I have gotten the important things I want in life.
_____ If I could live my life over, I would change almost nothing.
_____ Total

Now check where your level is.

31–35 Extremely satisfied
26–30 Satisfied
21–25 Slightly satisfied
16–20 Neutral
15–19 Slightly dissatisfied
10–14 Dissatisfied
 5–9 Extremely dissatisfied

So learn to rate your experiences on what went right rather than on what went wrong.

Consciously Shift Away From Negativity

Another way of changing the lethargy and disinterest in life is to consciously shift away from negativity. Although changing endogenous depression requires lifestyle corrections that are made over the course of time, it is possible to nudge your depressed self into a more active, positive state of mind immediately. Try reciting the following statements (or make up your own):

- I can think what I want. And I want to think I have many good traits.
- I don't have to leave my negative brain on autopilot. I can override it to think something positive.
- What I think affects what I do. I will think about using my strengths.
- Even if I don't feel the energy to do something, I can choose to do it anyway.

These statements are helpful for people suffering from other types of depression as well, as negativity underlies all forms of depression no matter the original cause.

In the long run, a person with endogenous depression will use methods that will help engage the prefrontal cortex to deliberately shift away from negativity and act in opposition to lethargy while making lifestyle adjustments that help build a healthier or more resilient brain. Although these changes involve many different methods to mobilize energy and generate health, in the short run, avoiding triggers by making small changes can avert the lifelong tendency to sink under the weight of yet another failed expectation.

Make a "To Do" List

Making a conscious effort to move from negative thinking to positive thinking is perhaps the most effective nonpharmacological approach to combating endogenous depression. However, as mentioned earlier, making this shift can be difficult for people who have spent their lives focusing on the negative. When dragging your mind into a positive frame seems too daunting a task to accomplish, try simply distracting yourself instead.

A good way of doing this is to engage in a simple, productive activity. It's wise to keep a list of these little things you want to get done so that you do not have to come up with them on the spur of the moment when your mind is in a negative place. What kinds of things are on a list like that? Put a photo in a frame; sort out a closet; read a magazine article; call a friend you have not talked to in a while; clean out the car; weed the garden; clean out the refrigerator; watch that documentary you saved for a quiet hour; sort the recycling; take a bath—the possibilities are numerous. The only requirements are that the activity be relatively easy to accomplish—thinking about retiling the entire bathroom, for example, is likely to make you feel more exhausted, not less!—and that it doesn't require you to shift into a positive frame of mind *before* beginning the task—although you'll probably find that you're feeling more positive after you finish!

Plan to Get What You Want

As mentioned earlier, although an insufficient supply of neurochemicals might be at the heart of endogenous depression, triggers often include life stressors that evoke the feeling of exhaustion: extra work that unexpectedly needs to be done, disappointment of expectations in work or social life, failure to achieve what you expected. Even a simple thing such as getting a C on a test when you expected a B can trigger the thought that nothing you do will ever be good enough and put you on the path to feeling depressed.

When you know that you are about to be in a situation that typically challenges you, you may prepare to feel depressed, essentially rehearsing your depression and thus increasing the probability of triggering it. It is always tempting to plan to be disappointed and tell yourself, "See, it always goes this way." For example, you may expect that others won't come through to help you—your colleagues will fail to do their part of the work, or your fellow students all assigned part of a group project will blow it off—and you start to feel low. At that moment, the trigger is rehearsing how past experiences may recur.

Respond differently. Stop planning to be hurt and hopeless. What do you do instead? First of all, delay thoughts of failed expectations. This is not pie-in-the-sky thinking. It is a simple refusal to think ahead about inevitable failure. Tell yourself instead that you will "face it when it happens." If you are going to be disappointed, there will be time later to deal with it.

What you think about next is up to you: You might just push off negative thoughts and change your focus to whatever you are doing at the moment, or turn on some music to listen to, or call someone up to chat about a different topic. If you can, deliberately imagine that instead of failing you, everyone has done his or her part.

If it is hard to imagine that others will come through, switch your sigh of depression to a vision of yourself adequately responding in a stressful situation. Envision yourself being resilient. For example, if you are imagining that your date is not going arrive or will not call when expected, go right past that moment in your mind and instead think about what you will do with your time if it is not filled up with that activity. Maybe the unexpected free time allows you to get some Christmas shopping done or to drop in to say hello to a friend who works in the area. Perhaps it gives you time to catch up on emails or call a family member you've been meaning to talk to. If you can act as if you have better things to do, even for a few minutes, it can prevent the lethargy from overwhelming you.

Delaying thoughts about disappointment can eliminate triggers to feel depressed because often in the moment of *expecting* to be disappointed, your neural networks light up as if you *already were* disappointed, which leads to inaction. You want to get out of this vicious trap as soon as possible. Taking action is the opposite of depression, so any small action may avert the triggering sensation of ineffectiveness.

There may also be things you can do ahead of time to help prevent others from disappointing you. For example, if you worry that your co-workers will let you down on an important project, try sending an email, text, or phone call stating that you are looking forward to seeing what they have gotten done and remind them of their part and the deadline. If you are expecting a friend to show up late or completely miss a social function, send a message ahead of time that you are looking forward to seeing the person and name the place and time.

Endogenous depression with its lethargy can lead you to develop bad habits of refraining from doing these small things to avoid disappointment. And the less you do to help people to please you, the more they disappoint you. In this way, your depression ends up tricking you into believing that your negative thinking about others is valid—when in fact, if you hadn't succumbed to your lethargy and inaction, these disappointments may never have come about.

DEPRESSION AS A CONSEQUENCE OF ATTACHMENT PROBLEMS OR ABUSE

Among the most challenging symptoms of depression that I observe are in people with a history of childhood neglect or abuse. They frequently display a tendency toward remarkable, dramatic shifts of mood from feeling okay to feeling seriously depressed. Such depression also manifests itself in a cognitive "default mode" of negative expectations about the world—no one is going to surprise this person with a positive outcome. People with this type of depression also appear unable to calm down or "self-soothe" in times of challenge. They tend to plunge into despair whenever minor upsets occur. And when they plunge, they may engage in impulsive self-injurious behavior such as drinking, gambling, risky sexual escapades, or even suicide.

When I observe a person plummeting from relative equanimity to abject misery and hopelessness, I look for an early life history of adversity that might explain this, because it will affect our treatment choices. Not only are these people not expecting much of others, but also their plunges into despair are like "falling off a cliff" and are very difficult to interrupt. Therefore, treatment has to focus first on preventing destructive actions, as described in Chapter 9. Once a measure of safety and self-control are assured through symptom management, the longer-term psychotherapy to resolve early life adversity will become more effective, ultimately eliminating those plunges into despair.

What Causes Depression in People With Attachment Failures in Their Histories?

This type of depression stems from serious and repeated adversity very early in life, created by the very people who should have protected you. It is quite likely that early adverse events in life, particularly abuse but also repeated neglect, "contribute significantly to the potential for a depressive episode" (Kendler, Thornton, & Gardner, 2001, p. 582). This risk is based in several potential outcomes of repeated adverse stress early in life:

- One cause is due to changes in the stress response (Bergmann, 1998), exaggerating the effect of small stresses due to a permanent overreactivity to stress.
- Cellular changes occur when a child does not receive comfort for distress. Over time, those changes result in diminished effectiveness of responses to new stressors (Kendler et al., 2001). This is observed to be a genetic predisposition coupled with a "dose-specific" impact of stress (Nemeroff, 2004; Shelton, 2007).
- A distressed child who is not comforted becomes frantic and then shuts down (Schore, 2003). The neurobiological impact of repeated neglectful or traumatic failures to receive comfort is a shutdown at the level of the parasympathetic nervous system, creating a state of biological and psychological despair. This biological shutdown of unabated sympathetic arousal has repercussions. The arousal will be shut down much faster when a similar arousal is felt at a later time.
- Memories that are implicit—felt physically rather than cognitively and without specific recall (Siegel & Hartzell, 2003)— result in fewer efforts to soothe oneself and contribute to negative expectations of the outcome of new experiences.
- Exposure to early life adversity increases the risk of depression due to the changes in the neurobiological responses to stress and also in the coping style, which becomes maladaptive later

59

in life (Felitti et al., 1998; Nemeroff, 2004). People who have suffered aversive early life experience tend to search for soothing via maladaptive means that can become self-destructive, such as poor self-care, poor eating habits, smoking, or risky sexual behaviors.

As the child matures into adolescence, the risks of feeling less reward and making less effort toward reward show up in the tendency to make poor social connections and feel more depressed. By adulthood this person may have a severe inability to use rational self-talk and natural calming down when facing trouble.

This is a likely outcome for a child who is repeatedly left when distressed without comfort by caregivers. That child first becomes frantic, then resigned, and then hopeless, in effect shutting down emotionally. Repeated experience of this kind of neglectful or even traumatic attachment failure can result in an adult mental default mode of hopelessness and low expectations of self and others, and cause self-reinforcing plunges into psychological despair.

Over the course of life, the way people habitually think about themselves develops into self-image. The self-image that emerges from an implicit memory of despair is an intrinsic sense of worthlessness. The trigger to plunging into this kind of depression can be any situation, inner thought, or conversation that elicits fear of being disappointed, abandoned, or neglected. In some cases, the trigger may be obvious, such as failure to receive a hoped-for promotion, but other times it can be something as small as not receiving attentive service by waitstaff at a restaurant.

What Helps?

The resolution of depression with this underlying cause obviously requires more treatment than just using some aptly applied interventions to manage symptoms. What truly sets the stage for people to trust therapy and develop responses that are not harmful is to work deliberately and consciously on safety. This means literal safety from any self-harm they may impose and also safety with a therapist, trusting the process of recovery. This occurs over time, but at first they need outside influence to hope for a better outcome in their lives than what they can envision. At the same time, depression management strategies can be powerful responses to depression triggers. Thus, the first focus should be on interrupting the default mode of persistently negative expectations and on counteracting feelings of depression, disappointment, and low-self esteem by building stronger networks of joy during times when the depression does not have the person in its grip.

Set Up Rewarding Activities Before the Depression Sets In

Make an effort to develop activities that are rewarding or exciting and that are ongoing obligations *before* the triggers occur—for example, prepay for regular tennis lessons or join a sports team or group that gets together to play cards, or participate in any regularly-scheduled activity. Then, if you are unexpectedly hit with a plunge, you may be lifted up by the obligation to participate whether or not you want to do so.

Build Positive Brain Circuitry

Responding differently to the triggers that plunge people into this kind of depression requires planning ahead. In the moment of freefall, creative thinking is impossible. Thus, the new response is to write down whatever plan you make. You can develop new self-soothing coping skills by addressing your habitual thought process, learning to leave the negative network and instead build positive networks that will compete with the negative for brain time and provide you with some resources for doing things differently. This could be as simple as a reminder on your door to notice something beautiful today.

You can also change it by actively challenging the negative scripts and the pessimistic expectations that you probably review excessively as a means of preparing to be disappointed. Plan to interrupt every negative forecast with a completely opposite, positive forecast. Although everyone needs some ability to prepare for trouble, decreasing the frequency of negativity should be a primary goal. So, when you catch yourself imagining how your boss is going to yell at you, for example, deliberately imagine what would happen if she were pleasant.

You can use the powerful executive decision-making function of your left prefrontal cortex to put changes into place that will help when you need to downshift the negative thinking that automatically happens when you are triggered. Repeatedly strengthening a positive way of appraising and responding to situations will make it easier to gain access to positive thoughts, and the less you dwell in the land of the negative, the less your brain will go there automatically. There will be more on this in Chapter 11.

Another way to boost your ability to access positive brain circuitry, again in a plan-ahead mode, is to *describe the good parts only* when you are talking about situations. Listen carefully to how you automatically describe things. Do you go for the bad part of an experience, playing the "ain't it awful" card as a way to get your point made with some drama or get sympathy from others? Many people with depression learn to relate to others via tales of sadness, loss, grief, disappointment, resentment, and unfairness. People listening to a sad story will be attentive and may join in, so you feel the comfort of social bonding. You feel connected when getting a sympathetic response. However, rehearsing stories of unfairness or loss won't contribute to feeing good over the long haul, nor does it cement friendships as well as fun does. You may need to learn how to get that kind of engagement around happy or cheerful stories.

Try noticing what was good about an experience. See what transpires if you tell someone about the experience without including the low points. What if you only told the high points? Try it on purpose. Chances are good that you will rate the experience as more pleasurable.

1. Rate your level of pleasure about an experience you recently had. Pick a commonplace event like getting an oil change or being at a party or going to a school concert or having lunch with a colleague.

2. Then tell someone about it, but mention *only* the good, fun, delightful, or amusing aspects of the situation. (Do not disguise complaining as if it were amusing.)
3. Now rate your level of pleasure in the experience immediately after telling about it.

Finding a way to gain access to pleasure may serve you well when trying to get out of the pit of depression, even temporarily.

Join a Self-Help Group

As discussed earlier, people with depression may attempt to self-soothe through destructive behaviors like gambling, drinking, overeating, and so on. If you find yourself engaging in these types of behaviors, it is a good idea to join a self-help group that addresses the specific behavior. Participation in this kind of group can allow you to make pre-trigger social connections that will help you when you need to respond differently. Calling people in your group is a first-line defense against a trigger to despairing depression. Self-help groups will also help you to acquire tools that you can practice ahead of time, such as reading literature that is soothing or inspiring. Such reading is, in effect, providing the missing voice of a caring parent. That kind of influence needs to come from the outside until you are farther along in recovery from depression.

SITUATIONAL OR STRESS-INDUCED DEPRESSION

The symptoms of this type of depression, especially pronounced physical lethargy and isolation, are natural outcomes of the prolonged exertion caused by chronic stress. The colloquial expression "burnout" describes the condition that precedes situation-induced depressions. It is typical to see sleep disruption and self-medication with alcohol or over-the-counter medications, which may become problematic over time. The symptoms are self-reinforcing because it is challenging to overcome sadness, discouragement, or a sense of meaninglessness when you remain exhausted and isolated. Situation-induced depression may occur following events such as serious personal loss (of a job or loved one, for example), work burnout, or exhaustion from long-term care of a sick family member.

Treating situational depression involves not just changing one's attitude but also changing the situation. If you are suffering depression because you are in an abusive relationship, for example, approaches such as "describe the good parts only," discussed earlier, not only won't work but also can even be detrimental if you don't remove yourself from the abusive relationship as well. Of course, many times people face challenges they can't avoid: the death of a spouse, the necessity of caring for a parent with Alzheimer's, long hours at work to keep a job. In these cases, people must make behavioral changes in the way they handle the stressful situation. The daughter caring for an elderly parent might, for example, seek relief opportunities such as having a person or an agency outside the immediate family take over for a while.

Changing the situation or changing the way one handles the situation can be exceptionally challenging for people with this kind of depression. Cognitive rigidity—a failure to see options to do things differently—sets in with burnout. The caretaker, for instance, may feel locked into the pattern of care-giving and unable to take advantage of relief opportunities. She may see only the obstacles and not the benefits in getting relief. For example, she may see the elderly parent disturbed by an unfamiliar face and fear it will worsen the illness but not recognize how her tension affects the quality of her time with the parent—or how getting relief could help her be more emotionally available.

Such mental rigidity may be evident in long hours a person puts in on the job or in repetitive approaches to solving problems that would be better fixed by other solutions—the burned-out person simply does not have the energy to consider or implement other ideas. It is important to note that situational burnout can be seen in any line of work and at any age, including in children, who may be overly involved in activities or may carry burdens of caretaking or housework when a parent is ill or dysfunctional. The lack of flexibility in thinking and the desperate fatigue that accompany this kind of depression are its most striking symptoms.

What Causes Situational Depression?

People who suffer from situational depression may have some predisposition to it—in other words, the depression was essentially just waiting for the right situation to trigger it. The neurochemical changes caused by chronic stress may be the culprit, but the physical and mental exhaustion of chronic situational stress can be a major causative factor as well. Chronic stress at a nontraumatic level damages health in many ways and affects the brain by depleting neurochemistry. Under conditions of stress, the brain uses up available supplies of serotonin, norepinephrine, and dopamine. As those neurotransmitters are depleted, the typical depression symptoms of less mental and physical energy, less sense of interest in the world, and loss of pleasure become increasingly evident. Rigidity in problem-solving sets in as the loss of mental clarity and low energy prevent a creative look at solving the stressful situation.

The symptoms one sees as the outcome of chronic situational stress are the kinds of symptoms present when you are sick: fatigue, loss of interest, loss of appetite, and so on. Those symptoms lead a person to rest, which is a great help in recovering from infection but doesn't help to treat depression. Nor does "pushing through" the symptoms and stress help—in fact, the more a person pushes through, the worse the impact of the stress on physiology. Again, the only way to alleviate the symptoms is to change the situation or the way you are handling it.

When people feel like they can't change the situation or they way they handle it, they may try to escape the stress and "recharge" by isolating themselves from people and activities they previously enjoyed, thinking that being alone will reduce the stress. However, isolation rarely succeeds in recharging the person, especially when the stress is ongoing. In fact, contact with social groups is a major salve to the wounds of stress (Jetten, Haslam, Haslam, & Branscombe, 2009). When people participate with others in rewarding activities, they increase the flow of dopamine, the "I feel good" neurochemical, as well as others such as oxytocin (a "soothing" neurotransmitter that flows when one is touched, befriended, or otherwise in pleasant contact with others). These neurochemicals make people feel soothed, calmer, and refreshed. In isolation you miss out on that positive reward. So, pulling back from social contact diminishes opportunities for the counterweights to stress: emotional experiences of comfort and joy. Isolation itself becomes a trigger for depression. Jetten's research suggests that isolation leaves people not only feeling alone but also less able to cope—cognition is affected and it is harder for them to make good decisions. "I can't" is hard for people with situational stress to say aloud, but they think it a lot. By establishing contact with others they will be able to gain access to help and be less overwhelmed.

What Helps?

These neurochemical changes are reversible with time, but if the patterns of behavior that develop out of excess work or lengthy care-giving are not specifically changed, the depression will not lift. Therefore, attention to behavior change is primary (see Technique #3, "Cool Down Burnout"). The biggest mental hurdle is the cognitive rigidity that emerges under these situations, and challenging that rigidity often requires the help of another person who can aid the depressed individual in identifying the problem and in generating solutions to it. However, when people are mentally stuck, coping in the best way they are able, they are often not likely to want to be told to do it differently. They may feel as if they are being labeled as failures. So any conversation about *how* to change, whether you are making suggestions to yourself or another person about the need to change, must not imply failure. Remember, too, that people with situational depression have probably been highly successful in managing the very situations that have exhausted them. They may only see that what they did before works, so some resistance to trying something new is normal. To help shift into a different mode, think about behavior change as trying something new or different to get a *similarly good result* with the stressful situation but with less pain.

Reestablish Good Self-Care

The triggers for stress-induced depression include letting go of self-care. To respond differently, addressing personal care—a major behavioral shift—is a good place to start, as people under stress have probably stopped doing the things that promote health. Lifestyle changes will be highly effective and won't trigger the fear of failure. These lifestyle changes are discussed at length in Chapter 5.

End Isolation

Although self-care is an important part of recovery, in the short-term, getting back to social contact is highly useful. Relying on others may seem impractical or impossible in your particular situation, but taking small steps toward reliance on others, even if it is simply to enlist their help to view your situation through fresh eyes, can immediately offer relief from the burden of aloneness. It is unlikely that any long-lasting recovery will occur without ending isolation first (see Technique #5). People who stay in isolation are living a life that has become out of balance, and that balance needs to be restored.

Reestablish Spiritual Connections

Many people with situational depression feel depleted in a way that might be called *bereft*: in effect, spiritually impoverished from neglecting formerly important connections to communities such as volunteer groups, churches, or social-action activities. These relationships gave them a sense of purpose and a sense of connection to something greater than themselves. Reforging a spiritual connection that they have allowed to drop is an immediate boon to the impoverished spirit of these overworked, stressed-out individuals. A cognitive component of recovery that leads to a much deeper feeling of peace begins with finding ways to connect to something greater than oneself. For some people this may mean using mediation or prayer; for others it may be spending time in nature or volunteering for a cause they believe in. Feeling connected spiritually is one excellent way to start the process of knowing how and when to rely on help, because one not only connects to a "higher power" but also finds spiritual support via connections to other people or communities.

POSTTRAUMATIC STRESS DEPRESSION

Posttraumatic stress disorder (PTSD) is another cause of depression. The depression of PTSD can be moderate or very severe, and even suicidal ideation can emerge. As a symptom of PTSD, depression is quite variable in its severity, depending on the pre-stress health and resilience of the person suffering the traumatic event. In other words, the presence of PTSD does not mean that the depression will be more severe than it is in people experiencing depression without PTSD. However, no matter what the overall severity of the depression is, it can manifest itself in sudden feelings of helplessness, which are set off by emotional or environmental events. In some cases these triggers may be obvious, such as a new sexual encounter triggering memories of an earlier rape, but other times they are much harder to recognize—for example, a subtle smell that subconsciously brings back felt memories of an earlier trauma.

Helplessness is often a feature of depression, but it is remarkable in the person suffering PTSD. It is a cognitive as well as emotional feature, because in this type of depressed state a person feeling helpless is less likely to generate solutions to problems. Victims of trauma may even feel helpless about having depression, which may be a replay of the helplessness they experienced during the initial trauma. They have a hard time believing anybody can help them, much less that they will ever be able to help themselves.

What Might Underlie Depression Stemming From Posttraumatic Stress Disorder?

Overcoming or ignoring feelings of helplessness is especially difficult because the feeling is so believable—it's hard to get motivated when you believe that any effort you make to try to feel better will be futile. This makes sense for a couple of reasons. First, traumatic stress sensitizes memory so that recall of trauma is easily triggered. This is related to the impact of dopamine in combination with norepinephrine, both of which flood the brain during the experience of trauma, forming powerfully etched memory associations. In other words, the trauma is vividly learned and easily recalled after it is over. Second, the concept of neural networking makes this even more evident. Recalling the trauma causes one to enter the network of memory that holds all of the details—including physical sensations, all of the environmental stimuli, all of the thoughts, and all of the affect that accompanied *both* that situation *and* other similar situations. In this way, helplessness is self-reinforcing.

Another feature of this type of depression is that even small stressors are mentally and physically experienced with disproportionate power. Rachel Yehuda (Yehuda, 1997; Yehuda, Harvey, Buschbaum, Tischler, & Schmeidler, 2007) speculated that the person who is vulnerable to developing PTSD may well have a risk factor of low cortisol, creating a problem in *turning off* stress. Investigating the minority of traumatized persons who develop PTSD after an event, she found that biological risk factors such as lowered cortisol contribute to the emergence of PTSD.

However, we also know that trauma resets the brain's stress response system to a more intense level, leaving in its wake a perpetually higher level of norepinephrine, which means a more sensitive trigger for stress and more intense physical reactions (Bergmann, 1998). Small stressors are now experienced physically and mentally as if they are big. These conditions all contribute to the development of depression. A person's genetic risk for depression and the impact of trauma, which changes a healthy, balanced brain to a less balanced and more vulnerable brain, are both possible underlying reasons why traumatic stress can result in depression.

Identifying triggers is a difficult task for a person with PTSD. That's because our clever brains, in an effort to protect us physically and psychologically, begin to associate all kinds of new situations to the former traumatic situation if they are even remotely similar. This process is automatic and sometimes outside of your conscious awareness; you do not need to be thinking about the trauma for new associations to be formed. The brain responds to new associations—cues or triggers—so that in a new situation your emotional brain will recognize risk fast enough to protect yourself. The trouble is that you might not realize that this has happened. You might not consciously see a new situation as problematic yet still plummet into a mode of feeling depressed (helpless and fearful). There are therapy methods, such as eye movement desensitization and reprocessing (EMDR), that are effective in finding and eliminating responses to triggers, even when they are not intentionally formed. There are also steps you can take outside of therapy to deal with identifying and responding differently to triggers.

What Helps?

Recovering from depression associated with PTSD involves a two-pronged approach, including becoming aware of what is triggering the trauma associations and therapy to work through the traumatic stress.

Bring It to Your Conscious Attention

People with PTSD-related depression may find themselves reacting to a situation with a sense of helplessness or depressed mood that only hours or even moments ago was not so strong. When this happens, it is time to "stop, look, and listen"! Pause and reflect on what has just been happening. Do not discard the possibility that something in the situation has triggered this feeling. As explained earlier, some situations will obviously be reminiscent of a trauma. For example, after a car accident you may notice that any time a car speeds past you or tailgates, you start to get agitated. (A common response to triggers is nervousness.) That agitation may turn to a sense of depression fairly quickly. Other times the trigger isn't so obvious. It can even be something internally felt rather than existing in the environment, such as an emotion or thought that reminds you of the traumatic situation.

Then, write. If you are not a writer or cannot write at the moment, can you talk to yourself instead? If you need to talk aloud, call a friend just to describe, not fix, what just happened to you or what you just did or thought. Do not get overly concerned about *why* that situation should be a trigger. Just notice that it *is* a trigger. The idea is just to grab as many details of what just happened as you can. When you hit on the detail that was the trigger, you will notice a shift of intensity in your emotions. You might feel worse or you may suddenly feel better because you *consciously noticed* what your brain was trying to alert you to.

Once you notice, all you need to do is ascertain if the situation is genuinely dangerous to you. Is a bad outcome of any kind likely to occur because of the situation? In all probability, you will find that there is nothing you can determine as a problem. For example, Douglas was a client of mine who got very depressed after a serious car accident in which he was hit from behind while at a stoplight. After the accident he would sometimes feel as if he could not get out of the house; he felt helpless when asked to run simple errands and was losing interest in life as he stayed closer and closer to home. He started to feel overwhelmed by simple activities—going to the grocery, going to a movie, or shopping at the mall with his wife. After practicing "stop, look, listen," Douglas was able to identify that he felt overwhelmed if asked to be anyplace where people could walk up from behind him. He could see that his brain associated all experiences of "coming from behind" with his accident, regardless of whether they actually posed a threat. Once Douglas saw that, he could talk himself into entering some activities and he no longer felt so helpless.

Therapy

In the long run, therapy will be necessary to work through the traumatic stress. Yehuda (Yehuda, 1997; Yehuda et al., 2007) has done a stellar job of examining the implications of PTSD for successful treatment of the depression that is part of the syndrome. She observed that how a person subjectively interprets the event of the trauma influences whether he or she develops PTSD, and she noted that exposure to a prior trauma has a powerful influence on the interpretation a person makes. This suggests that cognitive change in many forms is of critical importance. Cognitive-therapy concepts such as reframing understanding, observing actual outcomes, and working with neural-integration techniques (such as journaling) are very important. It is unlikely that a person can do this kind of reworking without assistance. Yehuda also commented on the need for social support to ameliorate depression symptoms. No one technique to help eliminate depression symptoms is exclusive of the others, and social support is a good example of this. How one uses the support may vary from one situation to another, and in PTSD getting help to identify triggers is a good place to start utilizing support.

With this range of underlying issues, all of which demand appropriate and probably longer-term treatment, is it any wonder that people with depression find themselves casting about for effective means of reducing the distress? Is it any wonder that therapists look for as many tools as possible to assist their clients in recovery? I have found that providing people with management methods for their specific symptoms may begin to correct brain function and facilitate psychotherapy for the underlying cause of the depression.

By beginning at the right place and managing symptoms that reflect the most likely underlying causes of depression, we create necessary changes in energy to move a person out of depression. Therefore, it is wise to start small and build on each step.

FOUR

Technique #2:

Start Where You Already Are

Two themes predominate in depression: feeling inadequate and feeling worthless. And two signs of depression—lethargy and the inability to feel rewarded—make those beliefs seem true, although they may be far from the truth. The belief that one is inadequate particularly plagues people with burnout or situationally caused depression because they know they coped before but are not coping well now. They are very conscious of the difference between earlier assessments of themselves as capable and current feelings of being overwhelmed and thus inadequate. These people may castigate themselves as worthless—specifically with regard to the current situation, but then it spreads to other areas of their lives as well. For people with endogenous depression, physical or mental lethargy can drag down motivation, and the often lifelong presence of depression can affect one's sense of identity, making these people believe that they are just not worth as much as others.

In either case, a vicious circle can begin. Believing that you are inadequate or worthless depletes your energy to do or try new things, to take up a challenge, or to overcome lethargy. And the less you do or try, the more inadequate you feel. Motivation wanes in these conditions, and low self-esteem emerges—or predates the depression. In any case, it impedes recovery.

How do you start to feel motivation when you do not feel the physical energy to start moving? How do you begin to overcome lethargy and feelings of inadequacy when that task seems insurmountable? Surprisingly, it may take less effort than you think. The key is to "start where you already are." If you look closely at your life, you can begin to recognize things you appreciate about yourself and strengths you've previously overlooked, as well as see that there are positive aspects of experiences you're already having. Increasing awareness of your own best self and of the things that are going right in your life will stimulate both mental and physical energy to overcome the lethargy that stops you from doing more and feeling better.

If you are feeling the pervasive lethargy of depression, it might be easiest to just *stop doing* something you are already doing instead of starting to do something else. Consider the following possibility.

FOCUS ON WHAT YOU APPRECIATE ABOUT YOURSELF

In depression, neural networking (the way the brain clusters memories of physical sensations, emotions, details, actions, and thoughts that compose an event you remember) links the memory of one unhappy situation with other similar memories. Networking causes the tendency to tumble from one miserable thought to another. It pulls you to think about things that are not right about yourself, reinforcing feelings of inadequacy or worthlessness.

Interfering with that network is a start in the realm of motivation. How do you do that? It is very important to stop speaking the language of negativity. This is a small change, and one that almost any depressed person has the energy for because it is just *stopping* one action, not starting a new one. Anyone who pays attention to the way things work out in life knows that you can construct your own reality by what you say about yourself and your situation. So:

Stop saying bad things about yourself. Don't say them to yourself and don't say them to others. Notice if you are thinking things like "I am just no good at . . . " or "I made a mess of . . . " or "I can never . . . " and then stop thinking or saying it the moment you are aware of it. We all have deficits—a depressed person is not unique that way—and we are all more than our deficits.

Then do something different. It is small and won't take much more energy than stopping, but you have to do it on purpose:

Notice what you appreciate about yourself. In the world of business development, there is a process called "appreciative inquiry." Some companies became roaring successes by following the appreciative-inquiry approach. In the first phase of this business practice for improvement, they do not evaluate their problems. Instead, they look at what they do really well. It seems to me that this has a direct parallel to developing motivation. To pull out of depression, it is not very motivating to look at all of your problems and flaws. It is much more helpful to begin by taking some moments to appreciate only the best in yourself. No matter how depressed you are, there are things about you that are good, and they are part of you, even if, at this very moment, you believe no one else knows about them.

Literally make a list of those things, no matter how small or big, important or seemingly insignificant. Try to list 25 or more things that you appreciate about yourself. (If you find fewer that is okay. You may not have the energy to notice all the good things about yourself—yet.) Think about your character in particular. Some examples of things you appreciate about yourself might include:

- Kindness
- Courage
- Being considerate of others
- Gentleness
- Good cook
- Intelligence
- Work ethic
- Liking to read
- Handy around the house
- Generous

- Good eye for decorating/art
- Enjoying bike-riding
- Good at your job
- Kind to children
- Polite driver
- Following through on what you commit to
- Keeping workspace organized
- Being easy to get along with

As you make your list, be specific and don't worry if you don't seem to be *acting* on all these good qualities. It is not about what you are doing, but rather what qualities you have. Depression pushes memory into what is negative. This step—appreciating yourself—is a departure into the memory of things about you that are *good*. If you are having trouble with this, ask a friend or two to tell you a few things that they think of as your good qualities. Do not listen to that voice in your head that might be saying, "This is not humble." We have all been encouraged to make the most of our talents and abilities and to strive to be of good character. You cannot maximize your potential if you have no idea what your potential is. It is helps motivation to think about your real potential, so first you will want to remember what that potential is.

After you've made the list, carry it with you. Take a moment several times a day to look at the list and to remind yourself that whatever else you might have thought on this day, these things about you are true.

This technique may seem minor, but really it is not. There is a reason this is one of the first methods for extinguishing depression. When you focus on what you appreciate about yourself, *you are constructing a reality in which you are adequate and worthwhile.* The point of this exercise is not to give you "warm fuzzies." It is a significant way to make what is good about you more evident to you and to make this way of your being in the world real. Also, although it takes little effort to do this step, it will help increase your energy. Appreciating what is good is an essential level of motivation. We tend to do what we rehearse in our minds. If you want to have the energy to do good things and fulfill your potential, begin by imagining doing it. This is the start.

Appreciate Yourself

1. Stop saying bad things about yourself.
2. Make a list of what you appreciate about yourself.
3. Carry this list with you.

STOP COMPARING YOURSELF TO OTHERS

One of the problems in depression is getting a clear view of oneself. The negativity of the depressed brain casts a pall over everything, including your self-image. When you're in this negative frame of mind, it can be easy it is to find examples of people who are doing more or better. But this just reinforces your tendency to see yourself as inadequate or worthless. To combat this habit, it is easier, again, to *stop* doing something than to start—to just *stop* comparing yourself to others.

You can't stop comparing yourself to others until you notice you are doing it, and once you notice you are doing it, you will probably realize you are doing it a lot. Many of us in the U.S. immediately focus, for example, on whether others are thinner or fatter or fitter than we are. Some women do this every time they see another woman. Men compare too, but they are often more focused on status: what kind of car the other guy drives, who has the more expensive watch or better job. Adolescents are particularly prone to comparison. They desperately want to be simultaneously unique and seen for who they are while also being enough like everyone else that they are not dismissed by their peers. How depressing these comparisons are!

The pervasiveness of seemingly "perfect people" in the media only makes this tendency to compare even worse. Movies, television programs, magazines, and billboards and other advertisements feature Barbie-doll proportioned women with flawless skin and men with ripped abs and bulging biceps. What you don't see is how much editing and doctoring those images undergo before they are put into print. Photo editors call it "touch up," but in reality it's common to completely replace body parts with more attractive ones, or alter people's bodies in radical ways, such as erasing extra pounds or wrinkles.

If you rely on being "better" than others to feel good about yourself, you are going to feel bad—inadequate, unattractive, worthless—whenever you cannot be on the topside of the comparison. Comparison is a risky way to build self-esteem, because it's unlikely that you are always going to be better than the people you observe. The reality is this: There will always be people who are better looking, wealthier, and more successful than you are. And when you are already depressed, you will only make it worse because you will err on the side of negative assessment, seeing others as better than they are and yourself as less adequate and worthwhile than you are.

To change this habit, make a conscious attempt to interrupt yourself every time you catch yourself making comparisons. Literally stop your thought in your head, or your words as they come out of your mouth, and change the thought to one that does not involve comparison. Instead of "she is so much better-looking than I am," try "she is good-looking." Make it into a simple compliment. If it is a status comparison, try, "Boy, oh boy. He drives a great car. I'd like one like that too." Acknowledge the desire for the status but do not judge yourself for not having it at this time in your life.

After you stop the negative thought, substitute a positive thought about yourself. "I am lucky to be so healthy and strong." "I am grateful to have a good brain." "I don't know what that guy's life is like, so I cannot know if he is happier than I am." Then (a) avoid reading magazines or watching shows that put you into a comparative mode, (b) learn how doctored the photographs in those magazines are, and (c) practice remembering that you are fine as you are.

USE YOUR STRENGTHS

Those two themes of inadequacy and worthlessness that undermine action on one's own behalf are equally evident in looking at your actual strengths and how you are already using them. It is almost always true that depressed people are still functioning in the world, although perhaps not as well as they want to or are able to when feeling good. (It is only in the most severe depressions that people are completely inactive, and if you are that depressed today, you probably do not have the energy to be reading this book!) But your depressed brain makes you focus more on what you *aren't* getting done than on what you *are* doing. To overcome lethargy, it is very important to notice what you are already doing: you are reading, you are doing your job, you are caring for your family—you *are* already doing something!

When people are depressed they sometimes say that their work is the one thing they can keep doing. Of course, needing the income you earn is a powerful motivator to keep working even when you don't really want to. Homemakers often tell me they can force themselves to get up with the kids and get them to school and then they feel their energy flag. Responsibility to others is one aspect of this push to keep moving. However, there is another reason that people keep doing their jobs: We typically use our strengths and talents in our daily work. Doing what we are good at is a motivation booster—it helps us feel worthwhile and adequate at something, even if not in all ways.

Several researchers support this notion. Martin Seligman (2002), who has done considerable work in the area of positive psychology, and Buckingham and Clifton (2001) focused on the component of strengths in a person's wellbeing. Their research indicates that people who do what they are good at feel better about themselves. Csikszentmihalyi (1990) wrote about a phenomenon he called "flow," in which people profit emotionally from experiences in which they feel simultaneously challenged and capable.

What you *do* changes how you *feel* about yourself, and opportunities to do your best give you self-esteem of the most important kind. When you are depressed you may forget that you have strengths that you are using or could use.

Similar to focusing on what you appreciate about yourself, the "use your strengths" method will take you one step farther. In this exercise you will make another list, but this one has a crucial difference: In addition to identifying your strengths, you will also look at when and how you use them, with the intention of increasing your use of those strengths. As you do things that are intrinsically rewarding, you boost your dopamine level and subsequently feel better. And the better you feel, the more you will feel like doing more. That reverses the low motivation of depression.

Begin by drawing a chart, with each of your best strengths listed at the top of each column. Think about *how* you do your work as well as *what* you do in your work. Strengths are not only skills for specific tasks but also the way you do them. For example, you may be great at computer tasks but also patient when showing others how to use a computer program. So you identify strengths both as computer skill and patience. Other examples might include your ability to find just the right word for an ad or flyer *and* being good at how you design the page—so you might identify strengths as "being a wordsmith" and "visually creative." Perhaps your best skill is carpentry, and you are also meticulous in finishing a project. (If you cannot see yourself as having any strengths at all, turn to the "resources for work, abilities, and career" section in the Recommended Reading list at the end of this book. There are suggestions there for websites and books that will help you figure out how to identify strengths in yourself.)

On the far left, list the days of the week on each row.

Now, below the chart, make a list of opportunities to use your strengths: What parts of your daily life allow you to show or use those qualities?

Fill in the chart on a daily basis. Every day, ask yourself: "Did I use my strengths? How?" Figure 4.1 shows an example of a partially filled-out chart. (A blank chart can be found in the Appendix.) If the idea of using your strengths seems overwhelming, just remember that you are not being asked to do much and certainly not to do anything new. You are just tracking some of the many ways you are *already* using your skills.

As you notice and use your strengths, your natural energy will rise and you will have a greater sense of satisfaction with your life on a daily basis. And that is an antidepressant in itself!

Figure 4.1 My Strengths and How I Use Them

	KINDNESS	DISCIPLINE	CURIOSITY	LOYALTY
Monday Used in: work, home, with my girlfriend	*Monday's meeting—I encouraged the new staff member to talk*	*Tired—got my work done*	*Put that shelf together when I did not know how*	*Talked with my girlfriend about her problem*
Tuesday Used in: misc. activities, home, work	*Opened the door for the woman with the baby stroller at the post office*	*Paid bills and balanced checkbook*	*Started reading a new book on the history of the American Revolution*	*Stood up for my coworker when I was talking to my boss*

Opportunities to Use Strengths
At home
At work
With my girlfriend
With my family

Use Your Strengths

1. List your strengths.
2. List the opportunities to use your strengths.
3. Fill out the chart every day.

DELIBERATELY NOTICE WHAT IS GOOD, WHAT IS WORKING RIGHT

In Technique #1, Identify Triggers, we looked at how assessing satisfaction can help you recognize the ways in which depression has interfered with or changed your appraisal of your life. There are ways to improve your overall feeling of satisfaction and thus improve your motivation to take action in your life, because when an activity is satisfying, we automatically want to do it again.

One aspect of feeling satisfied is related to how you feel about the outcome of an activity, and that is highly related to what you remember about the experience. Research by Daniel Kahneman indicates that the *sum total of the experience* is in many ways more important than any moment within the experience in terms of whether it was satisfying to you (Coady et al., 2005). The example of raising children is a great one here. Many of the tasks of childrearing are onerous. I have never met a parent who loved changing diapers, getting up in the middle of the night, going to PTA meetings, never completing a phone call without an interruption from a child, and so on. Yet most people are glad they have their children and consider it both important and fulfilling to raise a family. The same can be said of your work life. Aren't there some tasks that you will never enjoy or that you would never miss if you never did them again? Sometimes it is not the day-to-day work but rather the overall experience of the job that is rewarding. So, to improve satisfaction about an ongoing job or responsibility:

1. Periodically note what you like. Mentally note and write down or say out loud to someone the highlights in your daily, weekly, or monthly review of the task. What parts of this experience are rewarding, fun, challenging, exciting, allow you to use your strengths, put you in contact with stimulating people, or are otherwise pluses?

2. Notice whether the negatives outweigh the positives. In depression it is too easy to notice what you do *not* like, so sort out the negatives. Of course, if you are living in a demeaning, vile, or destructive situation, as can be the case for people suffering from situational depression, you need to take it seriously and get out, but it is more likely that the situation isn't so dramatic. Ask yourself if the negatives are worth putting up with. For example, if you have a great job but have to travel away from your family 4 days of the week, is that worth it? If you are running a volunteer committee and everyone on the committee complains to you about the others, can you

stop the negativity or should you leave? Put your focus only on the negatives that truly affect the quality of your life, and pay less attention to the little, niggling things that could be ignored. If the negatives are only little things, shift your attention to the positives and don't think about the small stuff.

INCREASE CONTACT WITH POSITIVE EXPERIENCES

One of the most unfortunate outcomes of the neurobiology of depression is that it robs people of pleasure. Low on norepinephrine for energy and dopamine for good feelings, and high on pain perception with more aches and pains, depressed people tend to avoid contact with positive experiences. They disengage from doing what they would otherwise have enjoyed. Without pleasure, the downward spiral to a gray experience of life is unimpeded. Low motivation creates inertia and blocks you from moving in a positive direction. Enhancing contact with pleasurable experiences is a vital part of treatment for low motivation.

Awareness that something is positive is the first part of increasing contact with positive experiences. Try the following exercise:

1. Keep track of every activity you do for a few days. I would recommend a week, but that is a lot of energy output for someone with depression!
2. Answer this question for each and every activity: "Was it pleasurable or unpleasurable?" You must pick one. Even if you are inclined to say, "Well, it wasn't *unpleasurable*," the way many a depressed person might answer, the correct answer is "pleasurable."
3. For each pleasurable activity, rate the degree of pleasure from 1 to 10, with 1 being the least amount of pleasure and 10 being the most.

Notice: There is pleasure in your life no matter how depressed you are. You may take pleasure in a morning shower, or in watching your child practice piano, or in getting a hug—all without paying attention to it.

Now it is time to enhance the pleasure that is already part of life. This is not so hard—if taking a morning shower is pleasurable, can it be even more pleasurable if you make it 2 minutes longer, or play music in the bathroom, or add some fancy shower gel? This same technique can apply to meeting a friend for coffee (make sure to order a specialty coffee you enjoy), taking a short walk (notice the color of the sky or the neighbor's flower garden, or remind yourself how many calories you burned), talking to the kids after school (review in your mind your child's smile after the chat is over), and so on. By enhancing the pleasurable things you are already doing, you will boost dopamine and consequently feel even more rewarded. The downward lethargy/low-reward spiral starts to reverse.

Another form of pleasure is one's sense of accomplishment. When you finish a task, a project, or just something simple like doing the dishes, you feel a sense of accomplishment—you feel good about it. But when you are depressed and feeling inadequate or worthless, you may overlook these moments of accomplishment. Paying attention to what you are doing and giving yourself credit for what you do, no matter how small or large, will contradict negative beliefs you have about your worth. To enhance awareness of accomplishment, you can do the same kind of rating exercise:

1. Keep track of every activity you do for a few days.
2. Answer this question for each and every activity: "Did I accomplish anything?" You must answer yes or no. Even if you are inclined to say, "Well, it wasn't *much* of an accomplishment," the correct answer is simply "Yes, I accomplished something."
3. For each item you rank as an accomplishment, rate the degree of accomplishment from 1 to 10, with 1 being the least amount of accomplishment and 10 being the most.

Notice: You are getting things done, even if it's not as much as you'd like to do. Only noticing what you fail to accomplish defeats the antidepressing purpose of boosting motivation.

The next step is to plan more pleasurable and satisfying activities into your life. You may need help to accomplish this from a therapist or a friend, because getting encouragement may be just the boost you need to shift your activity level. Research into behavioral-activation therapy demonstrates that changing your activity to include more stimulating, pleasurable events improves depression from the outside in (Addis & Martell, 2004).

Increase Contact With Positive Experiences

1. Keep track of every activity you do for a few days.
2. For each activity, assess whether it was (a) pleasurable or not and (b) an accomplishment or not.
3. For each pleasurable activity and accomplishment, rate the degree of pleasure or accomplishment.
4. Increase the duration or quality of the pleasurable experiences and notice the accomplishments you are getting done.

Getting motivated is not easy. You want to do more or take action but depression interferes. You know taking action is important, but it is hard to do anything when you feel as if you are inadequate or worthless. But by starting where you already are—stopping some basic negatives and noticing what you are already doing or accomplishing—you will incrementally be able to do a little more. That will develop motivation. If you appreciate yourself, see how your strengths may already be in action, and notice what experiences already stir a sense of pleasure, you make it much easier to move forward when you are ready.

FIVE

Technique #3:

Cool Down Burnout

"I am so burned out!" This is the exclamation of someone who has been doing too much for too long. The phrase means what it sounds like—you have burned all your energy up and you feel depleted. Being burned out is not to be taken lightly. When it becomes your chronic state, you now have burnout—a serious risk for health issues, anxiety, and depression. Burnout is not a diagnostic category in the mental-health literature yet. However, it has been discussed for years in occupational health as an outcome of unremitting overwork and in addiction literature as the outcome of work addiction. Literature on codependency describes mental and physical fatigue and the risks of caretaking for family members with chronic or terminal conditions. The term *burnout* was used by Freudenberger and North (1985) to describe the outcome of persistently caring for others while not caring for oneself. It is also, of course, used colloquially by people who feel they need a job or life change.

WHAT IS BURNOUT?

Burnout is chronic affective state of physical, emotional, and cognitive exhaustion brought on by chronic stress, especially work stress. When the stress response system goes into action, the endocrine system goes into high gear, releasing adrenalin and cortisol, and neurotransmitter activity surges to cope with the demand. The more intense the stressor, the more intense the stress response. Chronic stress is so depleting at every level that it can cause damage to physical health as well as to mental health. It could be called vital exhaustion, because burnout is a predictor of heart disease, type II diabetes, infertility problems, and poor self-rated health, among other risks (Melamed, Shirom, Toker, Berliner, & Shapira, 2006; Toker, Shirom, Shapira, Berliner, & Melamed, 2005).

The outcome of chronic stress makes the meaning of the word *burnout* abundantly clear. Under conditions of chronic stress, the systems meant to be protective for short bursts of extra energy deplete the neurotransmitters you need for a healthy brain, so you run low on serotonin, norepinephrine, and dopamine when you really need them for mental energy, optimism, clarity of thought, and motivation. The excess of cortisol released in the condition of chronic stress also negatively affects physical health, as does the impact of glutamate—too much excitatory activity—at the receptor sites of the neurons, which is considered a potential cause of damage to brain cells (Yehuda, 1997). Death of cells in the hippocampus, where memory and context for new learning are key functions, is one impairment from chronic or traumatic stress. The old-fashioned phrase "nervous exhaustion" paints a good picture. You are irritable and lethargic at the same time, you are not thinking straight about your situation (which seems hopelessly negative anyway), you are distracted, and you lose interest in the activities that would normally please you. Burnout also appears to precede anxiety and depression (Toker et al., 2005).

Health risks rise as the immune system becomes less effective after chronic stress. Studies on burnout and its health impact suggest that levels of C-reactive protein (CRP) rise under acute stress; when CRP is activated repeatedly, as in burnout stress, it remains chronically elevated. CRP is a predictor of cardiovascular disease and stroke. Health takes another kind of hit in burnout because people under stress neglect self-care, often beginning to use too much food, alcohol, and tobacco, all of which diminish wellbeing and increase risks for cardiovascular disease and other conditions.

WHAT DOES BURNOUT LOOK LIKE?

As explained earlier, burnout comes as a result of too much work. By "work" I am not referring solely to one's career or employment, but rather to any activity in life that a person regards as essential. Burnout can affect children, adolescents, and college students, whose "work" is schoolwork, as it can affect homemakers, volunteers, caregivers, and so on.

A sense of desperation to "get everything done" may be the first emotional clue that you are burning out, but this is not necessarily an accurate appraisal of the situation. You *believe* it is true that you *must* get the work done or something bad will happen—even if you don't know what "bad" exactly means.

You probably have noticed that you have less energy when experiencing ongoing stress. Signs that burnout is starting are evident in physical indicators such as:

- A sense of depletion
- Exhaustion that cannot be fixed by one night's sleep
- Inability to restore energy despite a weekend of rest
- The tendency to get sick when a stressful period ends

As this goes on, you show more signs of burnout in your thinking and especially in your behavior as you make attempts to resolve and cope with the stress:

- A compulsion to get work done
- Changes in your personal care (to get more time to work, you may neglect flossing your teeth, sleeping, and exercising, or you may skip dental appointments and physical checkups)
- Smoking, drinking, and overeating (which function as coping mechanisms that contribute to the deterioration of health)

- Decreasing social interactions as work increases (your entire social life becomes the brief greeting of colleagues as you attend one meeting after another or see friends only in one organized activity after another, as children do in nonstop sports, scouts, dance, band, or other extracurricular activities)
- Isolation (you stop wanting to talk to family and friends, trying to grab a little time to recharge; you stay in and alone whenever you are not working or required to be at an organized social event)
- Lack of knowledge or failure to notice what is going on in the lives of others (soon you end up exhausted, isolated, and lonely even though you are constantly busy, and have no fun)
- Depression (which catches up to you when you no longer can fill your mind with work to avoid the empty feelings inside)
- Inability to continue the hectic pace that started the burnout cycle

ARE YOU SHOWING SIGNS THAT BURNOUT IS A PROBLEM IN YOUR LIFE?

You will know you are starting to suffer burnout if you see yourself in the key indicators just listed. Figure 5.1 shows a list of signs I have seen in my overworked clients. Check off ones that apply to you to see if you could be burning out.

Figure 5.2 lists the indicators for children and adolescents.

If you see many of these signs, it is time to assess the causes of your burnout and immediately begin to plot a course correction. You cannot get rid of the depression or any of the other symptoms that go with burnout unless you change the circumstances causing the burnout or change your behavior in response to them.

Figure 5.1 Indicators of Burnout: How Many Do You Have?

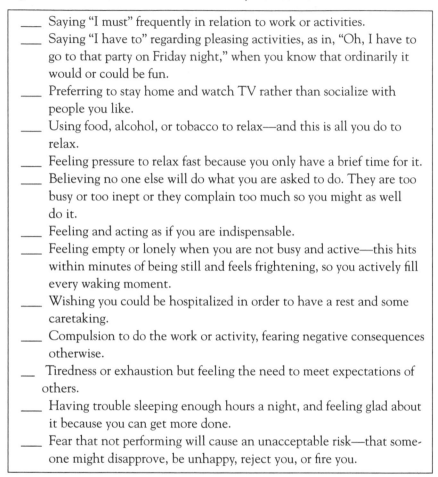

____ Saying "I must" frequently in relation to work or activities.

____ Saying "I have to" regarding pleasing activities, as in, "Oh, I have to go to that party on Friday night," when you know that ordinarily it would or could be fun.

____ Preferring to stay home and watch TV rather than socialize with people you like.

____ Using food, alcohol, or tobacco to relax—and this is all you do to relax.

____ Feeling pressure to relax fast because you only have a brief time for it.

____ Believing no one else will do what you are asked to do. They are too busy or too inept or they complain too much so you might as well do it.

____ Feeling and acting as if you are indispensable.

____ Feeling empty or lonely when you are not busy and active—this hits within minutes of being still and feels frightening, so you actively fill every waking moment.

____ Wishing you could be hospitalized in order to have a rest and some caretaking.

____ Compulsion to do the work or activity, fearing negative consequences otherwise.

____ Tiredness or exhaustion but feeling the need to meet expectations of others.

____ Having trouble sleeping enough hours a night, and feeling glad about it because you can get more done.

____ Fear that not performing will cause an unacceptable risk—that someone might disapprove, be unhappy, reject you, or fire you.

IDENTIFY THE CAUSES OF YOUR BURNOUT

Men, women, and children are all subject to burnout and the depression that stems from it. An important consideration is the objective degree of stress the person experiences. For example, an employee who has to assume the workload of a laid-off colleague may rightly fear also being fired and try to keep up. That is a lot of stress—two jobs' worth of work plus the fear of being fired—if it goes on for more than a few weeks. Over time, months or more, the stress takes a steady toll.

Figure 5.2 Burnout Indicators for Children and Adolescents

If you are a child or teenager, the burnout indicators for adults (see Figure 5.1) may apply to you but you will see them in:

- Doing your schoolwork
- Participation in sports, music, dance, and other extracurricular activities
- Doing more than you want to so peers will like you

Your mood will show it too:

- You may feel anxious, afraid you will fail or disappoint your parents
- You may become inattentive or crabby
- You feel annoyed at times when you change from one activity to another

Your behavior may change:

- You may act impatient or even aggressive when frustrated
- You may turn to substance use to change your emotions or get a mental break from the pressure
- You resist going to activities you normally like

Pressure to perform may cause a person to depend on the adrenalin rush of deadlines to fire up energy. As that pattern intensifies, the urgency of the adrenalin rush will obscure feelings of depression and anxiety that build up under long-term pressure. The adrenalin rush is particularly visible in men and women who work in high-intensity jobs that have deadlines for performance.

Children may end up depressed from a version of burnout that has to do with overstimulation. Our culture promotes a standard of parenting that believes children should be entertained or kept busy nearly every moment of every day with structured, highly stimulating activities and not allowed down time to rest, stoke their imagination, or learn to soothe themselves. Children who are kept busy from the minute they wake up to when they go to bed are not getting essential time for the soothing, rejuvenating, and brain development that occurs when they are allowed to rest, let their minds wander, and entertain themselves without direction. They may be so stimulated that they lose the ability to feel reward over small things and suffer anhedonia, which is the inability to feel pleasure (Hart, 2007).

All you have to do to spot the cause of burnout is make a list: What are you doing or what has happened in your life that you have to cope with? Big changes, even positive ones, cause stress. Taking out a mortgage, having a baby, changing schools or neighborhoods, getting a new job—all are positive and all count as stress. If you want a checklist, the Holmes-Rahe Life Events Rating Scale is available on-line. When you go over your list of stressors, put a star by any that you are currently dealing with so that you can discuss them with a therapist or helper to look for ways to intervene.

Technostress

Everybody gets stressed out by modern technology in one way or another. Figure 5.3 contains some true/false questions, which I created based on my clients' reports of what stresses them out, that will help you know whether you must pay attention to stress related to technology or communication technology. There are too many solutions to technostress to list in this chapter (a whole book would be helpful for that!). Just be aware that you will need to resolve the source of the stress in order to eliminate the burnout from it. The more true answers you give, the more likely it is that you will need a helper to identify and manage the stress of technology.

Once you recognize a number of stressors from life events or technostress, it is time to identify appropriate recovery, relief, or changes of behavior. Many of the ideas suggested in this chapter address recovery from stress in general; however, when it comes to technostress, because there are so many options for what to do, I suggest that you evaluate whether your stress falls into the category of (a) needing more skills-training, (b) needing more self-control, or (c) needing help with setting limits on communication. Then find a trainer or therapist who can help you find good options to relieve the stress.

Figure 5.3 Are You Suffering Technostress? Answer each question as "true" or "false."

T	F	
		Communication Stress
__	__	1. I have had fights with friends about what I said in a text or email message.
__	__	2. I have thrown my phone, iPod, or other technological device in frustration with it.
__	__	3. I have been upset by reading an email only to discover I misunderstood the message.
__	__	4. I have been upset reading an email that was not intended for me.
__	__	5. I have mistakenly sent emails to others and worried about the consequences (such as hit "reply all" by mistake).
__	__	6. I spend more time each day interacting through the Internet than talking directly with people in person.
__	__	7. I get upset over things I read about my friends or me on social-networking sites.
__	__	8. I have broken off a relationship or received a breakup message by text, email, or social-network communication.
__	__	9. I have had fights with friends, my partner, or family members via text-messaging or email.
__	__	10. I am expected to receive messages from work on my personal phone or I am required to carry a phone supplied by the office and answer it at all hours.
__	__	11. I am expected to respond immediately to instant messages, emails, or texts even when doing other work or at home.
		Skills-Related Stress
__	__	12. I get frustrated because I lose time trying to use my computer when I do not know how to do a task on it.
__	__	13. I do not know how to use my computer to communicate (fax, messaging, web cams, etc.) and I believe my work life would be easier if I could.
__	__	14. I have new equipment or software at work that I have not learned how to use and it interferes with completing my work in a timely way.

(*continued*)

Figure 5.3 Continued

T   F

___ ___   15. My office does not offer training for the software I am expected to use or the training is inadequate to teach me what I need to know.

Impulse-Control Stress

___ ___   16. I have gotten into trouble for the websites I visit on a work computer.

___ ___   17. I lose money gambling on-line.

___ ___   18. I visit pornography sites when it is inappropriate to my location or my relationships.

___ ___   19. I spend too much money shopping on-line.

___ ___   20. I lose hours of time browsing the web when I should be doing other things.

___ ___   21. I have been embarrassed by things I posted on the Internet and then wished I could take back.

___ ___   22. I have responded too fast to a message without thinking about how someone might take it, and the relationship suffered because of it.

___ ___   23. I got angry about a message and fired one back only to discover the other person did not mean what I thought.

___ ___   24. I have texted a person hoping to embarrass that person when he or she read the message or hoping the wrong person would see it.

___ ___   25. I have gotten into trouble for inappropriate text-messaging (which could include cheating, "sext-messaging," sending hostile messages, or texting at inappropriate times, as in middle of the night).

ASSESS THE INTENSITY OF YOUR BURNOUT

There are identifiable behavior patterns in burnout that precede the onset of mental-health and physical-health problems. Behavior that results in burnout tends to be compulsive, and it progresses in stages. One can see this similar progression in the development of an addiction, whether it is to a substance or to an activity like gambling or sex. It starts out with an attempt to diminish stress by doing something extra but manageable, like "I will just work this one weekend to get caught up." But such a solution rarely relieves the problem of too much work to do. You can see this in homemakers or caretakers trying to get caught up with duties in order to get a break from responsibility. The problem becomes a cycle of working too much, feeling tired, and needing to even work harder and faster to get the time to stop working and rest. One cannot solve the problem of overwork with more work.

The subrogation of personal needs to the needs of others is a pattern of behavior typical of people with burnout, and it is also evident in people with codependency and certain personality traits such as dependent personality. If you do this you may be trying to meet another person's needs in order to get your own needs met. Or, in other words, "If I take care of you until you are filled up, then you will have enough to take care of me." You might function like this whether you are relating to people at work, to your parents or your children, or your partner. Of course, trying to fill others never works, because any person who is willing to take so much from you is not going to give much back. Such self-deprivations become more intense and more compulsive over time. The more deprived and exhausted you become, the less able you will be to think clearly and change your behavior before your burnout causes depression.

You may want to rate your burnout intensity simply on a scale of 1 to 10, with 10 putting you into medical care for your physical or mental health. Figure 5.4 lists some statements that correspond with increasing intensities of burnout. Remember that "work" can include caretaking, schoolwork, maintaining a household, and so on.

Why You Need Help to Know If You Are Burned Out

The more burned out you are, the less able you are to see what you are doing. Unfortunately, denial of your situation makes it more likely that you will keep on doing what you are doing—heading for a fall. You may

Figure 5.4 Statements That Reflect the Intensity of Burnout

1 – I am working more than I want to and skipping things I enjoy to get it done.

2 – I cannot take a day off without falling too far behind.

3 – I don't have time to plan or prepare for a break, or I don't want to take a break from my work because there would be even more to do when I return.

4 – I am tired all the time.

5 – I could use a week in a hospital or a health spa to rest and be taken care of, but I feel like I can't go. If I ever get out of this mess I will start exercising again, but right now exercising takes more time than I have available.

6 – My best fun is being home alone with a drink and takeout food.

7 – I feel anxious and depressed all the time, and not even drinking, eating, or smoking is relieving the stress. My friends might be able to cheer me up, but I am too crabby to want to see anyone, much less talk with someone about how I feel.

8 – I am constantly getting sick (or my chronic illness, e.g., diabetes, is not controlled).

9 – I feel like if something doesn't change soon, I am going to die of exhaustion. And I wouldn't even care.

10 – Friends and family express serious worry or are angry at my mood and workload, but they don't know how hard I am working to keep them happy—and I don't even like them, or anyone, anymore.

need a therapist or a loving friend to help you look at your pattern honestly. Workaholics Anonymous meetings are also a great resource. Denial is a state in which you lie to yourself about your behavior or about the consequences of your actions, *without knowing you are doing it*. When you are burning out, the big lies you tell yourself are:

- "I will stop doing this soon."
- "I am the only one who can do this. I am indispensable."
- "I can't stop now."

If you are a competent person who is burning out, you may not want to know it. It is frightening to feel helpless or to think you cannot handle your situation. It may not fit with your idea of yourself, and you criticize yourself for being "weak," "incompetent," or a "failure"—which makes it even harder to change course. Ask yourself this: "If I were suddenly not able to do this—if I got sick or even died—what would happen?" It will behoove you to remember that cemeteries are filled with indispensable people.

You may also be unable to see *how* to change. Most of us see the stress we are under but feel we have no control over it. You may admit you are under too much stress but believe you have no choice but to handle it. In fact, you may believe you have no choice about how you behave in order to get your work done. People with good coping skills and high degrees of capability often fall into burnout because they *believe* they can handle anything—until suddenly they cannot. Someone else's point of view can help you to figure this out and to spot ways to start the process. If you are helping someone identify and stop burnout, remember that the person may not see it. Make sure that you note the signs of burnout in Figures 5.1–5.4 as a way to refute denial in yourself or another.

CHANGE A PATTERN

When people are depressed from burnout, they are unable to decide where to start reducing their stress or may not even be able to recognize a possible change. They may not feel the motivation to change, even though they know something has to give. The first step is to enlist some help.

Get a Burnout Buddy

This is essential. You need someone to help you select the changes you start to make and also monitor your progress in completing them. Pick someone who fully supports your effort to change, but who also supports your work. You want to know that the person understands your goals and the reality of the work you have to do. That will help the two of you select where and how you can make changes that will reduce your stress and start to cool down your burnout. Do not, however, expect this person to hound you, do it for you, or cheerlead. You are responsible for making the changes. The other person is just there to help you see yourself as others see you and to help you be accountable by accepting your reports.

People benefit from helpers. Mothers with newborns have less depression when they have support from experienced moms helping them adjust. Likewise, peer support helps people recover from posttraumatic stress (Yehuda, Golier, Halligan, Meaney, & Bierer, 2004) and the research of Shelly Taylor (2002) on the "tend and befriend" instinct demonstrates that people suffer less stress when they support each other going through difficulties. The idea that we are not alone goes a long way to decrease stress. And that is a great benefit to you if you are burning out and want to stop the process.

Choosing a Burnout Buddy

Consider the following questions:

- To whom will you be accountable for your actions with regard to changes you decide to make?
- Who will provide information on appropriate changes, such as nutritional information or healthcare professionals to see?
- With whom will you evaluate your progress?
- With whom will you process your reactions and the emotions you feel when you make the change? If you work less, you will have an emotion about it! This might be a reason to consult a therapist who can spot these issues. For example, if you feel pride in being able to refrain from eating for a day while you finish a work project, not wanting to give up that bit of pride could be an obstacle to establishing a healthy eating pattern.

The Workaholics Anonymous program can be a good choice for people who do not have the kind of family or friendship situation from which they can draw a person to help them. These meetings are available across the country. If excessive drinking or other addictions figure into your burnout, you can get support about how to manage them from your group and your sponsor. This is equally true for people who are in codependency with someone who has an addiction. See the Recommended Reading and Resources section for a way to contact 12-step self-help programs.

MAKE A SELF-CARE CHECKLIST AND FOLLOW IT

People with a compulsion to keep working may neglect their personal care. The most obvious kind of neglect starts with eating fast food instead of meals prepared at home, eating in the car while driving to save time, or skipping meals. A leading cause of obesity is eating food from a bag while driving. You eat high-fat, high-calorie food too fast to notice when your stomach is full enough. You skip the pleasure of noticing the taste of the food and there is certainly no visual pleasure from the presentation of the food, nor anticipation from the delicious aroma of food cooking in a kitchen. That is depressing all by itself!

However, there are many other ways to neglect your care, some of which are listed in Figure 5.5. Check off what you need to do and at what interval (I have suggested some intervals for you to consider), adding any self-care items that pertain to you personally. Then follow the list.

Sleep and Self-Care

Sleep provides recovery from stress if you can get the sleep, but if you have burnout, you may have trouble falling asleep, as your mind is spinning from work or you hop into bed without any transition. You may

Figure 5.5 Self-Care Checklist

Self-Care Need	Interval for Doing It	Check/Tally
Eat nutritious meals sitting at a table	At least one time per day	
Brush teeth	Twice a day	
Floss teeth	Once a day	
Aerobic exercise	Start where you can—minimum 3x/week and build to 5x/week, 25–45 min per time	
Dental checkup	2x/year—schedule it now!	
Eye checkup	Depends on your age and eye condition	
Physical checkup	Annually or biannually—schedule it now!	
Haircuts	Your discretion	
Monitor blood pressure	Are you following doctor's orders?	
Monitor blood sugar	Are you paying attention to this?	
Medications	Are you taking them as prescribed? Do you need a doctor's visit to renew a prescription?	
Flu shots, vaccinations	Are you taking these at the right times?	

awaken early, think about your work, and get up to get started. You cheat yourself on both ends of a night's sleep, which makes the onset of depression come on even faster. Sleep researcher Michael Perlis (Alspaugh, 2009; Perlis, Smith, & Jungquist, 2005) has reported that insomnia may trigger the depression. The question is whether the insomnia triggers the depression or is part of the brain's effort to fight against it. Several factors are involved.

Sleep is the way the brain tries to let go of painful memories. The depressed sleep pattern shows a pressure to get into REM, which is unusual both in duration and intensity. This is problematic, although the impact is not entirely clear. In sleep we consolidate memory, and REM is particularly important to emotional memory. It may be that people with depression are consolidating too much of the negative experience they are having, making them too prone to remember it. Another interesting hypothesis about why sleep architecture may get so disrupted prior to a depression episode is that sleep disruption may be the brain's attempt to raise serotonin. Extended wakefulness promotes functioning in the serotonin system and may also cause release of dopamine, so that not sleeping has an antidepressant effect.

The insomnia might also be an attempt by the brain to dampen the hyperarousal of the chronically elevated stress response. And there may be an interdependent link between depression and insomnia. When serotonin levels are low, as is typical in depression, the production of melatonin by the pineal gland can also be disrupted. That is the mechanism that governs getting drowsy and reawakening and is linked to daylight and nightfall.

Eventually, the sleep disturbance is problematic enough to leave you exhausted, and in that condition people are irritable and have problems with low energy and attention. It brings on the physical conditions that are hallmarks of depression. Furthermore, an exhausted person cannot get over depression, so attention to improving sleep must be a part of recovery from depression. Although there is a lot still to understand about the interrelationship between burnout, sleep disturbance, and depression, it is clear that sleep has a lot to do with handling your stress and minimizing burnout.

Setting a Pattern of Sufficient Sleep

People find it easier to fall asleep, stay asleep, and wake up rested when they are regular about the times they sleep. Sleep is part of the rhythm of the body, governed by the pineal gland, melatonin secretion, and circadian rhythm. Whether the depressed brain is forced out of its rhythm by neurobiology or by caffeine ingestion to fight low energy or by burnout when people stay up too late, those rhythms are disrupted and are hard to reestablish. Here is how to get back on track. Pay attention to how you handle evening activities, long before your actual bedtime, so you have enough time to calm your stressed mind, and then go to sleep and get out of bed at the same time every day. This will take a while to work, so keep at it and try not to be discouraged by trouble falling asleep or trouble waking up initially. Even on days off, try not to vary your sleep schedule by more than an hour.

Another aspect of sufficient sleep is making time for it. People in the U.S. seem to be of the opinion that sleeping is a sign of weakness, but most adults need 7 to 8 hours, adolescents need 9 to 10 hours, and children need more hours depending on their age. To start getting enough sleep, you have to go to bed early enough to stay in bed for a full 8 hours, even if you wake sooner than that for a while. Until you can sleep for 8 hours, you should plan to stay in bed and rest while practicing the sleep hygiene methods that will eventually help you fall asleep and stay asleep. When you are sleeping on a regular schedule, and fairly well, you will find that you awaken when you are rested, and you will discover exactly how much your sleep your body needs to feel restored.

Adolescents and Sleep

Adolescents are in a special category regarding their circadian rhythms. Biologically, they may not be ready for sleep until midnight (unless exhausted) and not ready to awaken until 9. School is at exactly the wrong time for the adolescent body! Adolescents will have to decide how to accommodate this problem, but most can sleep by 10 P.M. A bigger problem is establishing time limits on using the computer, phone, or playing video games in the evening in order to finish homework and school activities in time to sleep.

The Elderly and Sleep

Even though we may need less sleep as we age, there is great variability among older adults about what they need. The biggest key to knowing if a person is sleeping enough is to assess their daytime drowsiness. Older adults should feel alert and energetic enough to do daily activities, perhaps with the help of a midday nap. But sleep problems can interfere. Elderly people may sleep more restlessly for several reasons, including the need to use the bathroom or brains that no longer produce sufficient melatonin. Many older adults live in environments that may be too noisy or too light. Look at how environmental and lifestyle components can be made more conducive to sleep, and see if health will permit a trial of supplements to calm the brain or produce melatonin before using medications that promote sleep.

Helping the Depressed Brain
to Sleep Better

First address the environment where you sleep. Although a quiet room without TV or lights is generally better, many people say they *need* light or noise (like TV or radio) to fall asleep. It may be a good idea to look at your environment when considering how to address that habit. The amygdala functions in sleep as in waking, staying alert to warning signals that danger might be near. It responds to *variances* in sound, smell, and so on, waking the brain up when it notices a change. Screening out environmental noises (like people talking in another room or noise from the street) is very important to eliminating the amygdala's response to variation in the noise. When people live in urban environments or apartments where noises from outside are unpredictable, having a consistent noise that dulls down the impact of outside noise makes it easier to stay asleep. White noise blocks environment sounds, which, though not dangerous, still keep causing the brain to go on alert. If someone *must* use TV to fall asleep, remember most televisions have sleep timers.

Set the timer and then have a white-noise background to block environmental sounds.

You can improve sleep onset and quality by following these rules:

- Eliminate violent or exciting TV for several hours before sleep—that means even skipping late-night news! Television news comes complete with amygdala-jarring music, unexpected and often gruesome visuals, and overexcited voices. Its *sole purpose* is to keep people watching for *fear* of missing something important.
- Stop using the computer at least an hour before sleep. The light from the screen stimulates your wakefulness.
- Take a warm bath for 20 minutes before sleep. It relaxes tight muscles and stimulates oxytocin, a hormone that soothes.
- The brain heals itself from stress and rebuilds itself best during sleep. But it needs nutrition, too. People help their brains build cells when they eat well during the day and then have a *small* high-carbohydrate snack before sleep. That helps the brain to have the insulin and blood-sugar levels necessary to use proteins and nutrients that build neurotransmitters during sleep. (For additional help in this area, see the "the brain and methods to work with it" section in the Recommended Reading and Resources list for the work of Amen & Routh, and the "nutrition and supplements" section for the work of Brown, Gerbarg, & Muskin and DesMaisons & Weil.)
- Sleep in a room that is cool and as dark as possible. This helps establish a good circadian rhythm that will promote sleep on a regular cycle.
- Create a drowsy brain with herbal teas such as catnip or chamomile. To get the full benefit of the herb, steep the tea in boiling water for 5 to 10 minutes.
- Keep caffeine as low as possible, especially after noon, because it is a stimulant.

Sleep Hygiene

1. Set a pattern of regular times to sleep and awaken.
2. Make sure there are sufficient hours to be asleep.
3. Create an environment for good sleep, including a dark, quiet room.
4. Calm the brain down before sleeping, using quiet activities, baths, herbal teas, and so on.

IDENTIFY WHAT GIVES YOU ENERGY

It is important to assess what gives you energy versus what depletes you. Feeling vigorous and full of vim can take you far in accomplishing great tasks. Melamed and Shirom (2005) devised a rating scale for assessing vigor as well as burnout, and I have included it with their permission in the Appendix. However, you can assess vigor with a simple visual that illustrates what gives you energy and into what activities you send your energy (Figure 5.6). This immediately shows where you can eliminate outflow and where you must boost inflow.

Your energy is like a river collecting water from many springs and tributaries that flow into it. Make a list of the sources of your energy or write them on the drawing shown in Figure 5.6. It is also important to look at the major points of outflow. Like a river forming a delta as it flows outward, your energy spreads out, depositing itself into various activities. Note not only your major outgo (work or raising children) but also the little things like paying bills for the family or any activities you do regularly, like taking a child for allergy shots.

Now figure out if you can add some inflow positives if you do not have enough of them. This is another part of changing your usual pattern. Things that give you energy do not need to be lengthy, but they should be done with your full attention—that way you can get a lot in return for just a little energy. These inflow sources might include activities such as:

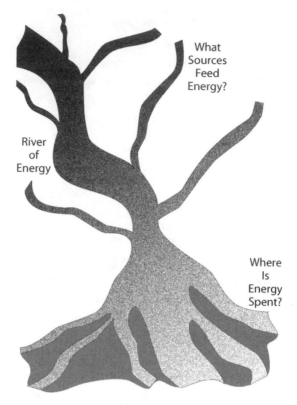

Figure 5.6 Your Energy Flow: What Supplies It and Where Does It Go?

- 10 minutes in the morning reading something inspirational
- Eating a little breakfast and doing nothing else but noticing it
- 15 minutes with the morning paper completely without other stimulation
- Leaving work for lunch break—even if it is just a 15-minute walk outside and a snack
- Walking outside for some time every day (dog walkers always get this energizer)
- Talking on the phone with someone you love (voice-to-voice is much more energizing than email—just keep it short enough to feel good and not drained)

106

- Watching a sports game with a friend or meeting a friend to chat over coffee

Then look for energy outflows you may be able to cut back, remembering that all those little things add up. For example, arrange a car pool instead of driving your child to soccer practice every day.

The good thing about diagramming energy outflow and inflow is that you can easily see if there is an imbalance and figure out how to begin correcting it. You can also use this visual for single aspects of your life, such as work if you have a job with many tasks.

Harold fit every description of burnout ever made. He worked 80 to 100 hours a week, and when he was not at his job he was working on his house or chauffeuring children to activities. When we assessed his outflow it was like a rushing river; his inflow was a mere trickle—limited to an hour of church each week followed by lunch all alone with no one bothering him. His idea of a perfect future was living a life where "no one would yell at him." When I asked what activities he thought were fun, he literally could not think of an answer. It was clear that he needed to first stem the flow of energy going out. After completing an intensive outpatient treatment for depression, Harold agreed to leave his office by 6 P.M. each evening (even though he could not imagine what he would do with all those hours at home and needed to make a list of possibilities to feel less alarmed about having free time). Then his recovery started with basics like taking a required lunch break, eating meals that included vegetables, taking vitamins, and sleeping. Only after that became habitual could he start to think of small activities he enjoyed: reading a magazine unrelated to his profession, seeing a movie in a theater instead of on TV, and so on. Gradually he was able to reverse his burnout pattern.

LEARN TO SET BOUNDARIES

Setting boundaries is a concept that puzzles some people. If you are one of them, think about whether this statement makes sense: *An exhausted person has nothing to give.* The implication here is that you have to keep something for yourself. The boundary is where you stop giving and start holding on to what you need to stay healthy. You might need to hold on to your energy, your time, your thoughts, your creativity, or other things people want from you that you *could* give but choose not to at this very moment.

People who are caretakers of chronically ill or elderly parents may have real trouble seeing how they can *not* do something for that person, and they may refuse to accept help from family, friends, church members, or professionals such as hospice workers. They believe they should wait "until they really need it." My response to this common comment is: "You need help before you *really* need help." If you wait until the point where you cannot do any more, you create an emergency.

If you are depressed, you may actually unconsciously crave emergencies because they boost your energy enough to make you feel alive and able to respond. You may not recognize it or want to admit it, but in these cases you get a perverse benefit when bad things happen—an emotional and physical charge from coping with an emergency. If this sounds like you, it's a good indication that you are suffering from burnout. A much better way of dealing with the situation is to address the core burnout and depression rather than relying on the "quick fix" of the emergency to boost your energy level.

The need to set boundaries can show up in many areas. Following are some key areas where boundary problems can appear and some ideas for addressing them.

At work. Work is a major outgo of energy flow, no matter what kind of work it is. It is important to set boundaries regarding your work hours. How many hours will you work per day/week/month/year? Establish maximums that you will *not* exceed, and decide how many days of vacation you will take every year without doing any work on those days.

Also consider boundaries related to accepting work duties or roles: Who will help you establish the priorities? To whom will you be accountable? For every work-related request, ask yourself, "How important is it?" You may need to differentiate an "urgent" request from an "important" request. Some important things can be done later whereas some are urgent; some "urgent" requests are not important. Some people respond to urgency with an energy surge but waste essential time needed for important tasks. Then they end up working longer to get the important things done. Once you've asked yourself how important the request is, ask others if they have a similar view of the importance and urgency of the job you are about to agree to do.

Similarly, notice the extent to which you use your cell phone to stay connected to work. Do you interrupt activities, such as dinner with a friend or driving the kids to school, to take work calls or messages? Set a boundary. Decide whether you are working or not working, and do not use your communication devices when you are off work—it will make the off-work times feel like more of a break. You may need to have a personal phone if you need to stay connected to family. It would be worth it.

Interpersonal relationships. Even friendships can end up being more draining than fulfilling in some cases. I once had a client who was very charismatic and gregarious—the type of person people naturally gravitated toward. Not wanting to disappoint anyone in her wide circle of friends, she packed her calendar so full of social engagements that she had no down time for herself and became severely burnt out. Another client, a college student, prided herself on being a loyal friend who could "always be counted on to help out." She soon found herself overwhelmed with requests to help friends with school projects, help them move into new apartments or dorm rooms, provide a sympathetic ear when they were having problems with parents or boyfriends, and so on. She gave so much time that her sleep and study were both disrupted. I did not see her until she had lost her scholarship because of poor grades and poor class attendance due to exhaustion: She was depressed for many good reasons!

Many times people who are burned out get that way by allowing others to take advantage of them. They get pushed into doing more and more when someone shames them or bullies them into it. This could be a husband complaining, without any consideration for his wife's tasks of childcare, "Can't you keep this place cleaner? If I have to work, then you should have time to clean up." There are many situations in which that kind of manipulation or outright demand comes complete with swearing, demeaning, or threatening, and you may have become too depressed to push back.

Creating a boundary in these situations requires learning how to say no to unreasonable demands and planning strategies to end conversations in which others are berating you, swearing at you, or shaming you. Learn to say, "I cannot continue this conversation right now. I will talk to you about it later." Plan strategies for walking away and also for returning. Think through the situations in which these strategies will be employed (on the phone or in person) and visualize doing them with:

- Family members, including your partner
- Friends
- Clients
- Coworkers

It's also important to set boundaries around accepting requests for your time and energy. It is a sign of burnout when you start to "double schedule" your time, hoping to figure out the conflict later. Never say yes immediately to any request (while you are learning to say no). Only and always say, "I will get back to you." You may give a time, such as: "I will get back to you within the hour." Then consult your calendar, your recovery plan, and your burnout buddy if you are in doubt about whether to take on the new task.

Parenting. How is your way of living as a parent a potential reflection of "workaholism" that could use some boundaries? For example, do your children's activities dictate your schedule and consume every moment of waking time they are not in school? Remember that children won't suffer forever if you say no, and they may benefit enormously if you do. Also, because you cannot easily walk away from the house or the children, set some boundaries around time for your self-care, such as exercise, and don't give up that time to bake cookies at the last minute or drive a child to the store for a forgotten item. You may also want to con-sider parenting classes to help with setting boundaries.

Leisure time. Sometimes people do not keep a boundary around time for pleasure. It just drifts away with the press of business. You might even find yourself irritable about taking time to do social activities. If this is the case, begin by protecting small amounts of time for leisure or plea-sure so that you can build a tolerance for "sitting around." That may sound odd, but knowing what to do with leisure time is scary at first. If your time is uncommitted for too long, fear or anger can sweep in, and you can easily retreat into work for safety. Try planning for leisure time in this way:

- Make "play dates" with your children—let them give you ideas for what to do.
- Make "play dates" with your partner to do short, fun activi-ties, and include other adults at times.
- Make "play dates" with friends to do things that you both consider fun: see a play, go to a game, get your nails done to-gether, and so on.
- Schedule times to do something relaxing and enjoyable by yourself, such as going for a walk, taking a bath, or reading a magazine. How much time you spend on solo activities, how-ever, should depend on your individual circumstances and your level of burnout, as isolation can be a major contributor to depression. If you are in the extreme, "empty-feeling" stages of burnout, or if your burnout has led you to withdraw from other people, be careful not to spend too much time alone. If, on the other hand, your days are packed with social and work- or family-related engagements, it is wise to take a break for a little alone time.

Gift-giving. Giving and receiving gifts is an arena in which some people have very poor boundaries. They habitually spend too much or are stingy because they are so overwhelmed that they don't think of others. Others who are self-depriving continue to give to those who do not reciprocate and that reinforces feelings of worthlessness. If this is an area in which you have poor boundaries, plan the amount of money you have available to spend and do not spend more, and explore your emotions about giving and receiving gifts with your burnout buddy.

Regardless of what area of life it is in—at work, at home, with family or friends—setting a boundary is not the same as yelling about something or declaring, "This has got to stop!" First put a boundary around your anger. Keep your expression of anger to yourself until you know why you are mad and what you want to change. Never yell about something or make a demand if you haven't figured out what you will do if that demand isn't met. For example, if you are angry with a coworker who continually neglects to answer email that affects your work, ask yourself, before you explode in an angry tirade: "What exactly am I angry about? What will I do if he continues to be nonresponsive even after I've asked him to do better?" Similarly, if your children persistently fail to clean up after themselves, leaving dirty dishes and clothes everywhere until you pick up, plan a consequence, such as losing their favorite video game for a week. Warn them once and then follow through with the consequence. In other words, have a plan about how you will respond if your request isn't honored, be prepared to stick to it, and don't express your anger until you've figured these issues out.

The effort you put into identifying problems with boundaries and gradually correcting them one at a time will pay off in reducing your stress from daily life and creating a more balanced, pleasurable life—the antithesis of depression.

INCREASE PHYSICAL CONTACT

Increasing physical touch and affection is another good way of combating burnout. Physical touch stimulates the flow of oxytocin, a neurochemical that helps you feel calm and soothed. Sexual activity or physical closeness with a partner is just one form of oxytocin-producing touch. The neurochemical is also produced by nonsexual contact and affection, such as hugs with children or friends, getting a professional massage, playing with or patting a pet dog or cat, and even swimming.

IMPLEMENTING STRATEGIES TO ALLEVIATE BURNOUT

The problem with alleviating burnout when you are deep into it is that every small change to help seems like it will cost energy you do not have. The changes you put into place therefore should be things that are small enough to imagine but big enough to make a difference either in your attitude or in your energy. Take Rita, for example. After receiving a bad evaluation at work, she was sure it was a trumped-up evaluation in preparation to fire her. She knew she was at the high end of the pay scale and that administrators wanted to replace her with a younger, less expensive employee. Then she was given a new job assignment that required learning a very demanding software program—on top of the work she was already expected to do. Terrified she would be fired, Rita began working 12- to 14-hour days without breaks and putting in time on weekends trying to get all the work done. She gave up social time, stopped working out, began to gain weight (very unusual for her), and got behind on house and yard work. Frazzled, frustrated, and exhausted, she kept putting one foot in front of the other as if she had blinders on.

Rita came to therapy when she felt very depressed and started having panic attacks. As we worked on her mood and her panic, we examined the stress she was under and evaluated whether she could change how she responded at work. It helped her enormously to see that there was no way to respond differently and the best solution was to look for another job while simply doing the best she could with the time she had available in a normal workday. Although it created some tension for her at first to worry about getting fired, she reminded herself that she had enough savings to be able to cover her living expenses for several months if they did fire her, and she might also be able to get unemployment. Although dipping into savings wasn't an ideal option, it was much better than dying from stress! Rita eventually found another job that was not nearly as interesting but far less stressful, so she changed jobs and gave herself a year to rest and recuperate before deciding if she wanted to look for a more challenging position. She needed to change her situation before she could really stop the burnout.

Jonas was in a worse predicament. His wife had cancer and they had not caught it early. There was very little hope that she would go into remission, but they wanted to do all that was possible to treat her. The two of them lived far from their children, who had busy lives of their own. Jonas took on responsibility for taking care of his wife and their home; his commitment, he said, was not to force her into the sterile atmosphere of the hospital for treatment. This meant driving her to the clinic for chemotherapy and doctor's appointments of various kinds, in addition to keeping up with work at his job and cooking, cleaning, and doing chores at home. Jonas had used most of his personal days at work to handle the doctor's appointments, not wanting to use family leave in case they needed it later.

Though all of these were tasks he was willing to do, Jonas was completely worn out, and adding to stress was the emotional storm of possibly losing his wife. He had given up all the things he previously did for self-care and pleasure, and was barely sleeping, eating poorly, exhausted, and very hopeless. But he did not want his wife to see him getting worn down. He wanted help to cover up his symptoms and maybe even get rid of them so he could keep up the work.

Jonas was clearly burned out, but his situation could not be changed. He needed instead to respond differently to it. "I just need to buck up and do what needs to be done" was his plaintive statement. The first thing we discussed was who could help. Because they had been nominal members in a church, he agreed to call the church and ask about volunteer assistance. He found there was a team of people who were willing to be available to drive his wife to appointments so he could stop using up his personal days at work. He found that this was good for his wife, too, because she had been feeling guilty about his carrying the burden. We discussed why he had not asked his children to help out, and he reluctantly called them to ask them to visit. To his surprise, they were glad to know there was something practical they could do, and they arranged some short visits to keep their mother company. These visits also gave Jonas a chance have conversations that were not all about illness but also about the fun parts of family life. His isolation had taken a toll that he had not recognized until the house was filled with lively people whom he loved.

Jonas was also able to discuss the situation with his wife. When he finally talked with her about it, he discovered that she worried about ruining his health, which of course was not helping her to feel better. Jonas had never considered that his wife might benefit if he were in better shape emotionally and physically. So he agreed to get outside and moving, and he began bike-riding on the weekends again.

Once he broke through his rigid idea that all the responsibility was his alone, Jonas was able to make changes in how he was dealing with this essentially unchangeable situation, and the cumulative effect of these changes shifted the balance of his burnout. His depression lifted, his health improved, and he was able to continue what would be a long period of providing care.

Cooling down burnout is a process that takes time. Making behavior changes isn't easy, but it will reduce your stress, diminish your exhaustion, and consequently help lift you out of depression. The hardest part is to pick small changes that you can succeed at doing and sustain over time. If you can do that, you will reverse the burnout process in a reliable way and learn how to prevent it from happening in the future.

SIX

Technique #4:

Mobilize Your Energy

One of my clients who was getting better but was not out of the woods with depression described what she called "depression dips," meaning that she would wake up some mornings feeling too sapped of energy to get out of bed. The only thing that mobilized her to get herself up was the knowledge that she would later be glad she got up and went to work (because it would mean she was still employed). Like so many people with depression, she needed ways to mobilize action when depression dragged her down.

In most types of depression, the lack of physical energy and not feeling excited about anything can make you feel immobile. Your response can range from dragging yourself through your day to actually not doing anything you know you ought to do. This problem is typical for people with endogenous depression or who are in the exhausted phase of situational depression. When immobilized, you probably think or even say out loud, "What's the use?" regarding any suggestion to try something. The feeling of hopelessness can ooze out of you. Even things that used to be interesting or fun or rewarding just do not seem worth the effort. You may stop doing the very things you *know* would make you feel better. What you lack is the energy to get started.

The neurobiology of depression—particularly the low levels of serotonin and dopamine in the basal ganglia and the prefrontal cortex—

causes low energy, the feeling of being physically "sick," and not getting a kick out of life. The interplay between low energy and not taking action results in a downward spiral in which emotional lows are made worse by physical lows. The less you do when you are depressed, the less you *will* do. Reversing that spiral is one of the first things to do in depression. Changing your thoughts and changing your behavior will have an immediate effect because both thought and movement stimulate the brain. If you can start thinking there might be hope, it moves you mentally, and if you can get your body moving, you will see surprising gains in improving depression.

When you feel immobilized it is a good time to enlist the help of others in reversing the downward spiral. Although you can turn to family, sometimes partners or parents don't react well to their depressed family member, especially if the depression has lasted a while. Family members react to your hopelessness. They might turn it against themselves or you, thinking you don't believe they are worth living for, or they might turn against you, angry at your helplessness when they know you are a competent person. They may throw their hands up in frustration (literally or metaphorically) when you don't get moving. You may work better with a therapist or counselor who will not take your depression personally. Besides, those of us in clinical practice are taught early in training not to throw our hands up in frustration! A therapist can see your immobilization and listen to your feeling helplessness while helping you ease into changes that will raise your physical and emotional energy. The point is that you may well need a jump start from someone else's energy, from their insight or encouragement. If you do not work with a therapist, by all means ask a friend or family member who is able to encourage you so you can use that person's external energy to help you overcome your lethargy.

Regardless of whether you tackle this on your own or get guidance and encouragement from others when feeling depressed, it is wise to *mobilize*. The following ideas are like many in this book: simple, but not easy! But simply attempting them will help you start to feel more optimistic about changing your depression.

117

TURN "I CAN'T" INTO "I WON'T"

You may want some help with this method, which will require confronting your own helpless attitude. Whether you are talking to yourself or someone is helping you, please remember: Confronting someone who feels helpless might seem unsympathetic, but if that person cannot mobilize, the most sympathetic thing anyone can do is to help him or her get moving. Being lethargic or sluggish, as people often are when depressed, is a miserable state, and it's even harder if you feel as if you have no power to change.

At many points in this book I discuss the impact of language on mood, thought, and action. Using negative language when you talk to yourself, especially when you tell yourself you are helpless and the situation is hopeless, will block any action you might consider. When you listen to the voice of a depressed person you will hear "I can't" quite often. Beginning the process of mobilizing is as simple as replacing the phrase "I can't" with "I won't." And I mean this literally and suggest doing it out loud!

- "I can't get up in the morning" becomes "I won't get up in the morning."
- "I can't feel enthusiastic" becomes "I won't feel enthusiastic."
- "I can't do my homework" becomes "I won't do my homework."
- "I can't make myself look for a job" becomes "I won't make myself look for a job."
- "I can't do the dishes" becomes "I won't do the dishes."

Try these out loud as you read just to see how different they feel to you as you say them. The point of saying it out loud is to create a feeling of power and choice. When you say "I won't" instead of "I can't," what you are really saying is: "My *actions and thoughts are in my own control.*" That is what the "I won't" is all about.

This is a small change with a big result. Even though the lethargy of depression is real and the physical aches are undeniable, people with depression *can* move. They just don't. Saying "I won't" is a way to get your brain to hear "I *could*," and this increases the ability to move. Changing the language mobilizes you, because your brain believes what you say to it. Saying "I won't" is acknowledging that you have the power to choose what you do. The feelings of power and choice are good counterweights to the drag of negative, helpless, and hopeless thinking. You can't passively wait for your life to change on its own. You must start with the thing you can do *right now* to feel more powerful. And just changing how you say what you are doing moves you into the position of choosing—you are in control, not the depression.

"I Have a Choice"

Another version of the "I can't/ I won't" change is to listen for the ways you talk about having no choice. The double-edged sword of inadequacy and worthlessness cuts away the energy to change unfortunate circumstances. You may need help to mobilize your creativity, problem-solving ability, and decision-making in order to know what to do. In depression, low mental energy means not thinking things over very well. Problem-solving seems impossible. Thoughts can get stuck and ruminative. But action comes once you know what to do.

When physical energy is low, a mental energy boost is needed. This occurs automatically when you perceive yourself as having a choice. If a situation like your job or your marriage is bad, you can change what you are doing. In depression, however, you don't see it that way. You tell yourself you "have to" keep doing whatever it is you do not want to do.

When you stay in a bad situation *by choice*, you recognize that you have some control and therefore feel less helpless. "I have to stay in this job" or "I can't move out of this town" feels helpless. "I choose to stay in this job" or "I choose not to move at this time" is a statement of some power. This may be obvious, but when you are depressed you do not see

119

it. The hardest part is to not just *say* "I choose" but to see that you really *are choosing* to do the thing you are unhappy about.

Do some brainstorming to see how you are actively choosing your current course of action—do not neglect *anything* you *could* do. If you feel trapped in a job, for example, go through the choices, such as:

- I *could* quit today.
- I *could* take the day off, stay home, and read.
- I *could* quit and get a job at the coffee shop instead, where people are nicer, and just live with less money.
- I *could* tell my boss I will leave unless I get a raise.
- I *could* refuse to take the overtime so I can have more time for myself.

When people brainstorm they tend to argue against each idea *before* getting all the ideas out. But hidden in the complaint about why the idea won't work is the *choice* you are making. For example, "I *can't* refuse the overtime! They would fire me and I need the job for the money," can be restated as "I choose to work overtime because I would rather have a secure income than risk being fired."

"I Don't Like It *and* I Will Do It"

Just because you recognize that you are choosing to stay in an unpleasant situation doesn't mean you have to *like* that situation. This exercise is not about making a silk purse out of a sow's ear. *You are allowed to feel bad about it.* Think about how that feels. In fact, say it out loud as you read: "I do not like it *and I will do it.*" That is affirmative. That is power. "I choose." It is a great mobilizer, opening the door to problem-solving and making decisions about handling difficult situations. Even if you decide to tough it out in bad circumstances, your choice is made from free will and that is powerful.

One of my clients, Chakita, worked in a physical-labor job she did not like but needed. She had to finish her associate's degree before she could look for an office job that would be easier for her. She felt depressed and as if the world were against her. But when she realized she was *choosing* this job over not having any job, and when she said out loud "I don't like it and I will do it until I get something better," she felt less dragged down by it.

Mobilize

1. Turn "I can't" into "I won't."
2. Recognize your choices. "I can choose to do what I am already doing or choose something different."
3. You do not have to like what you do if there are good reasons to keep on doing it. "I don't have to like what I choose to do."

TAKE A BREAK FROM THE PROBLEM

Many people hit a point in stressful circumstances when they become overwhelmed. Excessive stress impairs your ability to find solutions, to keep on making productive choices, and to mobilize the energy to continue going forward. For many people, excessive stress is the trigger for depression. Whether the stress is chronic or acute, it can still overwhelm your ability to cope with it and leave you feeling inadequate. Mobilizing the energy to deal with your problem may require getting a new perspective on it. But in depression, your brain tends to ruminate and your analytical, problem-solving left brain depends too much on your emotion-laden right brain. Those features of depression are detrimental to finding good solutions to stressful, sticky problems.

Have you ever been encouraged to just get away from a problem you cannot solve? As it turns out, this is a great way to get a new perspective and allow your logical brain to have a little space from the emotional brain. There are several ways to get away. You can get away by "sleeping on it" or letting your unconscious work on it for you while you do something else. Walking away from a problem can help you see a fresh solution that might have always been there or might be a totally new and creative way to resolve that stressful situation.

Herbert Benson and William Proctor (2003) called this process the "breakout principle." They stated that if a person under stress can just let go or surrender to the problem and then do something entirely different that severs the mind and body connections to the problem for 10 to 20 minutes, there is a literal neurobiological change that helps give you fresh ideas. The brain will release nitric oxide to counteract the stress response. That neurological activity results in mental and physical relaxation and sets the stage for a shift in your pattern of thinking.

Their work demonstrates the neurobiological basis of this kind of intervention into the ruminative, stressed-out behavioral and cognitive patterns of depression. In fact, Benson and Proctor believe that such a deliberate break out of your pattern causes a permanent shift in thinking and behavior that may be accompanied by a peak experience or high. If you get that result it can be a boon to your depression recovery.

Try the following exercise. When you are feeling overwhelmed and stressed out mentally or emotionally:

1. *Stop!* Just stop putting effort into solving the problem.
2. *Do something totally different.* Pick something you *want* to do, like sit on your porch, walk, swim, listen to music, pray, or meditate. It should preferably be a repetitive activity that can absorb your interest and attention. This shouldn't require much effort because the activity is something you already find pleasing and you probably do it even when your energy is low. Keep this up for a little while. (Benson and Proctor's research indicates that 10 to 20 minutes is enough.)
3. *See what happens* to your thoughts on the problem when you return your attention to it. It is likely that you will find a new perspective to solve the situation.

Take a Break From the Problem

1. Stop!
2. Do something totally different for a little while.
3. See how this changes your perspective on the problem.

UTILIZE YOUR FUTURE ENERGY: START SMALL AND STAY FOCUSED ON THE OUTCOME

It takes some energy to move, and getting mobilized when you are low on energy is a challenge in depression recovery. People avoid doing things when they perceive themselves as lacking energy. Depressive lethargy may be more mental than physical, but you may still feel unable to get going and do daily tasks. Eventually the sheer weight of everything that hasn't been done makes it impossible to move. Things left undone usually include phone calls and emails, housework, homework, paying bills, invoicing, expense reports, and so on. How does a person get out from under the "undone" pile?

First, pick something to do that will require only a small burst of energy to get you mobilized. Tasks that have to be done all at once are good—like emptying the dishwasher, paying the electric bill, calling a customer back, taking the car through the carwash, and the like. Even if it is small, it is important to pick a goal you know you can achieve, so when it is done, you get the intrinsic reward of meeting the goal.

Now, create an image of how it will be when the undone task is done. Ask yourself, "What will this feel like when I do it? How will I feel when it is done?" Be very specific and create an image of the feelings, thoughts, and physical sensations, such as your stomach unknotting or the sense of relief you will have. If you make those work phone calls, will you feel competent and secure in your job for now? If you call the credit company to arrange a payment plan, will you feel relief and stop dreading that it could be a collection agency whenever the phone rings? If you send one resume, will you feel like you just created an opportunity or feel as if you are no longer frozen? Make this image *as vivid as possible*.

123

Next, stay focused on the outcome. Don't worry just yet about how or when you will do it. Rather, just think about the outcome when it is done. Not only will you feel good, but you may get a reward in addition to the weight being removed. For example, "If I can just make myself pay bills, I can watch TV without guilt." "If I finish my homework, I can go on-line tonight." Then, with that goal of how you will feel in mind, just start the activity. Chances are extremely high you will finish it if you picked a one-shot activity.

Then, pay attention when you finish. If you are depressed, you probably have a tendency to overlook the small, good feelings that you get whenever you complete a chore or cross a task off your "to do" list. *Intentionally noticing* the relief or pleasure you feel after completing every small action will help to boost your motivation and move you further in the right direction.

Utilize Your Future Energy

1. Pick a small task to do.
2. Create a vivid image of how you will feel when it is done.
3. Focus on the outcome.
4. Do the task.
5. Pay attention to the relief or pleasure you feel after it is done.

Ryan was a good example of this: He could not make himself begin his math homework, because it always seemed like too much. Even the threat of failing that class was not enough to light the fire of his energy. The mound of assignments had piled higher all semester. We identified small steps he could take to change this. The first was to ask his teacher whether he could pass and what he had to turn in to do it. Knowing what he was up against would reduce his fear and possibly challenge his belief that it was useless to start. Sure enough, the teacher said that Ryan had done well enough on tests that turning in the old assignments would give him a C and a great final exam could raise it to a B. The palpable relief he felt upon hearing this was impossible to ignore. Imagining having a B gave him a very good feeling, but he was not done yet. He still had to do the assignments, so I asked him to imagine how it would feel if he had finished just one assignment. He would feel some pressure lift, he thought. Staying with doing "just one," he was able to sit down and complete it. Not unexpectedly, once he did one assignment he felt great relief, and by imaging that outcome for every subsequent assignment, he was able to do each. As he went along, the sensation that he could finish got stronger.

START THE TRAIN ROLLING: REWARD YOURSELF

A depressed brain has less dopamine, the "feel good" neurochemical, than a healthy brain, so life does not feel as rewarding as it should. Also, lower levels of serotonin mean less sense of accomplishment. To make mobilizing easier, give yourself a reward for the smallest movement toward your ultimate goal.

Think about the weight of a very long freight train with a massive locomotive to pull it. When that locomotive starts to pull the train down the track, the wheels move *very* slowly on that first turn around. The second time the wheel moves a *tiny* bit faster, and then a bit faster, and with each revolution the wheel turns over faster and faster. That is a good metaphor for the process of getting mobilized when you are depressed.

Again, the key is to start small. A big task can be too heavy for you to do all at one time. Cleaning the whole house, getting all the dishes done, paying all your bills, filling out your expense report for work, getting all your homework done—these are overwhelmingly heavy and complicated if you believe you must do the whole chore at one time. Instead, it is possible to do just one tiny part of that task at a time. For example, if you pick the task of doing laundry, begin by listing each small step involved: (1) sort laundry, (2) put one load in wash, (3) put load in the dryer, (4) fold that load of clothing, (5) put folded clothes away.

Then, reward yourself for accomplishing each small task. To figure out a reward, notice what you are already doing with your time. You might be watching sports all weekend or lying on the couch watching reruns. You might be playing computer solitaire, reading a book, or surfing the web. You are doing *something* even if it is not the productive activity you wish you were doing.

This *something* you are doing while you are depressed is the key to getting rolling. It does not take much energy to do it and it is rewarding enough that you keep on doing it. All you are going to do is promise yourself that you can lie on the couch or play solitaire as soon as you do just one little thing toward completing a task. This works really well if you let yourself do what you want to do for 15 to 30 minutes and then do the next small step. For example, sort the laundry, then take a break to play solitaire. Put one load in the washing machine and then take a break to play some more. Then put a load in the dryer and maybe switch to something else you like, such as watching some of the ballgame that has come on. And so on until you are done.

Finally, pick a way to be accountable for the task. You may be able to be accountable to yourself by writing a list you can cross off, but if you are really depressed, you may need a friend or family member to help you. Tell that person about your goal and ask him or her to ask you if you met it.

Carla, a mother and homemaker, was depressed and feeling very guilty for sitting on the computer playing games all day while her family was at work or school. She wanted to do the laundry and the ironing because they piled up fairly quickly and were visible evidence of how little work she was doing all day. We broke it down as just described, and she sat at the computer for 15 minutes between each step. Bear in mind that she rewarded herself by doing what she had already been doing while depressed. She just required of herself a small activity before doing it. When she got to the ironing, to her surprise she was able to do several items instead of just one at a time because she had started the train rolling just by getting started and she knew she would get a reward.

The reward of getting something done will energize and mobilize you. The more you do, the more you will be able to do.

PRIME THE PUMP, CHARGE THE BATTERY: USE YOUR HANDS, TIME UNPLEASANT TASKS, AND TAKE "COMMERCIAL BREAKS"

The principle of priming a pump—letting in a little bit of fuel to get the pump started—is a good metaphor for mobilizing yourself in depression. You have to put a little energy in to get a good flow of energy out—and you will get more out than you ever put in. Likewise, by charging a battery, you increase the energy to accomplish something later.

Use Your Hands

When you are feeling physically drained from your depression, the idea of doing anything is so overwhelming that you do not do anything at all. The buildup of work around you then further depletes your energy. It's like a battery being drained of energy. It needs to be charged in order to provide energy for it to make something else run. If your battery is drained, where do you get the energy to charge it up again?

One way is to start by doing something with your hands. You literally stimulate the reward center of your brain more thoroughly by a physical action than a mental one (Lambert, 2008). So find a task that is physical in some way (typing on a keyboard or Blackberry doesn't count). Wash the dishes, cook, garden, build or repair something, do something artistic like painting or knitting or tying a fishing lure.

It should be something that you like. Being able to do something when depressed is easier if you really like what you pick to do. Not everyone is depressed to the point of complete immobility. So pick something you will be likely to do even though you feel depressed. The more valuable the outcome is to you, the more beneficial the activity will be for creating a sense of reward. One person might get more benefit out of painting a picture than cleaning the garage, but perhaps for you it would be the other way around. Regardless of what your preferred activity is, you will feel the positive sensation that is the flow of dopamine from working with your hands. And that energy can supply what you need to keep moving—even help you move on to activities that are not quite as rewarding.

Time Unpleasant Tasks

Also try this: Time how long it takes to do things you are not very interested in doing but that would help reduce the disorder around you. How long does it *really* take to file the three bills that came in the mail? How long does it take to fold the cereal box and put it in the recycling bin? How long does it take to make a bed, empty a dishwasher, pick up the newspapers, brush your teeth? At the office, how long does it take to enter one invoice on the computer or open the mail or put those catalogues onto the shelf or the files into the cabinet? You will find that tasks take much less time than you imagine they will—probably seconds instead of minutes. Then, once you have timed a task, get into this habit: When you look at something and sigh because you feel like it is just too much, ask yourself if you can put in that tiny bit of time—just 30 seconds to do the one task—and then you can sit as long as you need to.

One client of mine had so little energy that she let groceries sit on the counter—sometimes for days—without putting them away. I asked her to time how long it took to put one can on the pantry shelf. "Why only one can when all the groceries need to be put away?" she wondered. I told her I would answer that later. "Just do one!" She was totally surprised to see that it took only 4 seconds to pick up one can and set it on the pantry shelf. Her instructions were to ask herself whenever she was in the kitchen if she had 4 seconds to put one item away. Of course the answer was always yes, and the counter got cleared of groceries in short order.

Take "Commercial Breaks"

The most powerful battery-charger is an activity I call "commercial breaks." This is an intervention for people whose homes are in disarray and who are depressed about living in a messy place. During the space of one commercial break on the TV, you can start making a less depressing environment.

1. Look around you and see the things you wish were done but that you do not want to do.
2. Make a list. It will only take a few moments to write down a list of things you see: dishes on the table, newspaper on the floor, laundry to be folded, shoes and socks strewn across the living room, papers to be filed, bills to pay, and so on.
3. Then, as you watch TV, every time a commercial comes on, start one of the things on the list, doing it only for as long as the commercial break continues. Then flop down and watch the show until the next break, when you will get up and do something for those 3 minutes. Follow that pattern until the whole task is done, cross it off the list, and then go on to the next one.
4. If you are really tired, do this just during one show and then sit for the entirety of next one, or the next several.

You will be *amazed* at how much you can get done in one evening of watching TV. Those 3-minute breaks add up, but you never feel as if you are putting in a lot of effort at one time. This can even be a fun family activity (yes, really!—like a little competition) if you have everyone get up and do something during the commercial. One woman I know makes it a game by declaring "blitzkrieg!" and her children all get up to rush through the house tidying up. They challenge themselves to get all the dishes cleared and loaded in the dishwasher before the show starts. Even if it is just you alone, you will feel better as your environment becomes less cluttered or dirty or as small jobs get done.

EXERCISE

There is no way to overemphasize all the ways exercise is vital to your health. I won't even begin to list everything here, but I do want to talk about why it is of major importance to mobilizing energy. Exercise is probably the single most effective depression-defeater you can do. It is the best way of overcoming lethargy—as long as you do it.

Exercise Is Effective in the Same Ways That Medication Is

Like SSRI medications, exercise raises levels of serotonin in the brain, though it does this through different means. It may affect serotonin levels more positively in people who have problems with serotonin, as seen in research with depressed persons (Kiive, Maaroos, Shlik, Toru, & Haro, 2004). Exercise also enhances BDNF to encourage the production of new brain cells that can produce serotonin. Additionally, it increases blood flow to the brain, which is associated with many aspects of brain health, and it can affect your neurotransmitter levels as well as the overall functioning of parts of the brain. Therapists are beginning to understand that exercise is as important to recovery from mental illness as many other interventions that can be applied (Bartholomew, 2005; Cynkar, 2007; Penedo & Dahn, 2005). Furthermore, the sense of self-efficacy that exercise promotes in turn promotes the willingness to take charge of one's life in other ways (Craft, 2005).

Exercise Is a Prime Stress Reliever

A stunning amount of research demonstrates the many ways exercise is good for your mind and body, helping you maintain health and improving your ability to learn (Ratey & Hagerman, 2008). It also has a positive impact on reducing stress. For the depressed person with a lot of agitation, physical activities are better sources of stress relief than sitting still. Aerobic exercise is the best, because it is a great long-term relaxer. Also, it may help at moments of high stress to use up the physical energy released in the stress response. The vigorous activity uses up the adrenalin of the stress response and helps rid the body of toxic cortisol. It also helps the body avoid the likely weight gain of constant stress. And vigorous exercise promotes relaxation because muscles that are being used are stretched and relaxed afterward. There is no downside to vigorous exercise.

How Much Should You Do?

Although overexercising can be as damaging as underexercising (Talbott, 2002), the American College of Sports Medicine (ACSM) and the American Heart Association (AHA) report states that less than 50% of adults in the U.S. meet standards for minimum physical activity for heart health (Haskell et al., 2007). There are not yet standards set for brain health, but similar recommendations as those for physical health have a positive impact on anxiety (Manger & Motta, 2005). Michael O'Riordan quoted the recent ACSM/AHA study: "To promote and maintain health, the ACSM/AHA writing group recommends that 'all healthy adults aged 18 to 65 years need moderate-intensity aerobic physical activity for a minimum of 30 minutes on five days each week or vigorous-intensity aerobic activity for a minimum of 20 minutes on three days each week'" (2007, p. 2). Combining these routines is also acceptable, with people allowed to meet the recommendations by walking briskly or performing an activity that noticeably accelerates the heart rate for 30 minutes twice during the week and then jogging for 20 minutes or performing any activity that causes rapid breathing and a substantial increase in heart rate on two other days. The prescription for what enough exercise is: 5 to 7 days a week, for 25 to 45 minutes at 70% of your maximum heart rate.

If You Cannot Do Aerobic Exercise

Although aerobic exercise is good for both emotional wellbeing and physical health, some people cannot do it. You are not out of luck. Evidence shows that mindful meditation has excellent health benefits (Benson & Proctor, 2003; Seigel, 2007). Meditating twice a day for about 20 minutes will do wonders for your brain—and therefore for your depression. Yoga is another means of promoting mental health through balancing energy, encouraging meditation, and creating a strong, flexible body. Those who practice the martial arts also indicate the value of practices such as tae kwon do, which is surmised to raise endorphins and thus raise dopamine to improve wellbeing.

To sum up, exercise:

- Decreases the buildup of toxic stress effects
- Promotes healthy brain activity through increasing blood flow
- Keeps the body healthy and able to respond effectively to stress
- Improves self-efficacy

Getting Started With Exercise

For people who are not already regular exercisers, the biggest problem is getting started. Begin by getting educated about how important exercise is. That can help mobilize the willingness to do it. Thus, spending time in therapy on exercise is not only reasonable but also important to do. Remember that the anterior cingulate gyrus (ACG) and the orbitofrontal cortex (OFC), both of which are involved in creating new options to problems, fail to find new options when you are depressed. The ACG can get stuck on the "I can't" and the OFC can fail to generate new solutions. The brain thus needs a boost to feel the motivation to exercise. The answer is to use intention (the work of the executive decision-maker, the prefrontal cortex) to make a decision that even in the absence of motivation is a necessity to start exercising. Take time to develop both understanding and motivation to try this method.

A large step for someone who is not exercising might be to walk the dog for one extra block or 5 extra minutes, or it might be getting off the bus one stop early. It might be a commitment to walk with the therapist during the therapy hour to see what it feels like. Start by figuring out what activity will work and then make a commitment to trying it. If you are having trouble deciding on an aerobic activity, try the following:

- Ask yourself: "What physical things do I like to do?" (If the answer is "nothing," try to remember what you have liked doing in the past.) Don't exclude anything at first. Remember playing sports? Playing in the yard as a kid? Remember riding bikes for fun? Did you play tennis or racket sports or swim?

- What are your opportunities to do it? Look for something that is like what you enjoy even if you cannot do exactly that. Maybe you played basketball when you were in school. Can you shoot baskets in the park? In your yard? Join a community team for adults? Get creative about what could work. Talking it over in therapy, or with a friend or family member, can help you come up with ideas.

- Who would do it with you? Often an exercise partner increases both motivation and accountability. This can be problematic if you are starting from scratch. You might feel some embarrassment, especially if you have some social anxiety, at the thought that you are not as good as someone else. But even agreeing to meet a friend at the gym or local track to start and finish at the same time will be a big help. If you can afford it, working with a trainer can be a great place to start, because that person will know how far you can go physically and will encourage you. Even if you can only make a commitment to your dog to take longer walks, having someone depend on seeing you will make you more likely to get out and do it.

- Decide! What is the largest possible step you can take in the direction of exercise? Answer this question each week until you have achieved the goal of 25 to 45 minutes of aerobic exercise at 70% of your maximum heart rate. The weekly goal should increase incrementally, even if the increases are slight. This will also promote motivation, as success makes people prepared to do more.

- Make a commitment to an action plan. It is best to do it with another person, who will ask how it went. This can be a therapist or a friend or family member—anyone who can be counted on to ask about whether the commitment to exercise has been kept. What will you commit to this week?

- How will you be accountable? One way to be accountable is to simply keep track of what you do on a paper calendar or even just on an index card posted where you can see it.
- Evaluate your success and set the next week's goal in writing.

Duane felt incredibly guilty: He got depressed over losing his job and had become a "couch potato" during the winter. He had gained 30 pounds and stopped walking his beloved dog in the cold weather. He believed that exercise would help everything: his depression, weight, and guilt. We used his motivation to walk the dog to get him exercising. He agreed that this was necessary (intention) and that he had the ability to do a little. So he started by walking once around the block. Seeing his dog's delight at being out motivated him to walk a little farther, and he made a commitment to increase the walk a little bit each day until he was in the aerobic range. As that felt good to him, he added a short jog at the end of the walk and within several weeks was seeing and feeling everything improve, making him more energetic to go out job-hunting.

Exercise

1. Educate yourself on the importance of exercise.
2. Find a type of exercise that you enjoy.
3. What opportunities do you have to do it?
4. Decide the largest possible step you can reasonably take in the direction of exercise.
5. Get a partner if possible.
6. Commit to an action plan.
7. Be accountable. Keep track of what you do.
8. Evaluate your progress and increase your goal regularly until you hit your target for the prescription for exercise.

EAT SOMETHING—ANYTHING! THEN EAT RIGHT

Another very important means of acquiring energy is to eat. Although a small number of people with depression overeat, most tend to skip meals. Depression is perceived in the body as if you are physically sick. The chemical changes that occur—possibly as an outcome of stress, possibly as an outcome of an illness or surgery from which you are recovered, or possibly due to other causes—leave the brain producing neurochemicals as if you are sick when in fact you actually aren't. How do you feel when you are sick? It can be a beautiful day, perfect for a game of tennis or a day in the garden, and all you want to do is lie on your couch. You do not feel like eating and you may have little desire to even watch TV or play a video game. But you *aren't* sick. You won't get nauseated if you eat, and you don't need to conserve energy to fight infection.

When you do not move—and especially when you do not eat—you lose energy. If your blood sugar goes too low because you are not eating, your motivation level and your mood will reflect that. You will feel more negative and it will be harder to shake that feeling. Your situation might begin to look hopeless. This is very common when people have an important emotional loss, such as the breakup of a relationship, loss of a job, or death in the family. They stop eating, lie on the couch, and feel literal, physical pain in their heart and stomach.

Not eating makes a loss hurt more, and—even worse than that—makes it seem like you will never get over the hurt. Without food to keep blood sugar at a normal level, everything seems bleak. And people in these kinds of situations of loss need to be able to think in a new way, to see the world as having other possibilities. They need motivation to go on. So it is time to eat. Eat anything. Don't worry about nutrition—the last thing someone in this state will want to do is prepare a well-balanced meal. This may be the only time I advocate fast food or even sweets! Just reach for the easiest thing and eat it. If it's an apple, great, but usually it will be a drive-through burger or shake or a candy bar from a vending machine. Once the blood sugar starts rising, the world won't seem quite as grim, the heartache not quite as unbearable. And the motivation to go forward will become a little more accessible.

For longer-term recovery from depression, however, a healthy diet is needed. Your brain needs vitamins to operate properly and produce neurotransmitters (Amen & Routh, 2003; DesMaisons, 1998; Weil, 1998). The best route is to get nutrients from food. Remember that calories and nutrients are not the same thing. When it comes to brain health, what you eat is much more important than how much you eat. Folic acid from dark green vegetables like spinach is essential to producing serotonin (Delgado et al., 1994; Wolfersdorf, Maier, Froscher, Laage, & Straub, 1993) and, if you are on SSRI medication, for making the medication work at its optimal level. Make sure you get other vitamins from the colorful orange, red, and yellow vegetables and fresh fruits. Multivitamins can also help give your brain the building blocks it needs. Healthy fats from olive oil and from fish, like the Omega 3 oils, have a good reputation for helping your brain do its work.

Your brain makes neurotransmitters from the nutrients in the food you eat. And most of the production of brain cells and neurotransmitters occurs while you are sleeping. Your brain needs available protein while you are sleeping, and due to the digestive process, as well as the way the body uses proteins, it takes 12 to 15 hours for the proteins to become available in the brain (DesMaisons, 1998). This is yet another reason why a good breakfast is a good idea! To make protein available throughout the night, you must eat it three times a day, but you only need 3 or 4 ounces per serving. That portion is about the size of a deck of cards.

Then get some sleep! Your brain wants 8 hours a night, not just to manage stress but to repair and grow new cells. See Chapter 5 for information about sleep and depression and what to do for better sleep.

You can mobilize your energy by taking small steps at a time, identifying small activities that you can imagine doing even though depressed. The idea is that the small activities will have a big payoff: Once you start to feel mobilized, you will find it increasingly easier to keep on going. You will be able to more that is fun, more that is productive. And with each new level of activity, your depression will recede. Be sure not to criticize yourself for making small steps. Especially if you have endogenous or stress-induced depression, you get into trouble when you think you must do a lot. The whole idea is to stay mobilized by doing small things at a time so you will not become overwhelmed again. This can become a life strategy for beginning and completing the tasks of life without suffering exhaustion. Your energy level will thank you.

SEVEN

Technique #5:
End Isolation

Isolation is both a cause and an outcome of depression. When you are alone it is very easy to sink into the rumination that deepens depressive states, and when you are not communicating with other people there is no one to challenge your view of things. At the same time, people who are depressed tend to lose interest in things—including other people. And when you do not seem interested in others, you are not sending out signals that you want to be sociable, and consequently others do not tend to pursue your company (Zeiss, Lewinsohn, & Munoz, 1979). People begin to isolate themselves for several reasons and the ability to reverse the isolative behavior once it is in place depends on understanding the cause-and-effect relationship of isolation and depression.

When people are under stress, especially chronic stress, they eventually pull away from social interactions. Their families may notice and urge them to participate in social activities, but they refuse. The activity may seem too tiring; merely leaving the *house* may seem to require too much energy. You need some down time when you are under stress, but there is a point at which isolation just reinforces the depressed, empty feeling you have.

Isolation can particularly be a problem for people suffering depression consequent to early childhood adversity, as these people don't easily trust or rely on others. Being alone feels safer to them—or at least more familiar. But withdrawing in this way compounds the problem, as it prevents you from realizing how much being with others could relieve the depression. It is important in these cases to work on developing a sense of safety and trust with others who can support you when you need it.

People suffering from depression caused by traumatic stress may be more at ease connecting with others than people with early life adversity. However, isolation can be comfortable in that reminders of the trauma can be better avoided. So isolation can become a habit. In either condition, the depression is reinforced by aloneness.

A VICIOUS CYCLE

Isolation intensifies depression in a vicious cycle for some. If you are unhappy and find being around others to be a source of irritation, you are probably radiating signals that you are irritable. Especially at home, where there is less social constraint on your behavior, you may be grouchy, complaining, or impatient—all indications of your depression. Although you want to be soothed, you are unlikely to receive that response. Family and friends will pull away if you are crabby enough to be unpleasant to be around. As you have less contact with people who could support you—who could mitigate your mood, offer you some perspective, divert your attention away from yourself—you go deeper into your depression, making you less enjoyable to be around. See Figure 7.1 for a visual of this circular reinforcement of depression.

Extroverts and Introverts

Knowing whether you are an introvert or an extrovert is going to make a difference here. If you are an extrovert, you feel energized by others and turn outward for problem-solving and relief. When an extrovert starts to pull back due to depression, other people notice and let the person know that he or she is not behaving as usual. People ask what is wrong. An extrovert often has a variety of activities or a wide circle of acquaintances, so when he or she stops showing up, more people wonder what is wrong.

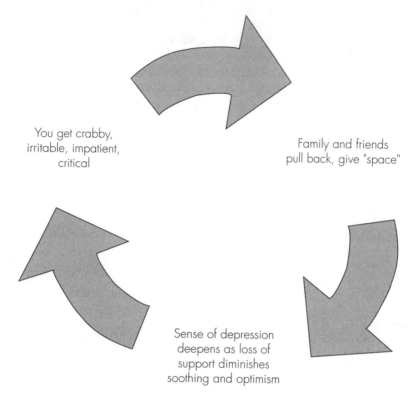

You get crabby, irritable, impatient, critical

Family and friends pull back, give "space"

Sense of depression deepens as loss of support diminishes soothing and optimism

Figure 7.1 The Circular Reinforcement of Isolation

When isolation happens due to something not of the extrovert's choosing—as in the case of a romantic breakup or period of unemployment or illness—it can *cause* depression. Extroverts are energized by contact with others, so when they become disconnected socially, they may feel as if they are meaningless or ghostlike. They often feel that if there isn't another person to share an experience with, the experience might as well not have happened. This means that normally interesting situations lose their delight. In these cases it is important to work at keeping social connections, no matter how hard that might be.

If you are an introvert, you restore yourself by turning inward for peacefulness and relish alone time to restore yourself. Introverts typically feel more exhausted after too much socializing, especially with a group. As an introvert, you need to get away from others to cope with stress and recharge yourself. But being an introvert does not mean you want *isolation*. That said, it is easy to slip into when you are depressed. People who are friends with you may not notice so quickly that you have pulled back. Your friends know that you appreciate alone time. The difficulty for introverts is knowing when they have crossed the line from restorative alone time to isolation.

ADDICTION, DEPRESSION, AND ISOLATION

The issue of addiction should also be addressed here, especially addiction to alcohol. Although many alcohol-addicted people drink in public, and many people use drugs at parties or with friends, addiction is not a social activity. Process addictions like Internet pornography or on-line gambling are typically done alone. Addiction is essentially a self-centered process as a person seeks immediate relief from an unpleasant emotion and finds that relief in using the substance or engaging in the addictive behavior. No matter what type of mood-altering activity is pursued, when people turn to an addictive substance or behavior to relieve stress, addiction may develop. And it may be easier to be alone to use the mood-altering substance or behavior, so feedback from others does not interfere with the use. Alcohol use in particular may not seem to the user to present a problem, and thus addiction to alcohol may burgeon in isolation without the check and balance of social appropriateness.

Socially isolated people do not turn outward for relief of depression. As drinking, on-line gambling, pornography use, or other addictions develop, people hide the signs of that addiction. This contributes to isolation from genuine social contact, which reinforces the process of addiction.

The interrelationship between depression and drinking was a huge component of Shannon's poor response to treatment. For several months, she complained of isolation but minimized how much of the time she spent drinking alcohol at home alone. Every attempt to get out with friends or use the health club seemed to fail; the alcohol use was rewarding enough to block efforts to end her isolation. The very thing she was using to soothe her depression was blocking her recovery. When we realized she was going to have to stop drinking entirely and treated her drinking as an addiction, her full recovery from depression became possible. This experience made it abundantly clear that exploring the use of alcohol, drugs, or addictive behaviors should be part of the assessment of every client's depression.

CONNECTING TO OTHERS: START SMALL

For isolated people with more severe depression, the thought of making the effort to connect to others can seem overwhelming. But you don't have to turn into a social butterfly to begin chipping away at the isolation that is reinforcing your depression. Start small.

Get Out of the House

If you are not getting out of your apartment or house at all, the first thing you need to do is go outside. Put on some clothes and take a little walk. This is not for exercise but just to notice that people are out and about and living their lives. Notice the wide variety of people and see if their clothes or demeanor give you any clues about what they may be doing.

Say "Hi" on Purpose

On your short walk, when someone looks back at you, nod and say "hi" as you go past. You are not starting a conversation, just acknowledging the moment of connection. Depending on where you live, you could find a park to stroll through, or go into a store to buy a small item—even just a package of gum—and say hello to the cashier, or greet someone in the elevator of your building.

If you are isolated, it's likely that you are not only staying inside as much as possible but also avoiding eye contact or social interactions that might occur when you *do* leave the house. Getting out of the house and saying "hi" on purpose are very small but potent ways of helping you realize you are not a ghostlike presence in the world. Do them every day.

On-Line Communication

There are certain risks to communication over the Internet and through social-networking sites for people with depression. Many end up feeling more isolated than when they began their session on-line. Social-networking sites can increase feelings of loneliness as you see that others are interacting in person, attending activities, or dating. Maybe they have more "friends" or respond more to others than they do to you. Additionally, if you are prone to negatively interpreting ambiguous comments—as is common for a depressed brain—you may get your feelings hurt from comments in emails or chat or instant messages that come without vocal tone and facial expression to clarify their meaning.

That said, reaching out to others via an email or a post on a social-networking page is a small, low-risk way to start connecting to others. Whereas meeting for coffee or making a phone call requires energy if your friend picks up the call to talk, an Internet communication can be brief and doesn't require getting out of your pajamas, taking a shower, or pasting on a smile. And it sends a tendril of connection out into the social realm that could lead to a reply from another person. That reply can remind you that others are happy to hear from you, and you might derive some good feeling from that.

COMMENT ON THE POSITIVES IN OTHERS: AWARENESS AND ACTION

Another possibility for a small step with big results to end isolation is to become more aware of others' positive qualities or actions. Although you cannot control what other people do, you *can* control what you pay attention to. No matter what caused it originally, once your depression is present, it alters your awareness, filtering life experiences to catch all the negatives while the positives go unnoticed. And that altered awareness can lead you to withdraw from others, because if all you see is the negative in people, why would you want to be around them?

There is only one way to start reversing this trend: *Look for positives on purpose.* Noting what is good or pleasing in others requires purposefully replacing the negativity filter with a positivity filter. When you comment on the positives you see in others, it has the double effect of boosting not only the other person's self-esteem but also yours. When your deliberate action of saying a word of praise or appreciation causes the face of the person you are appreciating to light up, you will feel reciprocal pleasure. You will know you did something good.

Commenting on the positives in other people has other benefits for relieving depression:

- It increases your sense of control—you are in charge of what you observe and what you say in this exercise. You do not need to rely on anyone else to make you feel better.
- It enhances gratitude—you cannot help but feel grateful when you are noticing the good in others, because their goodness is benefiting you in some way.
- It increases self-value, as you do something nice and note that others are pleased.
- It makes others react more pleasantly to you, so more nice exchanges occur. This is the positive social impact of kindness to others.

The exercise entails three simple steps:

1. Pick a week to try it. Then, make a commitment to yourself that on each day of the week you will make five positive comments, without caveats or modifications or holding back, to someone you encounter. It can be a family member, friend, colleague, or stranger. It can be a personal compliment or a

statement of appreciation, such as, "You are so well-prepared for this meeting. Thank you." Or, "You were so kind to that child. I was glad to see it." Or, "How nice of you to help me. I really appreciate it."

2. On a piece of paper, list the days of the week, and write down the numbers 1 through 5 under each day. When you make the comment, write the name of the recipient of the comment under the appropriate day.

3. Review your list in the evening and see if you can remember the five comments you made.

See the Appendix for a blank form for this exercise.

Another version of this exercise is to do five acts of kindness. Replace your awareness of positives in others and your five comments each day with doing kind things. Because what we put into action is more rewarding than what we do with mere words, acting kindly toward others will give you a "bigger bang for your buck" when it comes to fighting depression. It is wise here not to think too big and not to try to do the same thing every day (Lyubormisky, 2007). Small and random acts, like offering to help someone carry a bag or paying the tollbooth charge for the driver behind you, are more effective. Looking for opportunities to help others will build your awareness of others' ongoing needs, and when you help out, it makes you feel good. Small spontaneous acts of kindness for strangers won't frighten you about whether you can maintain the energy to keep doing them, and small acts of kindness at home for people you live with reap huge rewards of reciprocal kindness, improving your connection to people you are with daily.

JOIN A GROUP

If you are depressed, one of the best ways to break out of isolation is to get some social support right away. However, if you have been isolated for some time, you may not feel connected enough to individual friends to "impose" on them to help you. You may have wandered away from community or church activities and feel disconnected from them. However, social support is critical to reversing the spiral into isolation. Get into therapy. Join a support group. What kind of support group? Any group that remotely fits your circumstances. Join a job club. If you have any kind of addiction, join a 12-step group. (See the Recommended Reading and Resources section for Web site information.) If you are not addicted, it is highly likely that you have a friend or family member who has an addiction of one kind or another. Join a support group for them, like Al-Anon or the family groups for addicts to cocaine, narcotics, spending, gambling, sexual addiction, and so on. In the world of addiction, you name it, there is a group for it. Other ideas: Join a book club through the library. Take a class at a community college, where you can find an abundance of adult-education offerings for very little money. Go to the health club and take an exercise class. (That would give you a double bang for your buck.) A therapist may be key, though, because someone has to encourage and support you to get out of your isolation, and getting into a group might be too hard without the push from a concerned other person monitoring your progress.

Paul had become isolated from every person and group that had ever been meaningful to him. A military man, he had left his wife and daughter in the community where they could stay close to her family while he deployed. After two back-to-back tours, he left the service, but he had been away from civilian life for so long that his disconnection was complete. He loved sports and had coached soccer, but now his daughter was older and not playing soccer anymore. She was involved in dancing, which left him without a way to engage in her activities. He had been part of a men's group in his church, but that had been a long time ago and he felt odd about reappearing. His wife had developed a social life without him and he felt intrusive wanting her time. He had the depressed view that everyone was doing fine without him. So he stayed home and gradually sunk more deeply into the depression he brought back from the service.

Talking about it in therapy helped him generate some ideas. I asked him what was going on in his park district, community college, and church. All I wanted was a list of some things he might be interested in. (This step is often hard to for people with depression to do alone, as their negativism slows or stops investigation. Don't give up if you feel resistance in yourself or in someone you are encouraging.) After hemming and hawing, he started by volunteering as an assistant coach for his church's basketball team. This allowed him contact with other men around an organized activity and gradually helped him feel connected to the church community again. Because his family was still involved at the church, Paul was gradually able to participate more with his family and started the reversal of his isolation.

CREATE A CIRCLE OF INTIMACY

In what other ways can you start to move out of isolation when you are depressed? This happens in an "unwinding" kind of process as you undo the patterns of spiraling inward and begin spiraling outward again. Isolated people get more and more self-centered. Their lives become all about them and how wounded they feel. This is a dangerous time, when people can slip into thoughts of suicide. If you are at that point you need to get professional help with your depression right away! But if you recognize the "woe is me" attitude creeping into your thought process— such as "Who cares, anyway?" or "No one would notice if I . . ."—it is time to take a look at the fact that you are not alone, even though you have been working at getting that way through your isolation.

I think it is best to make a visual depiction of this, to make it more real and easier to hold in your mind. You are going to make a list of every person you know. If you interact with groups (students you teach, your PTA committee, the office staff, the patients on your unit at the hospital), identify the group rather than each individual within it, unless you have a special relationship with one of them. If you are an extrovert, list only people you have regular contact with, as your list of every person you know might be way too big to be useful.

Once you have the list, identify the level of intimacy you have with each member by putting a number next to the person or group's name. For the people you love or who love you, *no matter if you are feeling the love at this moment*, put the number 1 by their names. Sometimes you have an important relationship but "love" is not the right word for your feelings. A close or involved connection—someone whom you value and who values you—also gets a 1. Then, for all the people with whom you are friends but not the closest of friends, put a 2. Also put a 2 next to the names of everyone you see on a daily or near-daily basis, such as coworkers, even if you are not good friends. Give a 3 to people who are acquaintances but with whom you have predictable interactions, such as a health-club trainer, a regular server at a restaurant you frequent, or other parents at the bus stop.

Then enter these names into the diagram pictured in Figure 7.2. The center circle is for your closest loved ones, the middle circle for friends, and the outer circle for acquaintances. What do you do with it now? Remember, depression can get you very self-oriented. This method is intended to break that mindset and help you shake up the isolative behavior. You are going to answer the question "Who cares?" in a very literal way. Place this circle where you can see it daily or carry it with you. As you look at it, tell yourself, "These are the people who care." You want to remember that they care, even if you do not feel it right now.

If appropriate, you might add, "These are the people who would be hurt if I hurt myself by any form of self-destructive behavior." You could be specific about what that behavior is—addiction or self-harm, for example. This is not an addiction recovery strategy, however. It is a reminder that you are living a life that affects others, even if you are isolating yourself from their presence at this time.

Use this list to encourage you when you do not want to go out, get exercise, take care of yourself, or do other recovery goals. Tell yourself, "These are the people who would be better off if I get out of my depression." And every time you look at the list, tell yourself, "I am not alone." You might write those statements on the diagram.

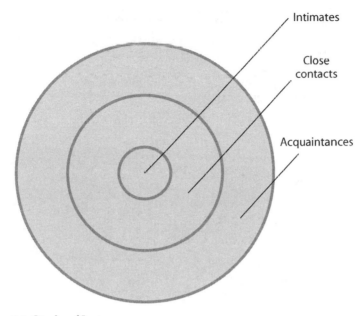

Figure 7.2 Circle of Intimacy

PLAN SOCIAL ENGAGEMENTS

In depression, people do not show the signs of interest in others that keep social life interactive. This starts a spiral in which you withdraw, which reduces the number of people who could draw you out, which leaves you even *more* alone, which leads to even *fewer* people to draw you out, and so on until you notice you don't see anyone anymore. It is time to show signs of interest, even if you have to feign interest for a while.

You can effectively feign interest by being deliberate about putting yourself into contact with people. Make appointments for contact.

- Tell someone you will call to chat at a specific time.
- Ask someone to join you for a small activity, like a coffee date.
- Make a meeting into a lunch appointment so there will a social component to it.

- Don't just expect to see family eventually—invite them to your home for small events that don't involve a lot of preparation.
- Make these plans in a way that would be hard to cancel later—be specific about the date and time, tell people you are looking forward to it, even go so far as to tell them you won't be reachable just before the meeting (so you cannot cancel easily without losing face). Do whatever it takes to ensure that you will be there.

Karl got sucked into social isolation as the result of long hours trying to save his business from failure. As he let go of employees and buried himself in work, he had no energy at the end of day to do anything but watch TV alone until he fell asleep. He was so grouchy his wife finally stopped trying to talk with him in the evening. He found himself irritated when his adult children came over on weekends expecting him to show his previous interest in family cookouts or watching football together. He barely showed any interest in his grandchildren. His self-reinforcing isolation was not unusual, and his family began to lose interest in drawing him out and grew impatient.

Karl needed to end his isolation, so I did a circle of intimacy with him. It was evident that his young grandkids were at the heart of his circle. He genuinely wanted a relationship with them, even though lately he did not feel much pleasure seeing anyone, even them, and he thought he could get enough energy to invite them over every week or two. I wanted Karl to pick activities that he couldn't skip once he invited the children to do them. We planned specifically what he would invite them to do—for example, walk to the playground in the park or play tee ball. Karl was genuinely devoted to his grandkids, even though at that moment he did not *want* to be around them. Yet he felt a responsibility to try harder for their sake than he might for a social acquaintance. Interacting with his grandchildren soon gave him more opportunity to talk with his children about their mutual interest in the kids, and this began to reverse his cycle of self-reinforcing isolation.

Strengthening Your Circle of Intimacy

1. On a piece of paper, draw three concentric circles (see Figure 7. 2).
2. Make a list of others in your life and enter their names in the appropriate circles.
3. Look at the diagram daily and tell yourself these are the people who care and who would be very hurt if you injured yourself. These are the people who want you to recover from depression.
4. Make appointments for phone calls, meetings, and brief social engagements that you can't cancel.
5. Plan deliberate activities, especially with family, that are hard to excuse yourself from.

IMPROVE YOUR SOCIAL SKILLS

Although we generally think of learning social skills as something that happens in childhood, it is never too late to get better at getting along with other people. If you are not as comfortable with other people as you want to be, or if you do not get out as much as you want to because you feel awkward about attending social engagements, it is a good idea to come up with a plan to develop your skills. As an adult, developing better social skills takes a little ingenuity, which you might not be able to muster due to your depression. This is where therapy can help. Your therapist can advise you about how to handle social circumstances and help you plan ways to practice your social skills. There are also several suggestions for books on this topic in the Recommended Reading and Resources list at the end of this book.

Although it takes some time to get practiced at social skills, there are some simple things you can do right away that will help you feel more connected and also receive friendlier responses from other people. Most of these things you already know, but you might not realize how depression stops you from doing them. So, consciously:

- Smile at other people—you can do it whether you are planning to talk to them or not. A smile encourages people to greet you or speak to you.
- Make eye contact. Although this is different from culture to culture, in the U.S. we like eye contact. We have lots of personal space, so the eye contact is safe and feels friendly.
- Shake hands when you greet someone and say a simple statement like "Nice to see you" before you go on to converse further or turn to greet another person. This establishes a moment of personal connection.
- If you are avoiding someone because you do not remember the person's name, remember that is actually *friendly* to acknowledge that. Say something like, "Forgive me for forgetting. Can you tell me your name again?" Often the person you are speaking to will want to have a reminder of your name as well, so you may not even have to acknowledge forgetting if you offer a handshake and just say your name: "Hi. I'm Margaret." Other people usually will offer their names in return.
- Try to start a conversation with a brief question about the other person's wellbeing. Yes, it is de rigueur to ask, "How are you?" and most people respond with "fine," but it is also polite to ask it, and it allows you to transfer into the rest of the communication graciously.
- If you are worried about interrupting the other person, especially when you are phoning someone or stopping by a colleague's office, start by asking, "Is this a good time for you to give me a few minutes?" If you notice hesitation, immediately offer to call back or come back at a later time. This allows the other person to invite you in (figuratively on the phone) or make an appointment that will allow for a better connection later.
- Don't forget to end a conversation or leave a situation with a goodbye, and make sure you add a word of appreciation for the time together. I am convinced that we are all more re-

active to the quality of those moments of connecting and disconnecting than most people are consciously aware of. Although you may not realize it, people will miss you if you just disappear. A goodbye gently disconnects people so the shift does not feel abrupt. In conversation with one person, say something that indicates that you appreciate having had the exchange, with comments like "Thanks, that's what I needed to know" or "Okay, good. See you later" or "It was nice catching up with you again." If you are leaving a group meeting, say something to indicate it was good to see everyone. If you are leaving a party, address your goodbye to the host and thank him or her for the invitation, good time, lovely meal, and so on.

Technology and Impersonal Communication

People who have always had email, texting, Twitter, and other electronic media as part of their life do not seem to have the same need for the social "niceties" with others that older people have. For example, you may not feel the need to reply to an FYI message, but if the person on the other end does not know if you received it, he or she may spend mental energy wondering about it or feeling ignored. Likewise, many people do not appear to know that they should respond to an invitation with regret if they cannot attend.

Rates of depression are skyrocketing, and although I am not suggesting that electronic communication is the cause, I do believe it contributes. Differences in social niceties are not inherently wrong, but communicating electronically deprives people of immediate feedback on how their words are received. This contributes to the lack of social skills and to a sense of disconnection from others—both serious issues that plague people with depression. It is too easy to send a text message that you are not coming to an engagement rather than call and hear the disappointment in the other person's voice when he or she learns you can't make it. It is too easy to inadvertently hurt someone with an abbreviated text message, never knowing that the person felt dismissed by you. It is far too easy to berate someone in email and be mean in a way you would *never* be to the person's face. And it is too easy to take offense at an off-handed remark written in an email when you can't hear the voice or see the face of the sender.

The challenge of addressing this problem with electronic communication is that each situation is a little different based on your age and the communication technology you use. You may not even know you need an intervention. Initiate a conversation with your peers and also with people you know in another generation to check out whether your communication style works for them. For example, ask your mom how she feels about getting an e-card for her birthday. It may actually *increase* feelings of disconnection for her. Ask your younger relatives to please respond to emails from you so you feel less ignored. Checking it out is the first step to better connections with other people and less isolation. Then follow up with change based on what you learned.

You may need to adapt your style for different people and situations. Your parents or grandparents may feel entirely different about getting a text to cancel plans than your friends do. Your best friends may know what you mean by what you write because they can hear your voice in their heads, but your boss might not. Make sure you know how your workplace culture views appropriate electronic communication, and learn how people in your workplace, from peers to supervisors, handle setting up meetings, giving feedback, sharing ideas, asking questions, and so on. The world is getting easier in some ways thanks to instant communication, but social skills still need social feedback, and getting that is harder if you aren't in the presence of others.

A Word About Children, Depression, and Social Skills

If a child is living with a parent who has poor social skills or who is isolated because of depression, that child is not being given a good model for social interactions. Children develop social skills starting in infancy by observing and imitating their parents' models for behavior. They participate in their own interactions with their parents and they observe thousands of daily interactions between their parents and others. Michael Yapko (2009) has described how depression is contagious in this way, and he has suggested that improved social skills are the answer. Children with poor social skills can end up depressed as teens and adults because of the isolation they feel when they cannot engage successfully with others. To ameliorate this, parents and teachers can intentionally broaden the child's social awareness and repertoire of skills. It starts with teaching manners. The constant repetition of reminders to say "hello," "please," "thank you," and "nice to meet you" are necessary and appropriate. Other ways to teach social skills include:

- Helping children develop perspective. This might start with noticing whether your children overestimate their hurts or underestimate the impact of their behavior on others. ("Do you think Johnny *meant* to hurt you when he sat with someone else at lunch?" "Do you think you could have hurt Shayna's feelings when you told her not to play with you after school?")
- Discussing ahead of time how your child could handle a difficult situation if it happens. Your child might not get a role in a play or a chance to play every quarter of the game or an invitation to a party. Discuss various options for how to behave and how to deal the emotions that come up. Ask your child which option seems best and discuss why he or she thinks so. This encourages children to develop flexibility in behavior, which ameliorates depression.
- Helping children imagine positive outcomes of their actions.
- Teaching children to think before they speak. Rules like "count to 10 before you show anger" and "do onto others as you would have them do unto you" are small miracles of social-skills training.
- Being respectful at home with other adults and with children. You can be more effective at discipline if you speak respect-

fully and if you demand respectful responses from your children. Starting young works better than trying to change a pattern of disrespect in an older child, but no matter what point you start at, it is possible to be respectful.

Two studies conducted by Martin Seligman (Novotney, 2009) have special relevance for parents and teachers who want to prevent or alleviate depression in children and teens. One study showed that helping children to think realistically and flexibly about everyday problems improved their optimism and cut their risk of depression in half. How did they do it? They literally taught children to identify their goals and then develop several possible ways to reach them. Developing flexibility and learning that goals can be achieved by multiple means defeated the rigid cognition of depression and promoted optimism by lessening the sense of failure if one way did not work.

The second study used guided discussion of stories students read in class to explore the strengths of the characters. The students were helped to discover their own strengths—a key premise of Seligman's positive psychology (Seligman, 2002)—and put them to use in everyday life. Not only did the students improve their social skills, but they also got better grades over the course of their high-school years.

We live in the world with other people who have feelings the way we do. That message is the heart of social connections. Whatever it takes to help children master healthy ways of relating will decrease their risk of depression and enhance their overall contentment with their lives.

BECOME RESPONSIBLE

If you have been isolated for some time, it will be uncomfortable to break out of that pattern. You may have lost connections you once had or may not have developed enough connections in the first place. Especially if you are shy or do not need lots of contact with other people to feel like you are involved, you will want to experiment to know just how much connection is enough and how you prefer to establish social relationships.

Taking on a responsibility is a good way to start. It can provide a structured format for the way you participate, and it may also help you to honor an obligation to show up and participate. An easy way to start is to get a pet. The responsibility for feeding, grooming, and walking is clear. You can get instructions if you need them. Even better, you immediately feel good receiving and giving affection. And better than that: You won't be overwhelmed by needing to use social skills that you have not practiced lately. Your sense of isolation is ameliorated by the knowledge that your pet is waiting for you and will be glad to see you.

Do you have children in your life with whom you could make plans? Younger children in particular are happy to have time with an adult and they do not have expectations about how you *should* relate. In fact, children will cheerfully direct your play. Can you become responsible to take a niece, nephew, grandchild, or the child of a close friend out for an activity? The sense of responsibility to follow through so you do not disappoint may get you out of your isolation. The affection and delight of a young child will reinforce your pleasure in getting out of your isolation.

Become responsible to help with something to which you donate your time. Looks for ways to help your neighbors or colleagues and commit to doing it. Does a neighbor need help getting to the grocery store, or could a coworker use help stuffing envelopes? What events are going on around you that you could help with? If you are isolated, you may not be very aware of these opportunities, so you might need to ask a family member, partner, work colleague, or friend for ideas. The pull of responsibility is what will get you out, and the reward of being helpful is intrinsic. The possibility of structured involvement with others will connect you without a lot of demand to improvise socially. The same thing is true if you find a place to regularly volunteer your time—walking dogs at an animal shelter, serving meals at a homeless shelter, or wherever your interests take you.

Whatever it takes to get you into the world and improve your connections to others is worth doing. Although you will not initially feel ecstatic about getting out and getting involved, this process is an outside-to-inside change, and the more positive feedback you get from others, the more you will enjoy those connections. The feeling of interest in socialization is the reward that comes from intentionally disrupting isolation. Following the ideas for developing your social connections a little at a time will help you overcome the drag of isolation and increase your desire to keep at it. No matter if you prefer a little activity or a lot, knowing you are connected to others who care about you and want you to be with them is a major antidepressant.

EIGHT

Technique #6:
Balance Your Life

Why is balance in life an important consideration if you have depres-sion? It's usually quite obvious that a depressed person's energy is low—that kind of imbalance is easy to see. However, there are many other aspects to balance. In an important article, Wallace and Shapiro (2006) drew on their knowledge of Buddhism and Western psychotherapy to define wellbeing as an outcome of balance in four arenas: goals, atten-tion, cognition, and affect (emotions). If you are balanced you are not overthinking or ruminating—instead, you have sufficient concentration to focus on and think about your goals. You are able to tolerate events and form responses to them without becoming too upset or overwhelmed. A balanced person does not show deficits or dysfunction in the activities of daily life.

When people are depressed, imbalances show up in each arena. The more depressed they are, the more their goals, attention, thinking, and emotions get out of whack. They tend to have a loss of motivation or energy to achieve their goals. They may even have forgotten what their goals truly are. In the arena of attention, people tend to overfocus on negatives, be underfocused on the positives, and have a deficit of caring or energy when it comes to carrying out goals. Many of the methods in this book have an impact on attention, but mindful awareness (Chapter 12) in particular keeps the depressed mind in the place of attending to what is happening and what is necessary to achieve goals.

The third arena of balance is cognition. In depression, thought patterns are biased toward negativity. Depressed people not only overfocus on negative outcomes, but also tend to misconstrue the intentions or emotions of others, seeing disapproval or lack of affection when those are not present. They are also remarkably inattentive in their interactions with others, not seeing how they affect other people regardless of whether their influence is positive or negative. Any of the techniques that address changing negative or pessimistic thoughts will promote cognitive balance.

The fourth arena of balance is emotions, and there is no question that the depressive affect of sadness, hopelessness, and helplessness needs considerable balancing. Affect is strongly influenced by thinking. It is also affected by the physical lethargy and low pleasure that are biological outcomes of depression. Emotions naturally come into better balance when a depressed person is helped to become more energetic and motivated and less mentally negative.

No matter what started your depression, you are likely to be out of balance in at least one arena, and this may have led to imbalance in all the others. If you began with endogenous depression, chances are good that your lower level of energy led you to not pursue goals that fulfill your potential or caused you to slow down achievement. You may also have had a more pessimistic outlook that prevented you from making an effort to achieve goals due to the belief that they were not attainable. Imbalances like these can result in feeling depressed about yourself or the world and can reinforce the tendency to see life's negative side.

A similar process can be set in motion by the emotional imbalance that occurs subsequent to early adverse experiences. Lacking trust or optimism, you might not expect your goals to work out, so you might avoid setting them in the first place, fearing you will see too many indicators that people are not able or willing to help you. For example, one of my clients told me she was going to put off taking the LSAT because once she did take it, she would know for sure if law school was an option. "I am not ready to give up hope yet," she said. "It makes me feel good to know I might have that option, and I can't bear to know it won't work."

Depression as an outcome of posttraumatic stress can have similar features when that person feels the negative pull of helplessness and gives up hoping or trying for good outcomes, consequently reinforcing depression.

The good news is that you can plan balancing actions on purpose. That's what this technique is about: quick ways to shift the depressive out-of-balance state into a more positive, balanced approach to life. As balance in one arena improves, that in others will follow naturally, or at least be easier to achieve. We will start with simple ideas that balance your level of activity. Being underactive in expenditure of energy, contact with others, or contact with positive thoughts is something you can begin to change immediately.

GO OUTSIDE

Going outside was mentioned briefly in an earlier chapter, but it bears repeating for depressed people who are low on energy and have become used to isolation. As simple as this method sounds, if you want to increase your energy toward meeting your goals, getting outside can help. If your depression is keeping you indoors—at home without going out or only going to work and coming back—and you are not getting out into the world of fresh air and other people, the act of going outside is a good rebalancer. Being in the outside air, feeling the movement of the breeze (or wind!), and seeing the sky will open your mind and boost your energy. This is especially true if you can catch some sunshine while doing it, although being outside even on overcast days is more beneficial than staying inside under regular indoor light.

People with depression can find their energy rebalancing just by exposure to outdoor light, which is why the artificial full-spectrum lights that replicate outdoor light work for many. But going outside does more than just expose you to light. It also requires you to move your body around, which helps your stuck brain shift gears, and it puts you in contact with other people, even if that contact is just a simple hello or momentarily meeting one's gaze. If you want to shake off negativity, moving yourself out of where you are will be a big help. Whether you are in the city or the country, whether you are experiencing the bustle of a metro-politan area or the quiet of nature, whether you are bundled up and moving fast in the cold or ambling on a hot summer day, you will get a physical and mental boost from being outside. Try strolling for 15 to 30 minutes a day, remembering to look at the sky and make eye contact with passersby.

BREAK YOUR ROUTINE

People with rigid, ruminative minds are probably engaging in repetitive behaviors as well. The imbalance in this arena has to do with dysfunc-tional patterns of activity or deficits in the right goals for activity, which may occur as an outcome of unbalanced, negative, and hyperactive cog-nition (rumination). This is one of the most typical imbalances in de-pression. What does this mean? It means that you don't see any reason to do anything new or different because it does not feel particularly ex-citing. So every day you come home from work and play video games or watch TV until it's time for bed. Or every day you stop at the sandwich shop and eat the same fast-food meal. Or you go back to bed the minute the kids leave for school and stay there until you have to get ready for their return. Or you sit with the paper and the puzzle section for 2 hours every morning, drinking coffee until sheer caffeination makes you feel like moving.

If this sounds like you, do something to break into your routine. You will have unexpected benefits—even if they are small—from just doing something different. The brain naturally locks into patterns because they are easy to follow, and you are even more likely to get trapped in patterns of behavior and thinking when depression depletes your physi-cal and mental energy, creating unnecessary routine. But the brain loves novelty even more! It finds it interesting and stimulating. This is why so many people complain about jobs in which they do the same old thing every day—especially jobs where they do not see their work as an impor-tant part of a process.

So what should you do to break your routine? Anything at all. Order tea instead of coffee. Walk a different route to work. Go into your build ing through a different door. Do your homework before you watch TV. Eat dinner early. Dress up for work. It doesn't have to be something big to have an effect. Then all you have to do is pay attention to what that difference is like.

DON'T SPEND ALL DAY DOING ONE THING

A corollary to breaking your routine is refusing to spend the whole day doing one thing. If you are very depressed, you might be spending the whole day passively lying on the couch sleeping or watching TV, but even people who remain "functional" during depression may be devoting the entire day to working, especially if their work allows them to be sed entary, such as people who enter data or develop software. They may spend most waking hours at their job and then just continue to be sed entary when they are home. One of my clients, a graphic designer, found herself spending entire weekends in front of her computer, surfing the web and playing games until the wee hours of the morning. Such mo notony reinforces patterns of thinking and contributes to isolation, shrinking down one's experience until it is out of balance with the rest of the world.

If you cannot think of a way to break your routine, you should get some advice from a therapist or friend. But there are also a few easy ways to begin doing it on your own. First, if you are still going to work, take an actual lunch break and eat different foods for lunch each day. If you are in couch-potato, TV-watching mode and truly have no energy to get up and go, at least change the channel. Watch something different than usual. Read a newspaper or a magazine instead of staring at CNN. Or read a magazine about something you have an interest in (or used to have an interest in, before you were depressed). Get a magazine about cars or gardening or cooking or celebrities (but be careful to avoid com parisons of yourself to the doctored photographs)—anything at all that is easy to read. Many people in depression find themselves reading fiction all day. In that case, sit in different rooms to read and change your genre to mix it up. When you are very depressed, these small changes make a shift in balance that will take you in the right direction. The eventual goal is to have balanced days that include work, relaxed time, exercise, contact with others, and so on.

These ideas are meant to stir up your level of activity, boosting the low energy of depression to a level at which you might be able to take more action on your own behalf. The next ideas are meant to look at balancing your emotions, or affect. In psychological jargon, the word *affect* comprises both the emotion you feel and the way you show it in face, speech, and body language. Depressed *affect* is often shown through dull, flat speech and facial expression, reflecting the dull, flat emotional tone of depression.

REMEMBER AND REPEAT PAST JOYFUL EXPERIENCES

When you are depressed, you do not naturally or easily recall all the great times of the recent past. You probably even discount good experiences by telling yourself they could have been better. But that is the depression talking. In reality, you've probably experienced many good moments—even if they were small—and your tendency to remember only the negative parts of your life is a faulty, imbalanced way of perceiving things.

The following exercise starts with thinking over what you have done in the recent past that gave you some pleasure and figuring ways of repeating those experiences. (A brief caveat here, however: If you are suffering situational depression due to a dangerous set of circumstances, such as an abusive relationship or work environment, you must acknowledge that reality and deal with it. This exercise isn't about looking at a truly bad situation with rose-colored glasses; it is about rebalancing the depressed brain's warped view of normal, everyday experiences as negative. Even if you are in a truly bad relationship or work environment, there are probably other, positive aspects of your life that you can focus on and work toward building—a friendship with someone you trust, or an activity outside the relationship or work environment that gives you pleasure. Building on these aspects of your life will help give you the strength to change your dangerous situation.)

This exercise is best done with another person, because the sharing of it deeply stirs positive emotions. Almost anyone you know would be *happy* to try it out with you. It goes like this:

1. Remember any experience that was pleasurable in any way, and then take a minute or two to remember the details.
2. Then take 3 to 5 minutes to describe the event in detail. Cover all of your senses—what you were hearing, smelling, tasting, feeling, and seeing. Recount the details of your emotions at the time and relate what the circumstances were. Get to all of it.
3. Now, think of how you can repeat this experience as soon as possible. If you are remembering something that is hard to repeat (like a vacation), pick some aspect of it that is easily repeatable.
4. Make a commitment to the person who is listening for when you will repeat this experience (or some aspect of it).
5. Decide how you will be accountable to that person for doing it.

It is a known fact that when you are depressed, you often fail to notice what is pleasurable. You may also tip the balance of pleasure to unpleasure by going past the point when it would have been wise to stop or leave what you were doing. Achieving appropriate balance in your thoughts and feelings about a situation may be as simple as exerting control over how you end things. This idea is addressed in the following method.

CONTROL HOW YOU END THINGS

Controlling how you end things can have a remarkably powerful impact on your satisfaction with an event, and you have more control than you might imagine at first. Remember the sayings "always quit while you're ahead" and "always leave while you still want to be there"? For performers, it's: "Leave your audience wanting more." These sayings imply that the quality of how you feel when something is over will determine how you feel about it later. "Wanting that again" is indicative of a pleasing experience. You can improve endings for your life experiences in several ways. Following are a few of them:

- When you are accepting a social engagement, always consider what the right time to leave probably will be. For example, if the neighbors ask you to stay for an impromptu party, know what time you must be at home to get ready for the next day without feeling pinched. Then tell the host you will be happy to attend but must leave at that specific time. If you are going to an event that will stress you, such as a family party with an alcoholic family member, ask yourself how long you can stay before it gets to be too stressful for you. Then leave at that time. *Don't wait until it gets uncomfortable.* As anyone who has seen *Who's Afraid of Virginia Woolf* knows, that is the point at which you lose your balance and tip the pleasurable into the unpleasurable.
- When leaving an activity with your children, don't wait until they are tired, crabby, or overstimulated. Also, don't pull them away in the middle of a game. Parents who leave at their own convenience without regard to their children's needs set up a bad ending both for themselves and the kids. Leave before they are too tired, and give them lots of warning that you will leave soon so they can finish whatever they are doing. How will it benefit you to end for the sake of the kids, you ask? Well, how much do you like whiney, crabby chil-

dren?! You will have shifted the balance from fun to misery in no time flat—what a reinforcement for your depressive point of view that nothing is fun anymore!

- Then there are the bigger endings: moving away, leaving a job, or finishing a stint on a committee. People don't like saying goodbye, but goodbyes are the best investment you can make in keeping a balanced memory of that part of your life. A bad ending can sour your thoughts and emotions about whatever came before it. You may have noticed that people tend to get artificially close or get mad or distant rather than say goodbye. First, don't take those things personally, as if the other person's behavior is about you. Not everyone handles goodbyes well. Rather, you should take charge of your own part of the ending. So even if you feel hokey doing it, when you leave a group (like a club, a job, or a committee) for any reason, make sure you tell each person what you valued about working with him or her, what you will miss, or what positive thing you will remember even if you lose touch in the future. You can do it at a farewell function or quietly on a one-on-one basis, but do it. You will feel much better later and the positive part of the experience you are leaving will not be overshadowed by a bad ending.

- Whole books are written about ending love relationships because these are some of the toughest endings. All I will say here is: Tell the truth *kindly*. The whole thing will be less disturbing to your personal balance. If you can do what you believe is right and do it kindly, you will keep some balance in your thoughts and emotions about it all.

ENHANCE SPIRITUALITY

Don't skip this section because you don't consider yourself religious or because you are not much of a "God person." Spirituality has less to do with whether a person believes in God in a religious sense and more to do with *how* a person lives with him- or herself and others. Many of us think about spirituality as that deep sense of connection and commitment to something greater than ourselves, and although that "something greater" may be God, it can also be many other things to which we feel connected and committed. Things that are greater than yourself may include a commitment to a political or social cause—the environment, healthcare, preventing child abuse, working for a cure for diabetes or breast cancer, building a park in a blighted neighborhood, or any other kind of cause that grabs your heart and spirit. Spirituality is reflected in living harmoniously in the world and living out the values you espouse.

Why has this method been placed in a technique aimed at achieving balance? People out of balance can be out of balance with their goals, not fully aware of what gives them a sense of meaning or purpose, and thus living aimlessly. A spiritual life can give life meaning and action a purpose, and it can be expressed in any kind of work. One need not devote a life like Mother Theresa to achieve this. In the 1950s, a wonderful writer, Anne Morrow Lindbergh, wrote a volume of contemplations called *Gift from the Sea*. In one of the reflections, she wrote about how out of balance it feels living a life of being "torn to pieces" with too many directions and too few things that center you. For many women, housekeeping, childrearing, and working for income can be a life of being torn apart, but it need not be, if the goal is right. Lindbergh then described how spiritual it can be to live a life centered in creating a home, if all the choices of what to do with time are oriented toward that purpose. She believed that working with her hands to create a healthful, happy environment is a spiritual act, centering a woman rather than fragmenting her experience. And she wrote this long before we became so driven to participate in outside-the-home activities for ourselves and our children. Achieving balance may not be as easy today with the outrageous demands we place on ourselves and our children to do something with every moment. However, if you ask yourself about each activity "Is this activity in service of my purpose in life?" it can help you decide whether to do it or not.

J.J. talked about having become a "human doing" rather than a "human being," and she felt profoundly depressed. Although she earned a good living, she did not have a goal that she was trying to fulfill. When she really thought about what gave her life purpose, she immediately knew that making a good home for her children was her top goal, but traveling 3 days a week for work and shepherding the children to activities all weekend to "fulfill their potential" was destroying their home life and their connection with one another. J.J. decided to change this by basing every choice about what they would do as a family on whether it furthered the goal of making their home a safe haven and secure base from which to move outward. It took some adjusting, but reducing her travel and creating an inviolable family time every Friday night allowed J.J. to feel centered. For her, this was a spiritual anchor. A life with meaning and purpose *is* a spiritual life, regardless of whether it includes religion. When we feel our life has meaning, we have faith in an optimistic future and faith in ourselves or others. And faith is at the heart of a spiritual life.

Getting more connected to something "larger than us" can, and often does, occur through religious practices. It also occurs as a result of meditation, even when meditation is not connected to God. There is abundant research that stimulating your spiritual awareness through meditation improves the function of your brain, promotes compassion and empathy, and diminishes depression as a sense of wellbeing ensues. Spiritual experiences are often described as transcendent and hard to put into words but nonetheless powerful in leaving people with a changed state of wellbeing and perhaps an altered way of perceiving or thinking about things. It is possible to seek those experiences without seeking God, as people may have those experiences connecting to the universe, to nature, or to others. An intentional spiritual practice can help you become aware of your purpose and envision your dreams, thus giving you a more optimistic view of the future. Such a sense of spirituality is the opposite of depression in its energy, forward-looking optimism, and motivation.

A highly underdiscussed issue in spiritual life is participation in community. Monks and nuns of all religious paths have chosen to live in communities in which others practice the same discipline and support them in carrying out that discipline. You may not have an interest in developing a spiritual discipline of such intensity—few of us do—but being in a community of like-minded individuals who support our spiritual endeavors offers solace and encouragement. People who practice with you care about you. This can create a balance between depressed self-absorption and a supportive interaction with others.

How do you find the right community? If you are not currently involved in any kind of community, you might want to consider joining a church, synagogue, or mosque. Try attending several services to see where you feel the most comfortable. If the idea of getting involved in a religious group does not appeal to you, consider joining a group who practices some form of meditation. You can find such groups through community centers, mental-health clinics, and even gyms. The Internet makes it possible to find just about anything. Searching for meditation or mindfulness training in your area will lead you to a group. Practicing a martial art, such as Tai Chi or tae kwon do, is excellent for body, mind, and spirit. Joining a martial-arts group can help you meet like-minded individuals who can support you. Any group that is committed to a cause you support can also be a source of connection to others. Finally, 12-step programs base recovery on community support and on reliance on a "higher power." These programs are an excellent place to find a spiritual path as well as a community to support you in following it.

Connect to Your Higher Power

The outcome of enhancing your spirituality will be obvious in your sense of wellbeing and balance in all arenas. People who pray and meditate report stronger feelings of connection to a "higher power," along with improvement in their health, mental clarity and focus, and relationships with others (due to stronger feelings of compassion and empathy). What you get out of this depends on what you want from it. Your focus or intention shapes what you do and what you derive.

Finding God (or a higher power) is a tremendous source of wellbeing and solace in times of trouble. I in no way here want to promote a specific religion or way of thinking about God; the spiritual means to feel connected to God are available across *all* religious lines. The great benefit to people with depression is that the practice of connecting to a higher power neurologically promotes balance and health. Of course, I'm not suggesting that people who go to church and believe in God don't become depressed—they do. Changing the way they connect to God may be a way out of the depression.

The 12th (and final) step in Alcoholics Anonymous begins with the words "having had a spiritual awakening as the result of working these steps" (A.A., 2001), suggesting that the behavioral, physical, and cognitive changes involved in the first 11 steps *culminate* in spiritual awakening, which then leads to living life with new meaning. This idea that taking action to enhance spirituality can precede spiritual awareness is not just found in 12-step literature. In the work of Andrew Newberg and Mark Robert Waldman (2009), *How God Changes Your Brain*, readers can learn about various forms of meditation to enhance spirituality (with benefits that result in balance in physical, emotional, and mental arenas). The point is that you can start doing things now that bring you more spiritual connection and allow you to gradually become more balanced in all arenas of your life.

Pray or Meditate

You can achieve a transcendent state through prayer or meditation with the intention of being open to the experience of God. The kind of prayer that provides this is not likely to be a petition prayer, which asks God to fulfill wishes, needs, or desires. Rather, it is the meditative kind of prayer that centers the person in a state of receptivity to listen. (See Eddie Ensley's *Prayer That Relieves Stress and Worry* in the Recommended Reading and Resources section for excellent ideas on several types of contemplative prayer for Christian readers.) How you conceptualize God will have an impact on the result of your prayer. People who pray with thanksgiving, who conceptualize God as loving, who ask for the highest good to be achieved, or who show and receive love feel the most blessed by the praying, whereas people who question God, see God as punitive or hostile, or who ask to know what they have done wrong do not feel better (Menahem, 2005). Conceptualizing a negative, punitive, or hostile god activates the limbic system instead of the parietal lobes where transcendent experience appears to be located (Newberg & Waldman, 2009).

Meditation is the most commonly used way to enhance your awareness of God or your higher power. Typically meditation starts with the breath (Newberg & Waldman, 2009; Siegel, 2007; Williams et al., 2007). Simply being aware of the in-breath and out-breath can be a meditation (see Chapter 12 for methods on breathing).

Next, you might select a specific thought to focus on while you breathe. You can pick a religious phrase that has meaning to you (e.g., "have mercy on me") or a single word (like "one" or "om," used in yoga) to add to your inward awareness. Many people find that playing pleasing, peaceful music while meditating deepens their experience of the transcendent.

Newberg and Waldman (2009) studied the outcome of a specific form of meditation that included movement—the use of finger positions shifting with sounds that were uttered. There are also other means to incorporate movement into meditation. Walking a labyrinth and praying with a rosary are powerful ways to bring movement into prayer.

Moving your body in a repetitive, noncompetitive manner can enhance learning, open the path to creativity, put you "in the zone" (Benson & Proctor, 2003; Glasser, 1976), and give you many of the benefits of meditation without necessarily creating transcendent possibilities. Creating transcendent moments is about having intent and mindful awareness while doing whatever activity you've chosen. You may try visualization, body posture, walking meditation, progressive muscle relaxation, and other similar means.

Practice

If you want to learn to pray and meditate, you must practice. Finding what works for you and committing to doing it daily is the only way to get the benefit. It appears that one or two 10- to 20-minute sessions of meditation each day is where you will find the right balance for yourself. Herbert Benson (1996) described the ways people could reap health benefits with 20 minutes of meditation that invoked a deep state of relaxation. Newberg and Waldman (2009) saw the benefits begin accruing after about 12 minutes per day. Different practitioners advocate different amounts of time, but all suggest a daily practice and one that can be done at the same time each day so that your brain and body develop a sort of rhythm and expectation that contributes to sinking into the state of meditation and benefiting from it.

DEFINE YOUR VALUES

I was an addictions counselor for many years. In the 12-step program there is a conscious, intentional focus on connection to a higher power, but a strong reluctance to define God to anyone. I came to see the wisdom in not asking people to believe in a particular definition of God, even when you encourage them to tap into their profound desire for connection to something greater than themselves. After years of conversation with people about how to define spirituality, I came to understand that most people could identify their own values as a place of connection—a place where they were connecting to something more than themselves.

For example, Katrina, a woman who was decidedly agnostic, was in turmoil and told me there was no way a spiritual point of view would help her. When I asked her about what she believed in that guided her actions and decisions, she listed her beliefs that she should be kind to others, be frugal with her resources, make sure that her choices did not hurt others or infringe on their rights, honor her commitments and fulfill promises she made, and so on. It was the first time she had delineated the values she held and examined how they defined her connection to other people and the world around her. To me that is a spiritual life. How you connect with others is a spiritual concern and your values are the way you define a spiritual life. Any person practicing a religion certainly has values and may ascribe the importance of those to their beliefs, but even people who don't practice a religion have a sense of values. When they live in harmony with their values, they have a spiritual path to follow.

The following exercise will take a little time, but it is a way to find your values, find what you see as an ideal balance, and examine if you are fulfilling the goals of a balanced life. You might see ways you can direct your behavior to better live according to your values, and that will give you a good start in restoring balance by eliminating unnecessary activities and increasing action toward fulfilling your goals. Identifying goal-directed action is best for the purpose of keeping thoughts focused and correcting negative, pessimistic thinking. Knowing where to begin a behavior change is very helpful.

Use the following exercise to help you set goals and target actions that will be helpful to restoring balance.

1. Make three columns on a sheet of paper.
2. In the first column, make a list of every activity you do in one week. You can start by listing everything you did today and continuing the list for a week before you go on to the next step, or you can go back in your mind over the week and list everything you remember. Include everything, including your sleep time. You will be the only one to read the list. Include activities like making love, taking a shower, and other things that you may think "shouldn't" go on the list.
3. In the second column, next to each item, write down why you did it. Let's say you stayed an hour later at work because your supervisor asked you to finish something today when you could have worked on it tomorrow. Why did you stay to do it? It might have been to earn the overtime, it might have been to please the supervisor or avoid conflict, or it might have been to demonstrate your effort to get a promotion. There are many possible reasons. Try to pick the most important.
4. In the third column, write the value that you associate with

the reason you did it. Figuring out the value may be the tricky part. In the example of staying for work, look at how your reason may reflect a value you hold. The overtime might be related to a value to have financial stability. Avoiding conflict with the boss might be a value to be peaceful, but it also might be to keep your job (which is ultimately about financial stability). It might be that you stayed because you agreed the work needed to be done and you have a value to be good at whatever you do (i.e., because you have a good work ethic). Here is another example: The activities "I walked to work," "I took vitamins," and "I ate my vegetables" might fulfill the value of taking care of physical health. Find a value associated with each activity on your list.

5. Now consider what your *ideal fulfillment* of each value would be. To start, pick a value and ask yourself, "If I were doing a behavior that really reflected my values, what would I be doing?" For example, if you value taking care of your health, and you were taking care of it perfectly each week, would that mean that you were preparing food at home instead of eating out, exercising three times a week, and brushing and flossing daily? If your value is to learn something new every day, would you be reading a paper every day or listening to a specific TV or radio show? In the most basic of ways, what can you do to fulfill your value? You may have many values or just a few. The number doesn't matter—what's important is that you have a representation of what different activities you do and what values they represent. You may want to write the list on a new piece of paper.

6. Next, prioritize your values. This should not be too difficult—you will probably find that some are hard to place as more important or less, because situations may dictate that decision, but try to get an approximate ranking. You will choose behavior change based on how important these are to you. Now you are ready for the next step.

7. On a new sheet of paper, create a wheel with you as the hub and one spoke going out of the hub for each value you identi-fied. (There is a form for this in the Appendix if you want to photocopy it instead of drawing one.) Don't draw the outer ring that would represent the wheel just yet. The spokes go-ing out represent each of your values. Label each spoke with the name of the value at the end of it. Each spoke should have 10 equally spaced divisions, like rungs of a ladder going from the center to the outer point of the spoke (Figure 8.1).

8. Rate the degree of energy you are putting into fulfilling each value, based on your ideal of fulfilling that value, and mark the degree of energy on the spoke, rating your output from 0 (none) to 10 (very excessive) with 5 being the ideal amount of energy. In this ranking, it is possible to put *too much* effort into one value. For example, you may have a value for a good work ethic but realize that spending 70 hours a week at your job is causing other things suffer. On the other hand, you might be putting in 40 hours but know that you could devote the 2 hours a day you spend on the Internet to your work in-stead. Put a mark on the rung of the spoke to represent the amount of energy you put into achieving that value this week.

9. Now draw a line to connect the dots. This will help you visu-alize the balance—or lack of it. A perfect 5 in each value will make for a smooth-running wheel. For most of us, though, there will be different levels of energy going into each value. A spiky wheel shows where you can increase or decrease en-ergy to improve balance in your life.

Make a Behavioral Change

Now that you have a sense of your values and whether they are balanced in your life, what do you do? If you are putting in the perfect amount of effort on each of your values, you probably feel pretty balanced. But if

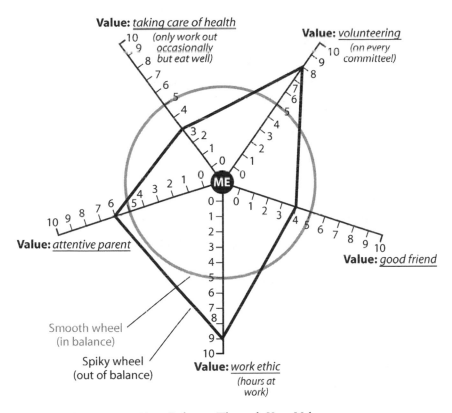

Value: *taking care of health*
.10 (only work out
.9   occasionally
 8   but eat well)
 7
 6
 5
 4
 3 .2
 1
 0

Value: *volunteering*
10 (on every
 9   committee!)
 8
 7
 6
 5
 4
 3
 2
 1
 0

10 9 8 7 6 5 4 3 2 1 0

ME

Value: *attentive parent*

0 1 2 3 4 5 6 7 8 9 10

0
1
2
3
4
5
6
7
8
9
10

Value: *good friend*

Smooth wheel
(in balance)

Spiky wheel
(out of balance)

Value: *work ethic*
(hours at
work)

Figure 8.1 Discovering Your Balance Through Your Values

you are depressed, you probably can see areas where you are not in balance. Identify the place where you are most out of balance, and look at your ideal fulfillment list. Find a small way to shift your energy output in an area where your balance is most out of whack. Try to stop output in one area and increase it in another. For example, if your wheel shows that the energy toward "being a good parent" is at a 9 and "being a good wife" is at a 2, you should think of things you can do to lower the expenditure of energy on the kids and increase it in the marriage. But think small.

Find one small change you can make and start doing it immediately. In the example just mentioned, you might decide to hire a babysitter once a week so that you and your husband can go out to a movie or dinner alone. Be very specific and write down your intention. Writing makes it more real and enhances your commitment to doing the one thing. And decide how to be accountable for it, too. Can you ask a friend to ask you if you actually went on that date with your husband? Can you ask your spouse to inquire about whether you flossed your teeth at night? Can you mark your calendar every time you go to church? Keep the chart you created in a visible spot and track whether you are coming into more balance.

Find Your Balance

First, define your values.

1. Make three columns on a sheet of paper.
2. In the first column, list every activity you do in one week.
3. In the second column, next to each item, write down why you did it.
4. In the third column, write the value that you associate with the reason you did it.
5. Then write down what your *ideal fulfillment* of each value would be.

Next, prioritize your values.

6. On a new sheet of paper, draw a wheel with you as the hub and one spoke going out of the hub for each of your values.
7. Rate the degree of energy you are putting in to fulfill each value, with 5 being the ideal amount.
8. Now, draw a line to connect the dots. A perfect 5 in all values will make for a smooth-running wheel. A spiky wheel shows where you can increase or decrease your energy.

Make a behavioral change based on what is most important to you.

9. Be very specific. Pick one small change you can make and start doing it immediately.
10. Determine a way in which you can be accountable for doing the behavior change.
11. Keep the chart you created in a visible spot and track whether you are coming into more balance.

DO WHAT RESTORES YOU

It almost goes without saying that in depression, people stop doing what is good for them. Among the things you stop doing are those things that restore you. Becoming depleted has an impact on your balance, because whether you are torn apart or so pulled into yourself that you are isolated, chances are high that you are not feeling balanced in your goals, attention, thoughts, or emotions. There are many small ways you can start restoring yourself. I always suggest small things first—not because small is better than big, but because of the reduced energy level typical of depression.

A depressed individual might need help in simply *identifying* which activities are restorative. Look at what you used to do when you felt better, and try to remember which activities you really liked. What activities did you do just because you liked how you felt after you did them? Make a list, even if it seems you can't do those same things today, just to get a sense of what to restore. Then:

1. Pick something you intend to do.
2. Plan it into your schedule
3. Make a commitment to do it and be accountable to someone who will ask if you did it.

Activities that might be on your restorative list could include:

- Intellectual, creative, or spiritual stimulation (joining a book club, going to a lecture, play, or symphony, going to church or synagogue, taking a yoga class)
- Getting out into nature (taking a walk, sitting by a lake, watching a stream flow by)
- Physical activity (bowling, playing tennis, riding your bike, running, dancing, swimming)
- Creative endeavors (drawing, arranging flowers, building furniture, putting a model together, cooking or baking, knitting)

- Low-energy, high-emotional-return social time (taking the grandkids to the park, meeting a friend for coffee)
- And don't forget all the things you love to do but don't typically make time for (watching a football game all the way through, seeing a movie, riding your motorcycle out into the country, taking a bath with candles and music you like, reading a magazine, spending an hour in a bookstore perusing the shelves)

Now pick one (or more) of those things and do it!

If you have the impression that balance means going both inward *and* outward with your energy, you are exactly right. In depression, people may fling themselves into frenzied activity or withdraw so far into themselves that they are like a black hole, sucking all the energy out of the people who are trying to pull them into the world of connectedness again. Balancing life is especially vital for people whose depression may cause plunges into despair, as these individuals often engage in destructive behavior such as overeating or drinking in an attempt to soothe themselves. (This is discussed in detail in the next chapter.) The work you do to create balance in this kind of situation will lay the groundwork for healthier ways of coping and feeling calm.

In trying some of the methods in the technique of regaining balance in your life, you will find that movement in one arena of balance will help you to move in other arenas as well. This is truly a place where every change in the direction of balance promotes more of the same. So don't be afraid that starting small is not enough. You will tilt the balance in your favor even with the smallest of beginnings.

NINE

Technique #7:

Prevent Destructive Behavior

I have always been struck by how many of my depressed clients are competent people, doing jobs with impressive responsibilities, who hit a small obstacle in work or personal life and fell apart. They may not show it on the outside because they have developed self-control for external appearances, but they may go home and get drunk, overeat, or pace around feeling as if nothing will ever be okay. They may sink into a very low place without warning. Some of them become distraught enough to contemplate suicide at these times.

What is happening? How can these people become so unhinged by small things—a boyfriend breaking a date or a client canceling a meeting or a boss giving them a ding on a yearly evaluation—that they feel as if the world is coming to an end? How can they overreact so intensely, behaving destructively toward themselves or taking it out on others, yelling at their children or berating a friend or quitting a job? Both kinds of situations—sinking fast into a hopeless state or plunging into despair and responding with destructive behavior—can be eliminated by knowing how to slow and stop the rapid slide to depressed mood.

This sensation of being okay one minute and feeling awful the next is not the downward swing associated with unipolar or bipolar depression. Nor is it the slowly descending fog of endogenous depression. Rather, it is an inability at a neurobiological level to temper adverse emotions, allowing them to immediately and intensely worsen. When this happens, you might then find yourself doing things that make it even worse: breaking up with the boyfriend who postponed the date, mentally reviewing every horrible time this ever happened before; eating an entire pizza if you cannot have a dinner with a friend; drinking a bottle of wine when you are disappointed about a small thing. On the surface, it makes no sense that people would want to *worsen* a feeling by their negative thoughts or actions, but sometimes people who are miserable seek more misery. Although I have no idea of its origin, an ages-old ditty I heard when I was a child goes, "Everybody hates me. Nobody likes me. I think I'll go eat worms." It made no sense to me then, but I recognize it now: If it's bad, a depressed person has an apparently uncontrollable urge to make it worse.

There are several possible explanations for this based in the life experience of the person who is depressed. Perhaps during your childhood development you did not get much help from your parents in modulating negative emotions, which would have been very stressful. Perhaps your parents did not provide a model of how to "talk yourself down" when upset, or perhaps they themselves became overexcited and lost self-control over small problems. If your emotions were intense, your parents may have been unavailable or unable to soothe you, and their unavailability probably intensified your already intensely unpleasant state, causing you to become distraught. If any of these circumstances occurred often when you were a child, you learned at the gut level that bad emotions get worse and there is no way out. Today, your neural networking efficiently connects you to other experiences of being shut down (depressed, bad mood, negative expectations, sadness) and within no time you are in a funk.

This situation might have been intense as well, something we refer to as "early childhood adversity." The stress response needs relief, and intense stress is disturbing psychologically as well as physically. The impact of what might be called an attachment failure—a lack of security and safety with one's earliest caretakers—can set up the child to feel unsafe and insecure whenever stress occurs. This is not a conscious choice you make but rather the way your brain develops in the context of insufficient soothing or being frightened by the very person who is also the source of safety. Think of it this way: Infant stress response systems, capable initially of getting upset and calming down, literally become regulated for how to calm the upset through interaction with an available, responsive parent. Infants' brains are developing the wiring for how upset to get and how to calm down in different situations of stress. Infants and toddlers become extremely distressed by hunger, thirst, tiredness, cold, pain, and separation from parents. In a chronically frightening, unsafe, or unavailable parental situation, the child's stress response system gets extremely aroused without being regulated downward by soothing from a parent. At some point the upset is so intense that the child must *shut* down, rather than *calm* down. It is a physiological as well as psychological stop for what is intolerable, and this state can be learned before a child is verbal, so the emotional shifts are literally at a level where thought is detached from the process. Shutting down extends into later life as well, because it is the way your brain keeps you safe from overarousal. You may show the shutdown via dull, flat response or you may use destructive actions, like overeating, drinking, gambling, or other behaviors meant to stop painful emotions.

With a history in which you did not learn to soothe yourself, you now go into a tailspin when facing a stress. Without self-soothing skills learned from good parenting, the small stresses of life can trigger gut-level reminders of awful feelings, causing you to plunge into despair.

The worst problem associated with this sudden mood change is that people do self-injurious behaviors that worsen the problem. They may drink, gamble, or even attempt self-harm, so putting the brakes on this emotional shift is necessary for safety as well as recovery. The goal of this technique is to put the brakes on the swift downward plunge and gradually enable the depressed person to learn methods to modulate negative emotions.

BORROW SOMEONE ELSE'S SELF-CONTROL

If you are going to recover from depression, you must be able to stop intense negative thinking or damaging behavior. But you may feel unable to do that without strong intervention on the phenomenon that I call the "plunge into despair." Initially this is not something you can do on your own. But planning what kind of help you need and from whom you can get it is something you can take charge of and do at a time when you are not distraught.

If you recognize this tendency in yourself, you will need help to manage it, because when you are in the midst of this kind of intense mood, it very difficult to interrupt. You need to have someone available to connect with very quickly, as soon as you recognize it happening. Working with a psychotherapist is a good idea to make sure you learn to recognize the signs that you are headed for a plunge and interrupt them. Learning to observe yourself is an important first step in stopping your negative mood and behavior. Your therapist will be able to help you identify the kinds of circumstances that set off this sudden shift to despair and will make plans with you for how to stop it. Following are some ways to intervene.

Make a List of Distractions

To start out, you need to prepare yourself to do things that you like to do, or are at least willing to do, that feel soothing and are not in any way self-injurious. Read, walk, listen to music, watch a movie, play a video game or computer game—anything that will distract you from your distressed mood. Make a list of activities. You will need them as helpers to calm down. You need a list because it will be hard to remember what to do once you are in distress.

Call a Lifeline

Once you have your list, identify someone who can be a helper. When you are plunging to despair, about the most that can be expected is that you have the energy to reach out and grab a lifeline—a connection to another person who can help you up when you are not able to do it. This can be arranged in several ways.

- You might use your therapist as a lifeline. Many people feel most comfortable calling their therapist, so they should make an agreement about when or in what circumstances they should call the therapist and what kinds of fees might apply for a brief reality check or a longer conversation.
- You can identify a friend or family member who can be trusted to stay calm and focused on you in this type of situation. Ask the person ahead of time if he or she is willing to do this for you, and describe what you will need when you are making a "lifeline call" (more on that in a minute). If your lifeline is your partner, be sure to differentiate when you are talking as a lifeline versus when you are just talking. Agree on what times of day the person is available for this kind of call. It is important not to call outside of your lifeline's comfort zones, except in case of dire emergency, because you want the person's help over a fairly long expanse of time. You don't want to wear the person out.
- Make a list of others who might be resources for you when you cannot reach your planned lifelines; these can be other people you know or even community resources like a crisis help line. If you are in an addiction-recovery program, you will have an excellent source of lifelines from the phone list.

Next, work with your therapist to construct some note cards on which you write ideas to help you out if you are highly distressed. These cards can help when your lifeline and backup lifelines aren't available. These ideas should be attached to your list of distracting, soothing activities.

Sometimes a reality check is all that is needed, and sometimes a longer conversation with a lifeline is necessary. How does this work?

1. Figure out what you feel like when you are in this state. You must first know what you are feeling to see it when it hap-

pens. Regardless of whether you know *why* you feel that way or not, call your lifeline when you get the feeling.

2. The first goal of the call is to identify the trigger for the mood. You want to learn over time to identify situations that are problematic for you. How do you get at this? Talking with your lifeline, go back in your mind to a time when you were feeling pretty good, and then walk forward in your mind one conversation, one event, one thought at a time until you note when the negativity set in.

3. The next goal of the call is the reality check. Is this situation, from the lifeline's external point of view, as distressing as it feels to you? You must be willing to hear that your emotional reaction is sometimes bigger than would be expected. Just knowing someone else does not see the problem to be as serious as it seems to you can help you calm down.

4. If you're still feeling distressed, you can have a conversation to help you get a reframe on the situation. You may need to get your lifeline to offer you some alternative explanations for the distressing situation. For example, what if you fell into the abyss when you heard a voicemail from your boss asking you to come to the office first thing in the morning? In no time flat, you saw yourself fired and living on the street. Your helper may need to remind you that you do not know the nature of the meeting and it could be that your boss wants to ask for your input on a work project that requires prompt attention. You may also need a reminder that the time to worry about it is *after* you know what the problem is.

5. Make an agreement about when you will check in after the call to confirm that you are okay or that the situation is resolved.

How long should this use of a lifeline be included in recovery? As long as you need it. Depending on your degree of intensity and the frequency of these episodes, assess with your therapist how this is working for you. I would expect it to need months, at least. If the cause of your plunges into despair lies in your history of early childhood adversity, you need time to learn to purposefully calm your immediate stress response while you make use of therapy to heal that emotional injury of your childhood and reset your stress response to be less overreactive.

LEARN TO SEE THE EVENT FOR WHAT IT IS, NOT WHAT IT REMINDS YOU OF

In order to put on the brakes and stop mood changes that result in destructive behavior, it is important to manage your view of the situation. People with depression from PTSD or adverse early life experiences can influence their emotions today by not interpreting every reminder of the trauma as another trauma. Because early life adversity and prior trauma both result in overreacting to stress, the overreaction has a powerful influence on the interpretation of the current problem as serious. After trauma, your brain automatically makes every molehill into a mountain and you have to work hard to level that mountain before letting your behavior make it worse. For example, if you were in a bad car accident that happened on a rainy day, you may get distraught at the mere sight of a dark cloud while driving, which won't improve your driving skills. If you were subjected to bullying during grade school, you might misconstrue a colleague's innocuous remark as a slight and become defensive, turning what would have been a neutral situation into an argument. Another consequence of early life adversity is that you have an automatic tendency to feel inconsolably upset when stress occurs.

What's the Disaster?

As you look for ways to evaluate your current circumstances more realistically, notice how often you interpret the glitches in life as disasters.

This can help reduce the impact of stressors that send you spinning. You can learn to think through your feeling that a disaster has occurred and see the event for what it is, not what it reminds you of, by asking yourself these questions and writing down or talking out the answers:

1. "What is the disaster?" Literally explain why this is disastrous. Of course, the goal here is that you will see this is not a disaster in reality, but rather a disaster at the level of your stress response, which is overactive. Write down the problem.
2. "What is the worst that could happen here?" And: "What is the *most likely* outcome?" You may note how often you confuse what is possible with what is probable.
3. "Can I cope with the likely outcome?" You might also see that you could survive the *worst* outcome, but answer it for the *likely* outcome.

Next, write down a list of the resources you can call on for help should any of the outcomes occur. As the situation unfolds, contact resources like a sponsor or friend to help evaluate the situation before you take action on any solution.

MODULATE YOUR RESPONSE INTENTIONALLY

Another important step is to check in on the intensity of your reaction and modulate your affective response intentionally, using the power of thinking (prefrontal cortex activity) to control negative emotion (limbic activity). You are going to change your brain to change the response that your body is giving you. Overreactivity feels true ("Oh my God, my heart is pounding and I'm really distraught—this must be a truly bad situation!") and you must use rational thinking to dispute it if you want to diminish how intensely you respond to a situation. You want to move your feeling from "this is a major catastrophe/disaster" to "this could be just an inconvenience." To do that, answer the following:

- Is this a minor inconvenience?
- Is this a major inconvenience?
- Is this a catastrophe?

For each of these questions, write out the reasons why you think this is minor, major, or catastrophic. You are working on modulating intense feelings and calming them.

Your brain will gradually change as you repeat this process over the course of several events, and over time you will develop a less overreactive stress response. You are learning in adulthood to do for yourself what your parents probably did not do enough of when you were a child: Listen to you and soothe you. This is a little like the manual override on your furnace thermostat. Now you must intentionally do what was meant to be automatically programmed into your stress response system.

Rosa was a classic example of the person who plunges into despair. She would often disappear from therapy for 2 or 3 weeks and then return, saying she had gone into a funk. During those times she spent countless hours working or surfing the Internet, watched TV all night, ate pizza or takeout instead of cooking, didn't talk to friends, and rarely left her house. We set up the lifeline program using me and her best friend for times I was not available. At first the calls were infrequent, because Rosa did not believe they could help, but after several calls when she felt considerably better afterward, she started calling nearly every day for a check-in to see if her perceptions were accurate.

Rosa found that most of the times that she plunged into despair were times when she perceived others to be rejecting or disinterested in her. One time, her bowling team decided to disband and she *just knew* it was to get rid of her. After our conversation, she not only realized that she did not have all the information about their decision but also acknowledged that she did not even particularly enjoy being on the bowling team and had been wishing for a way to change that situation. She also began to notice that her boss was sometimes a trigger for her plunges into despair. Like her mother, he was an alcoholic and could be erratic and prone to mood swings and Rosa felt she had to walk on eggshells around him. Once Rosa realized that these situations were not desperate catastrophes but rather just manageable upsets, she found that her despair lifted.

We also worked on things Rosa could do to interrupt her destructive behavior and help her feel soothed if she needed it. Even though she didn't particularly *want* to do some of these things, she acknowledged that she could *decide* to do them anyway—spend 10 minutes on her exercise bike before ordering pizza, or make a plan to have dinner with a friend *before* the weekend so she would have an obligation to get out of the house even if she was upset. The combination of experiencing the willingness of others to be available to her (which helped heal the neglect from her early life experience) and learning that she could do soothing that worked gradually eliminated her plunges into despair. Eventually Rosa was able to talk to herself about different interpretations of upsetting moments and found an increasing number of positive ways to calm down.

Journaling

You can accomplish neural integration (connecting thinking with an emotion to achieve a more balanced inner state) from an old familiar process—journaling. There are different reasons to journal, but you can follow this path to work on your own toward understanding what is going on when you get swept away by negative emotions. In that state you may not only do self-harming behavior, but also hurt relationships with angry or impulsive behavior. You may be too harsh with your children, be short with a significant other, tell off your boss, or do anything that might be hard to repair once you have done it. Journaling will help you put the brakes on hurtful behavior toward yourself or others, learn what is going on, and integrate the new situation in a healthier way. In this process, you will identify affect, connect it with earlier life experience, and see if you can distinguish between past and current situations. Follow this process of journaling by fully describing the following points. (You can also do this aloud with a therapist.)

1. What do I feel in my body?
2. Are these sensations familiar?
3. What is the earliest age I remember feeling this way?
4. Can I get a memory of a situation in which I had this feeling or even just an image of myself, like a snapshot, feeling this?
5. Is there any similarity between the two experiences (former and current)?
6. What did others do then?
7. What did I do then?
8. What are others doing now?
9. What do I want to do now?

This "thinking brain analysis" of emotions and sensations will help your brain integrate feeling and thought, strengthening the function of the circuits in your brain that connect at that junction. You should experience a lessening of intensity when the feeling comes up in the future, allowing you to gradually reduce the plunge into despair and your unhelpful behaviors when you feel that despair.

REMEMBER THAT A FEELING IS JUST A FEELING

Feelings pass. What we experience physically and how we feel, think, and act are inseparable, but the sensations are transient. You know what you emotionally feel by recognizing physical sensations that accompany experience. If you feel flooded with warmth in your chest, you may recognize it and say you feel compassion. A flood of warmth across the face may be labeled as embarrassment. Your body is doing its work to give you important data via sensations you can notice. Once you have recognized and labeled the sensation for the information it is giving you, the sensation fades.

Knowing your emotions requires a complex process of noticing those physical sensations and then interpreting them based on prior experience. It is only afterward that you decide how to take action. For example, if you *feel* anger, you are aware of it because your heart rate increases, your face feels hot, your stomach clenches or drops, and the muscles of your face, jaw, and neck tighten. The energy of the anger is *felt* first; then you label it, and then you must decide how to act on it. You might very quickly calm yourself and elect to take action on a rational appraisal of the situation, but first you must notice and then interpret the physical sensations.

When you suffer depression, you are predisposed toward labeling every sensation as negative and coloring it all blue. To interrupt the automatic tendency to plunge into despair when a feeling is negative or uncomfortable means slowing down this stage of emotion and learning to notice feelings without becoming alarmed about them. Feelings are feelings—they are not facts! This does not mean feelings are not real. It simply means they are information and not all information is useful. You can decide about the validity, usefulness, or importance of the information after you weigh it against other information. To be able to do that, you have to slow down your tendency to move quickly from "normal" to "despair." This will allow you to see what is really happening.

Labeling emotions is a process you will need to practice before you will be able to notice a sensation without leaping to a false label for it. People who are depressed have a tendency to skip noticing and labeling and go straight from a sense of negativity to despair. This method is intended to help you slow down to notice a physical sensation just for what it is without deciding what it means. "Oh, I feel heaviness in my chest and my eyes are welling with tears." Do not decide what it is until you get the whole of the sensation noticed. This is referred to as getting the "felt sense" of something. Only then, when you get the sense of it, do you offer an emotion label: "I feel sad." It might bring, at that very moment, a sense of relief just to know what you feel. "Ah, it is sadness." By itself, that might be a profound achievement for the kind of person who has been avoiding feeling feelings. When you are clear about the emotion that goes with the sensations, sometimes knowing is enough.

You may be surprised when you notice what is happening in your body to see the emotion you ascribe to the sensation, especially when you notice it in the context of a specific situation. Those same sensations of tears welling and heaviness in your chest might be the sense of futility, or of anger, or of being pressured. Once you label it, your body will react to the label and immediately give you the sense of whether the label is accurate. This is not the same as deciding what the feelings mean about you, your life, your identity, your future, or about what other people intend toward you. Without correctly appraising the emotion, you cannot know what it means. The plunge to despair carries you fast into those kinds of appraisals, and the goal here is to *stop* before you go that far.

For example, Mary came to session one day feeling extremely depressed. She was also mad at herself for being depressed and went off on a rant that she was never going to feel better—that because she was depressed today, she would always be depressed, and that therapy was useless "if here she was, depressed again." I asked her to slow down and close her eyes and just notice what she sensed in her body. She identified that her shoulders were heavy and sore, as if she were carrying a heavy sack across them. She noticed that all of her muscles were tired and that she felt weak, even sitting in a chair. Then we explored emotion words that went with this sensation. She tried out "tired," "weak," and "sad" and finally settled on "burdened." When I asked what in her life was burdening her, Mary's eyes welled with tears and she blurted out, "I am so tired of fighting with my daughter." She had not mentioned her daughter before that point. As soon as she said this, it opened a discussion about her frustration with parenting as a single mom. After a while I asked how her body felt, and she noticed that the burdened sensations had dissipated. I asked about her depression, and she was surprised to note that she was not depressed. She stated, "I was just frustrated and did not realize it. If I had just talked to one of my friends about that issue with my daughter, it would probably have been enough."

Practicing the "a feeling is just a feeling" technique might help you stop the plunge into despair or interrupt you from sinking into a funk. For now, try to acknowledge "what *is*" and then let yourself know that at this moment you do not have to change your experience. You do not have to fix it, solve it, get rid of it, or understand it. Many people who suffer depression may experience a moment of sadness and turn it into a huge problem: "Oh, I am *so* depressed." Just because you feel sad, you do not have to make more of it than it is. In depression, there is a tendency to go off on a tangent about why you feel sad, and why this time is just like other times you felt sad, and how you will always feel sad, and how bad life is that here you are feeling sad again.

Instead, when you have a sensation that you label, try to just notice how you made the label. What sensation are you labeling? Is your stomach sore, your chest tight, your throat blocked, your eyes burning? The sensation has information for you. Ask yourself, "What in the here and now is contributing to that sensation?" Notice that the question has nothing to do with what happened in the past or what will happen in the future. By slowing down the awareness and labeling process, you may be able to see that you are responding to something in the now and that sadness is appropriate. What you will immediately experience is that feelings are temporary and if you do not struggle against them, they shift almost immediately. The act of noticing is often enough to help the feeling move along. What a relief!

Your brain is so efficient at connecting (neural networking) that you might struggle to stop automatic interpretations of your sensations. You may need practice to identify and then interrupt automatic negative connections. It is common to have a sensation but leap past the moment of noticing to interpreting. The psychotherapy method known as "focusing" devotes considerable attention to learning how to follow the felt sense in the body to first identify the sensation and then label the emotions. If you need some help with that aspect of knowing how you feel, read the work of Childre and Martin (1999), Gendlin (1998), or Cornell (1996) in the Recommended Reading and Resources section at the end of this book.

A Feeling Is Just a Feeling

First, turn your attention to the physical.

1. Feel the sensations.

Then intentionally suspend judgment.

2. Notice how you label the sensations. What emotional label do you give?

3. Do you know the emotion? That might be the first part of learning to deal with reality. Recognizing emotion is a valuable aspect of wellbeing.

Pay attention to the idea that a feeling is just a feeling.

4. Notice what is happening at the moment that creates the sensation.

5. Try to interrupt comparing to the past or worrying about the future.

6. Try to interrupt explaining this as part of your destiny or identity.

7. Give yourself permission to let the feeling go without fixing or changing it. Tell yourself: "I do not have to understand every feeling. I do not have to make up a story about the feeling. I do not have to take action on the feeling."

DO SOMETHING DIFFERENT—NOW!

One thing you can be in charge of is *what you do* when you are depressed, especially if your mood takes a sudden shift toward the negative. Not all depressed individuals plunge into *despair*, but they often feel unexpectedly blue in a way that seems hard to shake. You may notice that when things go wrong at work or you have a personal disappointment it is very hard to shake off. Instead of making it worse by contemplating all the other times you have been disappointed, this is time to do something different. This is a good time to use those notes about distracting, soothing activities.

Depressed behavior reflects the inflexible, uncreative, or stuck brain that does not easily generate new solutions. It's likely that you respond in the same way every time you feel the depression plunge. You might order pizza, head for the ice cream, drink alcohol, or stay in bed all day. Those do not relieve the plunge into despair; they just are rigid responses you made before to dull the feelings.

Preparing ahead of time to see things differently will help your brain function more effectively, so planning a different course before you are upset helps break the rigid, uncreative brain function that marks depression. In 12-step programs, the first thing you do to break your pattern is call your sponsor. If you aren't in a program, you can try planning to shift your behavior ahead of time. There are options for doing something different. Plan exactly what you will do *before* you reach for a drink, eat, or lie down for the day. It should be a small activity.

Bill O'Hanlon (1999) supported this notion about the power of *doing one thing different*, suggesting that the act of interrupting your pattern of behavior with a planned diversion can set you off on an entirely different (and less destructive) path. Even one apparently unrelated activity, like changing your shoes before you eat the ice cream, can help you stop and move in a new direction. Anything might work: singing along with the radio for one song, going for a walk around the block, taking a shower. Just choose something that is odd, unique, active, and completely unrelated to what you were about to do, and then *do* it before pouring the drink, plopping down in front of the TV, snapping at your children, or whatever it is that you normally do when you feel yourself plunging into despair or feel the blues coming on.

Then see what happens. Observing the outcome of your behavior should start to become a habit as you try to change your old patterns. See what really helped, no matter if you expected it to or not. Learn what works best for you to divert, soothe, or calm yourself. Discussing the outcome with someone like your lifeline will give it more power.

DEVELOP COMPASSION TOWARD
YOURSELF AND OTHERS

Depression often causes people to be harsh in their judgment of them-selves or others. The negativity and inflexibility of the overactive limbic mind combines with the tendency to fall into negative interpretations of events. Then, low on neurotransmitter activity, you miss the modulating influence of an active, energetic left prefrontal cortex for thinking things through. Even worse, your anterior cingulate gyrus functions ineffi-ciently, so the circuit for compassion and empathy is out of commission in times of distress, and you make bad decisions about yourself or others. How can you interrupt this? By practicing a method that deliberately activates that circuit for compassion. You will feel much better if you get into the habit of practicing compassion.

In this process, you will learn to focus on compassion purposefully as a way to help your brain learn what that is like. Talk with your therapist or an understanding friend, or write it down privately. Do you know what a loving parent should sound like when holding a crying baby? Can you bring to mind the crooning voice and soft pats that communicate, "There, there, it will be all right?" That is the voice of compassion. It is the voice of the empathetic parent who cannot fix the problem of your distress immediately. Sometimes you have to wait a bit to be fed or changed or for your parent to figure out what is wrong. If you missed out on that kind of empathy for your pain, you may not have the immediate gut instinct to be that loving toward yourself. And if you cannot empa-thize with your own pain, you surely cannot be compassionate toward others, either.

In this method, you are going to remember a time when you needed to put on brakes but were focused on what a rotten situation you were in or were ruminating on how the other person injured you. That inner focus on why it *should not be* and how *bad you are* or how *bad the other is* only intensified your negative mood. It probably made your behavior worse, too. Start by trying this out when you are calm, because it takes some practice.

Focus on something in yourself that you judge harshly or a situation in which another person can send you into the swirl of negativity. You may judge yourself for drinking too much or continuing to smoke or not getting started on your college degree or having a messy house or being too much of a doormat to others. Now:

1. Select a situation. Pick one in which you are struggling to do something differently—something you wish you could change or that makes you mad or frustrated with yourself. Or pick one in which someone else's behavior is bothering you and you feel impatient with that person.

2. Now, describe the behavior exactly, either in writing or aloud. Describe words or actions as if you are reporting on them from a completely objective, nonjudgmental point of view. If this is about *you* doing something you do not like, talk about the *part* of you that is doing that thing—it isn't the *whole* of you who is choosing to do this; if it were, you wouldn't feel conflicted about it. If it is about *someone else's* behavior, give the other person the same benefit and discuss the part of that person who is doing the actions you do not like. Do not talk about *why* you think you or the other person is doing the objectionable behavior.

3. Try to literally see the *part of you* that is struggling. What do you look like at that moment? Or try to see that part of the other person. Then imagine that part of you or the other person sitting across from you.

4. Now you are going to say an empathetic phrase with just the right tone of voice. If you are writing, imagine yourself saying it aloud. In fact, *do* say it aloud if you are in a private place where you can. Address that part of you or the other person with the equivalent of, "Oh, dear. You are struggling." Remember, this part of you (or of the other) is not the whole of you (or the other). *This part is having a hard time.* Take a bit of time to feel what happens when you create a moment of empathy.

5. Now you are going to make a sincere and interested inquiry. Ask that part you are talking to, "What is making this so hard?"

6. You are going answer this question by imagining yourself in the position of the part of you or the other person. Speak or write with the voice of the part that is having a hard time, explaining what is so hard. Remember you are now talking to the part of you that is "without compassion" and "impatient."

7. Listen to the answer. If you speak without a lot of self-censoring, you might hear something very interesting.

8. Now, switch back to the "you who wants to be more compassionate" and without judging, teaching, or arguing, simply say, "You are right. That is very hard." *Do not add anything to the end of that statement.*

9. Talk (or write) about how it feels to say that without adding anything.

What you discover is going to vary depending on the situation, but as you describe how it feels to just acknowledge "that is hard," you will begin to touch on the hurts, fears, or disappointments that led you to be less compassionate. You will open up a new understanding of yourself and others.

Practice Compassion

1. Find a situation in which you feel no compassion. Write or talk about the behavior but not the motivation behind it.

2. See the part of you (or of the other person) that is struggling.

3. Address that part with "Oh, dear. You are struggling."

4. Ask, "What is making this so hard?"

5. Listen to the answer.

6. Say, "You are right. That is hard." Stop there.

7. What does it feel like to end it there?

Meditate on Compassion

The ability to feel compassion toward yourself and others can be nurtured in daily meditations. In 12-step programs there is a specific process for not "taking someone's inventory"—the outcome of which is to step out of the role of judge. You can only know your own part in a situation, and when you stop trying to judge what others' motivations and reasons are, you move to a place where compassion is possible. The idea of not taking inventory is a daily intention to stop seeing what is wrong in other people. When you catch yourself doing that, remind yourself that your role is not to judge others.

You can also try a method that has worked like magic for many of my clients. When you find yourself ruminating on the wrongs done to you by others, and you are distinctly *not* sympathetic to their plight, try 30 days of praying for their wellbeing. It does not even matter if you don't feel as if you mean it. Try this: Pray for that person to have every good gift—wisdom, honesty, kindness, fulfillment of all his or her needs, and so on. Pray for that every day for 30 days. It will take away your resentment.

Barbara was furious with her ex-husband for ruining her life with his cheating. She had divorced him after she discovered his affairs, despite the fact that she had never wanted to be a divorcee living with her children 50% of the time and not having the happy family life she had longed for. The divorce had been finalized 3 years ago, and Barbara knew she had to move on, but she was having trouble. She ruminated and felt as if her life would never be happy again. And he was still a thorn in her side. His slow payment of child support was an issue, as was his ongoing nastiness toward her (he blamed her intolerance of him for their divorce). The fact that he had found a younger woman to marry grated on her.

Barbara was furious when I first suggested praying for her ex-husband as a way to stop ruminating on her losses, but she reluctantly agreed to try it. She reported later that she became very aware that she did not want him to be happy—she did not want him to have a good life; she wanted him to suffer. But she prayed that her prayers would be answered regardless of her anger. She realized that the way for her to get what she needed for him better behavior toward her and fulfillment of his obligations to their children—was for him to be content, honest, and able to be satisfied with his life. If he was, then he would be honest with her and would fulfill his obligations. She said she did not know exactly when it happened, but her resentment lifted and she was far less depressed about the divorce.

If praying does not feel comfortable for you, you can still meditate on developing compassion. The activation of your sense of compassion and empathy is a natural outcome of meditation. There are several ways to do this. An initial place to start is just meditating on a word or phrase, such as "peace" or "have mercy on me." Another way to do this is to meditate on an object you regard as sacred to allow yourself to feel immersed in the experience of sacredness. If you want to explore some different versions of meditation, the Recommended Reading and Resources section has books by Thich Nhat Hanh (1999), Daniel Siegel (2007), and Newberg and Waldman (2009), all of which offer a variety of means to meditate for developing compassion.

The person with sudden plunges into despair needs methods that help with self-observation and self-efficacy. The lifeline methods promote self-observation directly. The goal of the lifeline is to promote cognitive change through reframing, understanding, and observing actual outcomes. These cognitive changes then help to change behavior. Changing your interpretation of your sensations is another way to learn how to cope without being destructive. Working with neural-integration methods such as journaling helps heal the brain so that the plunge into despair can be removed from your repertoire of behavioral and emotional outcomes of depression. And finally, feeling compassion stimulates the part of your brain that missed out on empathy when you were young, helping you to be kinder to yourself and others. The desired end result of these methods is that you will feel more self-efficacy—that is, you will be more able to cope with the problematic situations of daily life in positive ways.

TEN

Technique #8:

Broaden Your Perspective

Depression shrinks your field of vision, causing you to focus on your problems without seeing much of anything else in life. And it colors *how* you see what you *do* see. It shades everything with negativity. And then you narrow down your interpretations to the two themes that predominate in depression: feeling inadequate and feeling worthless. Believing that you are inadequate or worthless depletes your energy to do or try new things, to take up a challenge, or to see things with a fresh perspective. You tend to see every event through the lens of depression, as if it is validation of your inadequacy or worthlessness.

Your frame of reference determines how you interpret what is happening in a situation. One of the problems with depression is that the negative frame you put on things often isn't very accurate, leading you to do things that may make the situation even worse. This is why broadening your perspective is so important. In the world of psychotherapy, we refer to getting a fresh perspective as "reframing" a situation. This refers to the way that you can choose what a situation means to you and what to do about it. What you do in response to events is determined by your frame.

Suppose, for example, that you are a teacher tutoring a student having trouble in math. During the tutoring session, the child has a temper tantrum, screaming insults at you. You *could* interpret this situation through a negative frame, seeing the child's behavior as malicious and manipulative (trying to get out of doing his schoolwork), or by assuming you are an inadequate teacher. Or you could interpret it in a different way, seeing the tantrum as an expression of the child's frustration and fear that he is not as smart as his classmates. If you use the negative, "he's being manipulative" frame, you will probably respond by punishing the child for his outburst—which, if the real reason behind it is his fear, will only make his behavior worse by making him feel worse about himself. If you take the perspective that he is frustrated and fearful, you can help him learn how to calm down and handle frustration effectively, creating a nice learning experience out of a bad situation.

Deliberately changing your thoughts will also have an impact on the way you feel. Getting a new perspective helps you look at your situation differently and thus be able to feel differently about it. To use the tutoring example again, getting a fresh perspective means going from feeling inadequate as a teacher to feeling empathy and compassion toward your struggling student. It should be obvious which set of emotions is going to have a more positive effect on the situation.

The technique of broadening your perspective is aimed at finding that new angle, that new way of looking at what is happening. Changing how you think is a brain-based intervention: You are using your brain to change your brain. You will make decisions about stopping your reactions, stepping back, becoming observant rather than reactive, and only then choosing how to act. Small changes in your observations can make big changes in your emotions and reactions to your emotions. Finding a place to put "the lever that can move the world" is a matter of changing your mental frame of reference for events, experiences, and interactions with others. When you make an intentional practice of observing before acting, you will find yourself in an entirely different place from which to move your world.

LEARN TO OBSERVE WITHOUT JUDGMENT

The ability to observe is something you can cultivate. Many times we are inattentive to the world around us, and it would behoove all of us to take time to see what we are seeing or hear what we are hearing *as if it were unique* to the moment we are seeing or hearing it. In fact, it *is*. But our brains help us think fast and learn easily by forming categories and sorting new information into those categories. This allows us to quickly respond without much thought. It would be remarkably inefficient if we had to do everything in life as if we had never done it before!

But with depression, the categories of experience are heavily overlaid with negativity. When a previous experience has left you saddened, hurt, or disappointed, guess how you will respond when a similar event occurs? You will feel sad and hurt, and you probably won't even think of taking a fresh look at the situation, unburdened by assumptions from past experience. Breaking that tendency by having an open mind can eliminate this problem that occurs for everyone with depression.

Deciding What Your Feelings Mean

There is a saying that in life "pain is inevitable; suffering is optional." Many situations may result in a feeling of physical or emotional pain. But that does not mean that you are *destined* to have pain or that your *identity* is wrapped up in having emotional pain. It means that at this time and in this place, you are experiencing pain. Unfortunately, this is something that people with depression tend to forget.

Many people fight against what they are experiencing or try to change what they experience to fit a preconceived image of what they think they *should be* feeling. As soon as they compare "what is" with "what should be," they are bound for disappointment and depression. When you are depressed, it is likely that thoughts like "this is not what should be happening" or "this is not what I should be feeling" or "this is not what I should be doing" are typical of your thinking.

Especially if you have had recurrent bouts of depression, you might fight against feelings of depression emerging and try not to notice those feelings or what they are emerging from. Instead of trying to stop them or push them away, try to be nonjudgmental and a little curious: "Oh, depression, here you are again! I *thought* I felt you creeping up. So what's going on—why are you coming today? What are you trying to tell me?"

You might be really surprised to find that often the feeling behind the depression isn't nearly as bad as you fear. Maybe you are sad about a houseguest leaving, or sad about having to say goodbye to your students at the end of the semester. Often people feel depressed when sadness arises at the anniversary of the death of a loved one. Once you recognize the feeling underneath the depression, allow yourself to feel it. If you can just allow yourself to be sad (or lonely, or let down, or frustrated) you will find that the depression will go away relatively quickly. If you try to "stop" the negative feeling, on the other hand, you might find that, ironically, the depression will get stronger as a result. It is trying to get you to notice! So be gentle with yourself. Don't judge yourself as bad or wrong for having negative, even depressed feelings. Gentleness and compassion for yourself do not come naturally to many depressed people, and the need to develop them bears repeating for this reason. (See Technique #7 for ideas to work on that.)

Depression can also make trouble for you when you move too fast beyond knowing what you feel to deciding what the experience means. People with endogenous depression—depression that neurobiology predisposes you to have—tend to give their physical feelings a negative interpretation, thereby starting a vicious circle in which negative thinking enhances the depression. When feeling pain, you may go from simply saying, "Ah, this hurts," to "This is the way it will always be. This is because I am inadequate. This is because I am worthless." Statements like that make it worse.

Just as important is remembering that events you don't like will inevitably occur. Assuming they occur because you deserve them, have rotten luck, will never get a break, or are doomed to be miserable forever will make you even more miserable. On the other hand, when you believe you should *not* have to experience that event, you may fight against it. It is amazing how depressing it can be to fight against reality: "I don't want to feel this!" "I am miserable because I don't want to _____ [fill in the blank: be dumped by my girlfriend, lose my job, have diabetes, get a C on this test]." The depression stems from the way you make the situation mean something negative about you. In effect, you are making up your reality. Although you may find that hard to believe, in point of fact, if you can see things from a different angle, your reaction will be very different. For example, "I don't want to be dumped by my girlfriend and it hurts and I don't like it" creates a very different response from "She dumped me and I will never, ever feel happy again."

Consider the many ways you construct your own version of reality. Everyone takes in information and then interprets what it means. How often has someone taken offense at a statement you made (or wrote in an email), making you have to rush to say, "I did not mean it like that"? Certainly you've experienced the reverse as well: You heard or read something entirely different than what the other person intended. This happens a lot in email. You read *words* and you impose meaning on them. If you *think* the sender was criticizing you, you *feel* criticized. And that becomes the "reality" you respond to whether or not the other person was intending to criticize. Or perhaps a friend of yours gave you "a look" from across the room at a party—and you then spent an hour on the phone with a different friend dissecting what the friend who gave you the look meant and why she did it and what you should do now—only to discover later that she hadn't even seen you and her look had nothing to do with you. All the misery of your interpretation could have been avoided if you had stopped your interpretation and investigated the basis for your emotion first.

Denise, a young woman who had been seeing me for help with her recurrent bouts of depression, came in one day furious with her friend Joanie. "She invited me to tag along with her and her boyfriend at dinner!" Denise said, outraged. "How insensitive is that?!" I asked Denise to clear her mind and then bring up the whole situation to watch what she felt in her body. "Terrible," she replied. But of course "terrible" is not something you feel—it is just a level of severity. So I asked her where in her body she was having sensations. She identified pressure in her chest and tension in her shoulders. When she asked herself, "What is it about this situation that is pressuring me?" she immediately knew: She felt jealous of Joanie's relationship, and she was tense because she either had to decline a night out with her friend or face being alone for the evening.

At that moment there was no judgment of Joanie as being bad or good. Denise could see that the problem lay in how she felt, and she realized she had choices about how to react. She could ask Joanie to meet without the boyfriend, she could stay home, or she could live with her jealousy and go out with both people. Simply realizing that she had choices made her feel much better.

In depression, much of what you notice is immediately judged through the filter of negativity. Breaking that tendency has to be done with intention and awareness. It is not going to be automatic until you practice intentionally for some time. So start by purposefully (1) turning attention first to physical awareness, noticing the sensations and labeling the emotion (for discussion of labeling emotions, see the "A Feeling is Just a Feeling" method in Technique #7), (2) suspending judgment on what it means, and (3) identifying what in the situation is triggering the sensations. In this way you can begin to shake free from automatic assumptions and be able to form a new perspective, accepting *what is* and deciding what action to take.

For example, if something happens like your car gets a flat tire and you say, "This is terrible! These things always happen to me! It has ruined my day!" then you just talked yourself into being miserable. But if you say, "Oh, a flat tire. I will fix it now," there is no automatic negative meaning associated with getting a flat tire. There is just an event to which you can choose a response. This is what one of my clients, Duane, did after discovering that his car had been totaled while parked on the street. A young driver, taking a corner too fast, had smashed into it. When Duane saw his car, he immediately took a breath and checked in with himself. There was absolutely nothing he could do or say to change the situation. He did not think the universe was sending him a lesson. He just asked himself, "Since this has happened and it cannot be changed, what do I want to do about it?" He decided to call his insurance company and get instructions about towing the car. When I asked if he really stayed that calm, he replied, "I refuse to believe there was a purpose in my car being wrecked. Certainly that kid did not want to wreck my car, so there is not malice to protect myself from. Therefore, getting upset, angry, depressed, or having any strong reaction was unnecessary. I am disappointed because the car could have lasted a while, and frustrated that I have to buy a new one, but this is why I have insurance." By not judging the situation to be his destiny or his fault, and by not seeing the other person's actions as an attack against him, he stayed calm and identified good responses.

Accepting what *is* requires an effort to *notice without judgment*. Then, using the left prefrontal cortex's ability to control your thinking and modulate your emotions, you can deliberately choose to handle your emotional reaction differently. The following four steps should help you remember how to do this:

1. Choose to remember that your emotional reactions stem from your *interpretation* of a situation or communication.
2. Observe: What is happening in this situation and what sensations are you experiencing?
3. Suspend judgment of why it is happening.
4. Focus on what possible responses will help you.

Deciding What Your Symptoms Mean

When people have symptoms, those symptoms mean something. When your nose runs and you cough, it probably means you have a cold. When you get bitten by a bug and that area turns red and swells, you probably have an allergic response to that bite. In depression, people similarly ascribe meaning to their symptoms, often seeing their lethargy and inability to take action as evidence of their worthlessness or inadequacy, or as proof that their situation is hopeless.

Here is the problem: Your depressive symptoms can mean a lot of things, and the "cause and effect" relationship is not as simple as it is with a bug bite. Why you became depressed is potentially due to a variety of different causes, which were discussed in Chapter 3, and knowing these causes will help you treat your depression. When you jump to the conclusion that your symptoms "mean" that you are inadequate or your situation is hopeless, you hinder your ability to find their true origins.

Figuring Out What Purpose Your Depression Serves

When people talk about depression, they usually say things like "he suffers from depression" or refer to "the onset of symptoms"—as if depression is akin to a smothering blanket that gets thrown on hapless victims, and once it's thrown off, everything will be fine. Of course, it's true that depression is often debilitating, and recovery from it is the goal. But your depressive symptoms may also be trying to serve a purpose that is actually helpful. Broadening your perspective about the depression itself can help you see what that purpose may be.

For example, suppose you feel too lethargic to go to your son's baseball game, or attend your sister's birthday party, or clean the house. What purpose might that symptom of lethargy be serving? Perhaps a part of you doesn't *want* to go to the game because you know you will compare yourself to the other parents there and feel inadequate. Or, if you're too tired to attend your sister's party, you won't have to deal with your mother's constant criticism of you. Perhaps wallowing in your depression when you talk with your friends makes them more attentive to you. There may be an outcome from depression symptoms that is not wholly unwelcome.

Understanding what purpose your depression symptoms are serving requires you not to judge your symptoms as negative. If you see your lethargy *only* as evidence that you are a bad parent, for example, you won't ever think broadly enough to realize that it is allowing you to avoid an unpleasant situation. Once you know what purpose the depression symptom is serving, you can find healthier ways to meet the same needs. You might brainstorm about ways of ignoring, deflecting, or neutralizing your mother's constant criticism, for instance, or find ways of getting your friends to listen to you without dwelling on depressing things, such as by talking about a movie you recently saw or a story you heard on the radio.

Maintaining an open mind while paying attention to your depression can teach you what you can do to change it. As my friend and mentor Paul Bauermeister taught me, "there are things you can learn in the dark that you cannot learn in the day."

STOP MAKING ASSUMPTIONS

Everyone makes assumptions about why things happen—it's the brain's natural way of trying to understand the world. But the minute you make an assumption, it becomes harder to think about what else the circumstance might mean. In the case of depression, this is particularly a problem, as the assumptions the depressed brain makes are usually negative and often wrong.

Notice how often you make assumptions. "I bet if I don't get a call by the weekend, they're not going to hire me." "I'm sure I didn't get an invitation to their party because no one likes me." "I know she didn't call back because she is avoiding me." You assume you know the reasons behind another person's actions or behind a specific situation.

A feature of not making assumptions is trying to avoid passing judgment. "No judgment" has to do with being loving toward yourself and others. It means noticing those negative assumptions that you are not liked or that others are acting with malice toward you and coming up with alternatives to them. Perhaps the friend who didn't call back never received the message that you'd called. Even if you don't *believe* the alternative explanation—if you still believe in your heart of hearts that she's avoiding you—the mere thinking of it requires you to admit that it *could* be true, which challenges your view of yourself as inadequate or worthless. Of course, there is nothing inherently wrong with being self-critical—acknowledging one's flaws and trying to work on them are part of self-growth. But there is a big difference between the self-criticality of the depressed brain and that of the healthy brain. When you are depressed, you tend to see yourself as *wholly* flawed, with the assumption that there's nothing you can do to change it. This is why it's important to take off the blinders and see yourself and the situation for what it really is or could be.

Another way of challenging assumptions is to try "dialing down" what you assume to be true. Let's say you have a bad horseback-riding lesson and you make the assumption "I am a terrible rider." That could lead down the depressive pathway of "therefore I should sell my horse and never ride again." *Disputing* the negative assumption would be to say, "Just because I had a bad riding lesson doesn't mean I am a terrible rider." But if you are really depressed, this disputation might be too hard. A better approach here is to just *dial it down*: "I was a terrible rider today. But that doesn't mean that I will be terrible again tomorrow. I can learn from what I did wrong and do better in the future." Or, for example, you had a bad interview for a prospective job. Instead of saying "I completely blew that interview and I'll never get a job," you could say, "I completely blew that interview and I won't get the job, but I can use that experience to do better in future interviews." Or if you had a bad argument with your girlfriend: Instead of thinking "this relationship is doomed," you could say, "We are in a rough patch now but there's a chance that things could get better in the future" or "She's been under a lot of stress lately, but once that gets better, we may not have so many arguments." Dialing down your assumptions about your worthlessness or the futility of your situation may make it easier to get a new perspective on what is actually happening and calm you down.

If you can avoid judging others in the same way, you might get more pleasure out of your relationships. Dan Siegel (2007) has used the acronym C.O.A.L. to sum up this mindful approach to suspending judgment. It stands for observing situations with curiosity, openness, acceptance, and love. In every situation:

- *Be curious.* Ask what is happening literally. What are you taking in with your senses?
- *Be open.* What might be going on and what might occur? Try to free yourself from making assumptions about negative outcomes.

- *Accept.* Accept that this is what is happening now.
- *Love.* Love yourself and others, which implies eliminating self-condemnation.

Being curious, open, accepting, and loving is not about suspending the ability to respond but rather about freeing yourself from harmful, inappropriate, or impulsive responses in favor of more balanced and helpful ones.

BROADEN YOUR EXPLANATIONS OF OTHERS

This is pretty simple to understand, though not so easy to do. The problem of how you explain other people to yourself lies in the depressive proclivity to observe others' actions and offer negative reasons for them. For example, observing a driver: "That guy just cut me off! I bet he's high!" Or observing a mother in a store: "She is so neglectful. Look, she's not even responding to her child crying!" Or: "She never returned my email. She must really be mad at me." When you catch yourself ascribing motivations to others, stop and think about other reasons for their actions. Perhaps the driver just made a mistake. The mother might be picking up a prescription for her child, who has a painful ear infection. Your friend may have deleted the email by mistake and did not know to return it. Changing the way you explain things can interrupt your negative default mode.

REMEMBER THAT SOME THINGS HAVE NOTHING TO DO WITH YOU

People with depression often seem very self-centered, as if every bad thing that occurs around them is caused by them or meant specifically to torment them. But in reality, many things happen that have absolutely nothing to do with you. Try, one situation at a time, to assume that what is happening around you *has nothing whatsoever to do with you*. This means not assuming that a situation is your fault or that you can fix it. You might suddenly see that other people have their own lives, with their own problems, and it might come as a relief to you.

Charlene had frequent bad days feeling inadequate at work. Her boss would come into work in the morning in a bad mood, and she worried that she'd done something to cause it. I asked what would happen if she just observed his mood without judging it as being about her, and what she might do or think differently. She realized that he might be grumpy about the traffic or be tired or mad at his wife—and none of those things related to her. She tried telling herself these ideas as he came into the office and discovered that her mood at work improved considerably. Although his mood remained grumpy, Charlene enjoyed her day much more because she stopped assuming responsibility for his bad mood.

INTERFERE WITH PESSIMISM: DISPUTE NEGATIVE BELIEFS AND EXPECTATIONS

Disputing negative beliefs and expectations is an important step toward broadening your perspective. Although it may take a while before you see yourself as an optimist, you can interfere with the pessimistic tendencies of depression if you use this list of questions when you notice yourself being pessimistic.

1. What is your pessimistic thought or belief in this situation? Look for thoughts that limit your options or demonstrate an expectation of failure, such as "I will never get ready in time." "I won't be able to finish this." "I could never get through 4 years of school." "No one could love me unless I _____ [lose weight/ get a better job/ find a nicer apartment/ etc.]"
2. Actively dispute negative and limiting thoughts by asking: "What is the evidence that the pessimistic belief is true? What is the evidence that it is *not* true?"

3. Find alternative causes for the bad events of life. It is not likely that all bad events occur because you are doomed, inadequate, or worthless. What is a more realistic explanation? (Come on, look hard. Is it possible that other people are doing things for reasons that have nothing to do with you? For example, perhaps the woman you contacted through the dating website didn't write back because she'd just gone on a date with someone she liked—not because she thought you were unattractive.)

4. Consider the implications. Will this *really* ruin your life? Is there a less catastrophic implication? Remember there is a huge difference between something you wish were not happening and something that will ruin your life.

5. Plan how to improve the situation. Ask yourself, "Does this negative belief help me?" You may find that it *does*! Maybe it helps you because it lets you off the hook for trying. If you are depressed, trying takes energy. Ironically, it takes less energy to stay depressed and pessimistic, but it won't make you feel better.

6. Find a positive expectation—something that you can believe about how things will get better. If that belief gives you a little more energy, you might be able to change your behavior or your thoughts and improve the situation.

TRY NOT TO OVERESTIMATE THE IMPORTANCE OF A NEGATIVE EXPERIENCE

If you are depressed, overactivity in your brain creates negativity. You may spend too much time wondering about what will happen if all your negative expectations actually come to pass. You "catastrophize" about future events as well as about how you will feel regarding them. Your brain may be overactively producing thoughts such as: "What if I can't ever finish school? I will feel awful!" or "What if I can't do a good enough job? I will feel so ashamed." You become afraid of how bad you will feel *then*. It is as if you are feeling bad now and you will feel bad later, too. Your depression is making you feel bad twice.

But you are more afraid of feeling bad than you really need to be. Here is an evaluation process for you to consider:

1. Identify an occurrence that you dreaded would happen and did. Your lover broke off the relationship, you failed the test, you lost the job, or some other similarly awful experience.
2. Ask yourself, "Was I miserable?"
3. Then ask, "How long did the misery last?"
4. Then ask, "Am I still miserable about it today?"
5. Reflect: "How did I get through it? Did it improve in stages? What did I learn?"

How miserable you were and how you got through it will vary depending on the occurrence and the ameliorating circumstances. For example, you may have lost an excellent job, and how long you stayed miserable probably depended in some measure on how soon you got another job. But even if your job hunt lasted for months, you might well have adjusted and felt better about yourself long before you were reemployed. Or, chances are good that if your heart has been broken in the past, you got over it. You might have recovered faster when a new love came on the scene than when you stayed single for a while, but, even without the new love interest, you got over the loss and felt better at some point.

You also might find it reassuring to search out stories about people who have faced adversity, survived it, and even thrived afterward. Newspapers and television talk shows and news programs are full of stories of people who bounce back after illness or hardship—a dancer who lost part of her leg in the Haiti earthquake who is getting help to dance again; a successful woman in her thirties who was sent to prison for a drug-related crime she'd committed in her youth and who, despite her terror, came through the experience stronger and wrote a book about it. There are numerous books of inspirational stories and Web sites that will send you daily inspiration. Check some of these out to help you feel courage when you think you cannot escape your misery.

The trouble is that when you are depressed, you try to avoid the possibility of a negative experience, remembering too much of the pain of previous experiences and not enough about how you survived that pain. Always point out to yourself that whatever you have gone through, you have survived it. In fact, many things that seemed awful are things you managed to deal with.

You may even try so hard to avoid pain that you end up stuck in it by devising mental and behavioral ways to not feel it. Depression often leads people to flatten out their emotions, trying to ignore feelings that seem unpleasant. Most people prefer not to feel sad or lonely or hurt or disappointed (or any of the averse feelings) and some unfortunate depressed people may even try to flatten out positive emotions—happiness, excitement, love, or joy. Whenever you make an effort, whether consciously or unconsciously, to flatten out what you feel, you run the risk of depressing yourself.

Or you may try to avoid feeling it altogether. Drinking is one behavioral way to avoid pain. So is overeating. So are any addictive behaviors, like gambling or Internet pornography. Mentally, you might engage in any manner of avoidance techniques, such as those provided by computers or video games, which are emotion-dampening and can suck up lots of time. Here is the problem with avoidance: The pain doesn't go away until you go through it. You get stuck in it. It stays there and you cannot avoid it forever. It just keeps breaking through your efforts to flatten or avoid it.

To get over your pain, you need to know that *pain expressed is pain made less*. However, you probably cannot do this on your own. To stop avoiding pain, you need some heavy-duty support—like time with a good therapist. It is courageous to face emotional pain, but don't think that doing it alone is more courageous. Being supported by another person while you feel your pain will help you stay with it long enough to pass through it. For therapists or anyone who is reaching out to a person with depression who is expressing pain, be aware that just being present is often enough for the person to stay with it. Staying present means empathizing — *not talking the person out of it.* A therapist cannot fix your pain, but he or she can stay with you while you feel it. It is almost miraculous how emotional pain is lessened by feeling it fully.

EXPAND YOUR SELF-TALK

One of my clients reported that she was talking with her primary-care physician about efforts to change her self-talk (what you say in your mind to yourself about yourself). She wanted him to know what she was doing to alleviate her depression. "Now, when I'm at work," she told him, "instead of saying to myself, 'I can't do that,' I say, 'I can learn anything in time.'" The physician off-handedly remarked, "Well, that should be easy!" She was taken aback. It is not easy to change a perpetually negative frame of mind. She was able to tell herself that for him, it might be easy, and it was clear he did not understand depression. I thought she did a great job of handling that perceived criticism and seeing that his remark reflected more about him than it did about her.

The depressed thinking mode of pessimism and negative outlooks is reinforced by your self-talk. Although there are many varieties of negative self-talk, I want to focus on the thoughts that keep you expecting the worst to happen. To change your inner negative dialogue, focus your attention on the way you use the "ifs," "ands," or "buts."

Challenge the Negative "Ifs"

When you are depressed, the "if____ then____" scenario typically ends with a failure, a loss, or a disappointment. For example, Amy was trying to imagine why her new boyfriend did not call for nearly a week. What she said to herself was: "If he has not called yet, then it must be because he does not want to see me again." She could not generate a single option other than the failure of the relationship. But Amy's inability to foresee a positive outcome was a failure of her *imagination*, not a failure

217

of the relationship. Her default mode went right to the worst outcome and made her first depressed and then hopeless.

Then he called. His mother had been in a car accident, and he had left town hurriedly, forgetting his cell phone in which he stored her number, so he just planned to call on his return. It never occurred to him that this woman, whom he really liked but had only just started dating, would fall into despair over a few days of no contact. Amy needed help in learning to stop defaulting to pessimism. With encouragement, she kept her fears to herself around her boyfriend (a good thing) and accepted the positive outcome that he called. To prevent future trouble with seeing only negative possibilities, we worked to change the process of her thinking to (1) stop the negative endings to her "if . . . then" scenarios, and then (2) develop some other options.

When the outcome of a situation is uncertain, like the outcome of an important test or a budding romantic relationship, it is time to build your imagination. First, when you don't know what is going to happen in the future, *stop assuming it will be grim*. This requires a cognitive decision. You must acknowledge that when you are depressed, you just do not see all the options. Yes, a bad outcome could occur, but so could a positive one. So after you tell yourself the grim outcome is not the only one, brainstorm for positives. Allow yourself to see that many possible outcomes exist. This takes imagination, so if you cannot imagine possible positive outcomes, ask someone for help.

The key word here is *possible*. As noted earlier, even if you don't *believe* the outcome will be positive or you don't *expect* it to be positive, you have to admit that it's *possible* that it will be. Shift your self-talk to "my *imagination* is failing me" rather than "my *future* is failing me." There is a world of difference between the two.

Another "ifs" issue of self-talk is this: "If it *can* be bad, it *will* be bad." It's crucial to remember that your negative thoughts *are not predictions*. Just because you are worried that something may not go well does not mean it *will* go wrong. Carli came into a session crying. When I inquired about why she was so upset, she said her cat wasn't eating well. "I just know that he's really sick. I'm going to have to put him to sleep!" Carli was acting as if her negative thought ("my cat could be sick") was a prediction that the cat would die. You must interrupt the assumption of a negative outcome and instead focus on what is happening *now*. Stop, look, and listen. Can you recognize the difference between what you fear versus what has not yet happened?

Another way to get at this is to challenge your assumptions of negative outcomes by reviewing past "exceptions" to your belief that bad things will happen. Did you ever get stopped by a police officer who did *not* issue the ticket? Did you ever have a child come home very late from school and only then realize that he had *not* been kidnapped as you feared? That the mistake you made at work *didn't* result in your getting fired? That the wrong turn you took on the way to the party *didn't* cause you to get there late and ruin the whole evening? I have many clients who got jobs after terrible interviews, passed tests they were sure they would fail, or had a good time at events they were dreading going to.

Avoid Saying "But"

The word "but" is your nemesis when it comes to broadening your perspective. Pay attention to how you use it to stop good feelings and stay focused on negative ones. "But" is a "word eraser"—it erases whatever words came before it. "I got a lot done on this project, *but* I should have started sooner because then I would have finished." "I enjoyed the evening, *but* I think it cost way too much." After you develop awareness of your use of the word "but," make a promise to try to stop following positive comments with it. Pay careful attention to what it feels like to just stay at the positive. "I got a lot done on this project." *Period.* This is one small, simple change that will have a big impact on your feelings. It is a mental decision to just stop one mental habit. It will be a while before this comes naturally, so don't worry that you have to do it on purpose. Just do it as often as you notice the "but" in your sentences.

Use "And" to Allow Yourself Contradictory Feelings

Too many people think they are bad or wrong when they have feelings that contradict each other. "I love my dog so I shouldn't get so upset when she tears up the furniture." "My life is good, so why do I feel so depressed?" "I don't want to get up at night to feed the baby because I'm so exhausted. I shouldn't feel that way because I wanted this baby." You may then try to make these contradictory emotions agree with each other, but that only intensifies the problem.

Your struggle to make all your feelings agree, to get rid of one side of the emotional equation or the other, leads to self-blame or being stuck. You defend one side of the contradiction and then the other, feeling guilty that you have negative feelings about positive situations. See what happens when you accept that both can be true at the same time. Accept contradictory feelings or situations as the norm by simply adding the word "and." "I love my dog *and* I get upset when she tears up the furniture." "I have a good life *and* I am depressed." "I am exhausted *and* I am happy about having a baby." Allow yourself to have the negative position and also allow the positive part as *completely true*. It will mean less rumination and less need to argue with yourself.

LEARN OPTIMISM

Stopping the negatives is an essential part of challenging depression, but to get out of depression for good, you will benefit from learning other ways to think. Life is not always kind, and having access to your positive emotions is an important resource when things don't go as planned. This method involves some mental energy, so you may need to ask someone to help you when you do not feel up to it. This is where an "optimism mentor" is a help. What is an optimism mentor? It could be a real person with whom you can talk—a therapist, a coach, a pastor, priest, or rabbi, a trusted friend, or an aunt or uncle who understands what you are going through.

It can also be an "imaginary friend." I do not literally mean that you should start talking to someone who is not there. However, you may know of a person from literature or a movie who embodies an optimistic view. (I often recommend that depressed clients read the works of Louis L'Amour or L. M. Montgomery's *Anne of Green Gables* series or *The Secret Garden* by Francis Hodgson Burnett. The characters in those works embody optimism and self-reliance in the face of challenges. Movies are a terrific choice for characters you can identify with. Sad or funny, old or new, films offer indomitable characters as diverse as Scarlett O'Hara in *Gone With the Wind*, Will Farrell in *Elf*, and Meryl Streep playing Julia Child in *Julie and Julia*.) Then ask yourself, "What would that character say in my situation?" If Anne of Green Gables faced the loss of her job, she might say that this offers her new scope for imagination, or that it gives her time to visit a dear friend or be of more help at home. Then she would set off on an adventure.

I recently did this exercise with LuAnne, a client who was laid off by her employer in a very disrespectful way. LuAnne came in crying. Of course, I listened to the story respectfully, but then we discussed whether there were other ways of looking at the situation. She had gotten a severance package and did not have to work again for 4 months, so I asked, "How would you feel if you were offered 4 months' salary to stay home and do whatever you want?" I then asked her, "What would a playful, carefree woman with an income do with her time?" She got a surprised look on her face and burst out with, "She would bake a pie!" By the time she finished imagining how a woman with money coming in would spend the next several weeks, LuAnne was laughing and had a long list of delightful things she would do that she rarely had time for. The distress about how she was fired was significantly less.

Get Enthused: Give the "Virginia Report"

Being enthused is one of my favorite ways to develop optimism, and giving the "Virginia Report" is the best way I know to do it. My friend Virginia has had much to be depressed about—losing an adult child to cancer, seeing her family break down from the consequences of grief, having cancer herself (twice!), and suffering severe, debilitating side effects from treatment. Yet I never speak with Virginia without hearing her talk about an experience she just had that was absolutely "the best!" She just had the *best* sandwich she ever ate, the *most* fun she ever had, she laughed *harder than ever before*. In the "Virginia Report," everything today is better than anything that came before.

Although to some readers this may sound like a disingenuous way of responding to life, it is actually an excellent brain-based intervention. When you make a comparison in this positive direction, you boost your sense of wellbeing. Depression intensifies when you let yourself be robbed of what is good because it is not *perfectly* good. For example, you might hear yourself saying things like, "Well, sure we enjoyed being at the ball game, but the team lost." Too often depressed individuals feel the good things aren't even worth mentioning. You might find yourself saying something like, "Well, sure, that was a good pizza, but it was not special—it's always good there." So, try this instead:

Keep a record. Keep a daily record of positive things. This is not hard. Carry an index card in your pocket or purse and when a good thing happens, no matter how small, write a note to yourself about it. This is where being in therapy can help. It will help you be accountable for doing it, and a therapist can help you find positives if it is hard for you to spot them. Also, you need practice time to learn out-loud enthusiasm. There is nothing more fun in therapy than reviewing positives and making a safe place to practice injecting that note of eagerness, enthusiasm, and hopefulness into the experiences of daily life.

Use Superlatives in Your Speech

Try using superlatives while talking aloud about a positive experience to make it "the best ever!" à la Virginia. This is best done when being with another person so you get the benefit of the social boost as well as the benefit of hearing your words aloud and being stimulated by your tone of voice, your laughter, and your facial expressions, none of which you get if you just talk to yourself! For example, talk about a restaurant meal and describe the food as if you never had anything quite that good. It is okay to do it as a joke, as long as you say it out loud.

Then notice how you feel expressing the excitement. It is likely that you will feel energized—a good antidepressant. Describing any event or experience as "the best ever" is an upward comparison that will reinforce positive emotion about it. You will also find social benefits, as other people like to hear about your "best ever" experiences much more than your complaints.

Expanding your perspective on your situation is very much in your control. Although you might need assistance, making a decision to try these ideas is something your depressed mind can do, even though it might not be easy to carry out that decision. The good news is that even just a little progress in this direction makes more progress easier to achieve. At first, coming up with just *one* alternative to the assumption that you are worthless or your situation is hopeless may seem difficult, but you will find that once you've allowed room for that one new perspective, other perspectives will begin to emerge more quickly. And although being purposefully positive may feel awkward at first, the more you do it, the more natural it will become. As discussed in the next chapter, increasing your mental flexibility is an important part of recovery from depression. But you can't be flexible if your perspective is limited to the narrow-minded thinking of depression. By broadening your perspective, you grant yourself the freedom to think and act in ways that benefit both you and those around you.

ELEVEN

Technique #9:

Increase Flexibility

If you have ever watched a professional tennis match, you've probably noticed how the players try to maintain a position on the court from which they can quickly leap to any other part of the court the ball may land in. Their goal is to remain flexible enough to be able to handle whatever the other player sends their way—and to get back to that optimal position as swiftly as possible. The same can be said of life in general. You may never be able to perfectly predict what life has in store for you, but being able to respond flexibly and in a timely manner will give you a real advantage.

In depression, however, that flexibility gets compromised. Your brain becomes stuck in rigid ways of thinking, your behaviors get locked into repetitive patterns, and your lack of physical energy just compounds the problem. Although broadening your perspective is a powerful antidote to depression, increasing the flexibility in how you see things and what you do instead of your current depressed way of operating is real healing. Your symptoms will change and you will be able to strengthen brain activity that defeats depression.

Several of the methods in this technique utilize the concept of neural networking to either identify or change your typical reaction. By interrupting negative networking and building circuitry for positive networking, your range of motion for thinking, emotions, and behavior will be wider, and you will move more flexibly between your choices for thinking and action. The easier it is to find a new mental position, the easier it will be to diminish depression.

STOP REACTING TO YOUR OWN MOOD

A good example of the inflexibility of depression is the way your current mood actually determines how you experience your life. Start observing how often you have a bad experience *after* you are already in a bad mood. Remember neural networking: You go from the current bad mood into a network of memories of how you felt, what you thought, and what you did the last time you had such a mood. Being in a bad mood, you are certain to feel bad about what is happening next. That is how depression creates rigid ways of responding. To interrupt the process you have to (a) know it is happening and (b) find ways to intervene directly on the bad mood.

1. When you find yourself in a bad mood for any reason, take a moment right then to notice and write down what you are thinking, doing, and feeling. Be a bit careful, though. Your brain will want to rev you up or get you ruminating. To minimize that, think of yourself as a "mood detective," writing down facts about your mood as if you are an objective observer.

2. Notice if some of your thoughts are about what is coming next in your life. Are you getting "pre-mad" about something, as in "I just bet my kids did not pick up their room as I asked while I was at the store" or "I just bet we're eating dinner out of a bag tonight because my wife was not home this afternoon"? Are you *expecting* to be let down? If so, your bad mood is dictating those negative expectations, making it impossible to be in a good mood later. This means that even if the kids *did* pick up their room, you will still have a hard time shifting into a pleasant mood. Here's a guarantee: It is much harder to be pleasantly surprised when you are in a bad mood.

3. Then H.A.L.T. If you are *hungry*, *angry*, *lonely*, or *tired*, fix that problem before you start thinking about your next activity and how bad it will be. This is the way to shake off the bad mood before it poisons the rest of your day. Ask yourself what you need right this very minute to feel better. If you are hungry, eat something. You can't be cheerful with low blood sugar. If you are angry, decide what you need to do about it and solve it. If you are lonely, call or visit with someone for a bit or make an appointment to get together as soon as possible. If you are tired, take a nap or at least plan to rest before you get mad at anyone and take it out on that person. You might need to consult with a therapist if you do not grasp how to fix these based on this small description. I cannot emphasize enough how important this one small intervention is!

4. Finally, "act as if" by deliberately cultivating an image in your mind of how you would look, what you would say, and what you would do *if you were in a good mood*. This is how you stretch your imagination to become more flexible. See it as vividly as you can. In your image, see how others react to you. See what would happen if you cheerfully greeted those children with messy rooms who were still watching TV and then cheerfully herded them to their task and even helped them. Do you like that outcome better than the one you were imagining? Good. Now go out and do it.

5. Notice the outcome of this process. See if you want to try it the next time you are in a bad mood.

IDENTIFY AND CHANGE YOUR EXPLANATORY STYLE

You make depression worse when you dwell on negative expectations of yourself and others to explain what is happening in your life. "I did not get the promotion because no one ever notices me." "I'll never get a good grade in this course because the professor doesn't like me." "No matter what I do, I can't get a fair shake." "I don't have any money because whenever I try to save, things at home break down." Your storyline blames you or explains the misfortune as exactly the kind of thing you are doomed to experience forever. Such negativity is a reflection of what is happening in your brain when you are depressed. Your "optimistic" left brain is not strong enough to tell you that you will survive and thrive. It fails to suppress negativity. Meanwhile, your right brain is overly busy in predicting failures and only visualizing difficult, frightening, and overwhelming aspects of every situation.

Your explanatory style (your *narrative*, or the story you create about "why") is thus derived from your right brain's contribution of negativity. To change this default explanatory style, the "nothing ever works for me" attitude, start listening to your own stories about why things happen the way they do.

- Notice how you create negative storylines about why things happen to you.
- Listen for words like *always* and *never* in your explanation. When these crop up they imply that you feel stuck. "This *always* happens to me!"
- Listen for expressions that imply that you have no choice or control. "In this bad economy" is a popular phrase implying you have no choice about the outcome of work or financial situations.
- Listen for blame words: "I should stop . . ." or "I shouldn't have done . . ." or "I ought to know better." Sometimes people with depression blame others more than themselves, but it is the same problem: Blame prevents change.

TELL YOURSELF: "THIS MAY HAVE BEEN TRUE, UNTIL NOW"

Once you start hearing your words, change the way you say them. You only have to worry about changing one storyline at a time, not your whole style. Just make one simple change: Add the words "until now" to your description of yourself. For example, Robert started many explanations with: "I have always been a man who. . . ." He would then tell me a story about how he *always* did something. "I have always been a man who gets committed to a woman by the second or third date," he would say, implying that his relationship style was set in stone. Yet it had led him to stay with some very unhealthy women who made him miserable. He needed a new explanation. Look at how different Robert's statement sounds when he started it with "until now." "Until now, I have been a man who commits too quickly." This small change gave him the option to start a new way of relating and a new way of explaining himself. Try using this simple shift in the way you explain yourself and see how it feels.

REMEMBER THAT DECISIONS CAN BE CHANGED

Many depressed people believe they are stuck once they have chosen a particular path, when in truth, very little in life cannot be altered if you find that it is a bad choice. Your ruminative brain may go over and over why you did what you did or picked the path you are on. You may also do this with "pre-rumination" about decisions, believing you will be stuck once you choose.

I often meet high school juniors and seniors, for example, who are plagued by the decision of where to go to college. They are led to believe there is one perfect school for their academic or extracurricular needs. They visit, they plan, they search on-line, they consult peers, and they are still afraid of committing to any one place. When we discuss that they could start at one school and transfer if it does not work, they often balk. Their idea that there is one perfect choice makes them rigid in their thinking about where to go.

Learn There Are Many *Good* Choices, No *Perfect* Choices

When people believe that once they choose the big things—a job, a house, a town to live in—there will be no way out, they often feel that they then must choose the *perfect* choice. Yes, it is harder to change a job than a pair of shoes that don't fit, but it can be done. If you are stopping yourself from doing things because you believe you will be stuck living with your choice forever, learn to talk differently to yourself to improve your mental flexibility. Stop and remind yourself that (1) *no choices are perfect* and (2) *most decisions can be changed.* If you do not like what you chose as much as you expected, you can figure out whether it is worth it to change.

Randy had been trying to buy a car for 2 years but could never put down the money because he was so worried he would not get the best deal. He knew what car he wanted, but he could not decide if it was the best price. When I suggested that even if he made a less-than-perfect purchase he could view it as the best he could do at the time and next time could do better, he looked horrified. We started to discuss what he would suffer if he went without the car versus what he would suffer if he paid slightly more than the "best deal possible." He was then able to start evaluating the benefits of having the car now over waiting and being unhappy with his current decrepit vehicle for even longer. Randy needed to get past the idea that a wrong choice was "awful, terrible, and unrecoverable." He might even find later that he got a great deal, but not taking action wouldn't even allow that to occur.

Sometimes people make temporary choices—options they know will not be 100% fulfilling—because they can't get what they want at this time. They may purchase a house that's smaller than their ideal because they can't afford something bigger, or move to a less desirable area of the country because the job market in the city they want to live in is too tight. In these cases, it might be good to choose something less than your ideal—but it is not a good idea to tell yourself you are settling for less. You may be disappointed that you cannot have exactly what you want, but remember that it's a good *temporary* solution. It is better to view the option as a *good enough* option for now.

When considering choices, try the following:

1. Identify your need, goal, or desired outcome (e.g., a job that will give you Saturdays off, a house with a good backyard, a car with low mileage).

2. Identify your options—list every one of them, no matter how far-fetched.
3. Identify every option that is good enough. (You might need to address your false belief that a perfect option exists. It is good to see that you have chosen from among many options at this stage.)
4. Tell yourself that you can choose any of these options because they all are good enough. No matter which you choose, all the others would have been good, and so will this one. (This is the opposite of telling yourself that you cannot find the perfect option.)
5. Then remember that you can change your mind if you want to later on.

DON'T TAKE YOURSELF SO SERIOUSLY

Of course, everything in life *could* be serious, but what if most everything was not so serious? Telling yourself that things are awful or terrible makes you feel as if they are. Do people say to you, "Don't get so bent out of shape," when you are reacting? They want you to think, "So what if the brownies burn?" or "So what if it rains on the day of the picnic?" or "So what if the price of gas is higher in the summer?"

You may overestimate your own importance in unexpected ways. If you are depressed you probably agonize over your impact on other people. For example, you might have to miss a meeting and spend all night worrying about how others will be upset if you are not there. Or you might be fretting over the fact that you didn't have time to make the dish you promised to bring to a potluck meal, and now there isn't going to be enough food at the get-together. Or you might be agonizing about not continuing to date a person you recently met over the Internet because you know he wants to see you again but you aren't interested in him. In depression, you might overestimate how awful others will feel. Well, what if you are just not that important? Your choice not to attend the meeting, bring the potluck dish, or go on a second date might *not* ruin anyone's life. Other people can deal with whatever happens in their own lives, just as you can tolerate yours. Being flexible enough to remember this will take a weight off your shoulders.

FACE DISAPPOINTMENT

Disappointment is an interesting feeling. Your experience may be that it is an easy emotion to feel and express, but many people with depression cannot tolerate disappointment. This emotion is often shoved aside because it is so hard to know what to do about it.

Disappointment is a sense of loss. You feel disappointment when others let you down or you do not get something you powerfully desired. Those kinds of losses may seem minor to someone else, yet you feel them keenly. Some examples? You miss a movie you were looking forward to seeing because your friend cancels or is late. You feel devastated—as if you can never again see the most important movie ever made. Or, you really wanted to see the art fair but it was raining, and you feel as if you just lost the chance to buy the one and only painting you would ever want to own in your whole life. Somewhat bigger losses are even harder. You do not get the promotion and you react as if you have lost your current job and will never work again. The pregnancy test comes back negative again, and you feel as if you must accept being barren and dying without anyone in your life to take care of you.

Whether you feel it acutely or try to push it away because you think you can't handle it, the emotion of disappointment contributes to depression and feelings of being stuck. "I'll never find a new boyfriend." "I'll never make it as a writer." "My relationship with my daughter will never get better." And when you feel your situation is hopeless, you're less inclined to be flexible in the way you think about it and behave.

There is only one way to fix the disappointment. Feel it and express it. To whom do you express disappointment? Typically, you either talk to the person who let you down, or you talk with a sympathetic friend or family member who wants you to feel better. I have found that neither of those possible listeners works very well. The person who let you down feels too guilty to listen to your disappointment, so he cuts you off or hears you say "I am angry" when you actually say "I am disappointed." Then he argues with you about why you should not be angry, and you have no chance to release the feeling of loss that is disappointment. The person who wants you to feel better may rush past the loss to tell you why you should be happy about something else, as if there is a scale on which to weigh "happy" and "sad" and feel whatever the balance is. She may try to cram optimism down your throat when your throat is still filled with tears.

Even therapists may respond to your expression of disappointment in unhelpful ways. It's a mistake we sometimes make because of our training to get to the positive. Therapists may hear your disappointment as pessimism. When that happens, you may feel as if you are being told that disappointment is wrong. And when you believe that your feelings are wrong, the emotion goes underground and gets frozen. You may decide not to mention it again in therapy, or to others, and try to avoid feeling it. You may feel misunderstood or even alone and isolated, believing that not even a therapist can understand. If you are not ready to get to the positive, speak up! Your sense of loss deserves a hearing! A good therapist will immediately shift to help you with that. Also, that therapist can help you figure out whether you really are moving through it or getting stuck in the loss, which is a risk for a depressed and ruminative brain.

Managing Disappointment

1. Identify the loss and express how it feels to you.
2. What would you hope for if you were not afraid of being disappointed again?
3. Sit with the feelings you have without trying to change them. The reality is that *you may not get what you want in this situation*. That is disappointing.
4. Acknowledge reality: Not getting what you wanted is a loss.
5. Validate your emotions: It is appropriate to feel sad about any loss.
6. After you have done all of that, think about what you need to move on.

KEEP A BALANCE BETWEEN HOPE
AND DISAPPOINTMENT

Becoming more flexible means learning to understand that whenever you hope for something, the possibility exists that you might be disappointed. It also means not anticipating that a negative outcome is inevitable. Staying flexible might feel a bit like sitting on a teeter-totter in which balancing your hope and disappointment hinges on skills that help you to cope with loss or negative emotions as well as with success (Figure 11.1). Approaching this issue with some preparation is a good idea.

- Set reasonable goals to hope for. Make them small and achievable. If you do not see how the goal could be met in light of your current level of physical or emotional energy, then the goal is too big. Better to pick a tiny step and succeed than to pick an ambitious goal and fail.
- Learn cognitive skills that will stop rumination about the

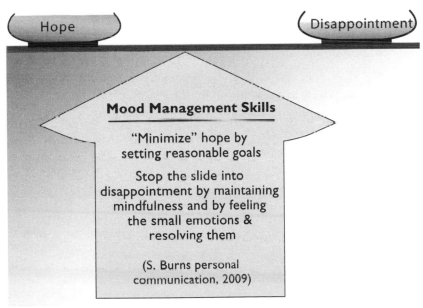

Figure 11.1 Hope and Disappointment Balanced by Skills

outcome or about setbacks. For example, learn to *reframe* a setback as new learning. This is look-for-the-silver-lining in action. When Thomas Edison was asked about his hundreds of failed attempts to find a filament for a light bulb, he reputedly answered that he had no failures. He had learned hundreds of substances that would not work. Most difficult situations allow a person to learn a new skill or learn a way that won't work and still have another chance to try. Ruminating can be helped with many techniques, but among the best is *thought-stopping* and *thought replacement*. In this method, you refuse to think the repetitive thought and plan to think about something else. See the Recommended Reading and Resources list for more about cognitive techniques to control worry, such as *The 10 Best-Ever Anxiety Management Techniques* (Wehrenberg, 2008).

- Learn to identify the small feelings and resolve them before they get big. You might need help to learn how to sense your feelings and identify the emotions you have (see Technique #7). Often in depression people don't feel enough energy to take action until the emotion is huge, and by then it is overwhelming. You will feel less helpless when you can identify and discharge emotions and resolve problems when they are smaller (S. Burns, personal communication, 2009).

- If you cannot yet hope for positive outcomes, at least stop projecting that you will have a negative outcome. Negative expectations of how things *might* go wrong in the future lead to bad feelings now. Anticipation of negatives can lead to relapse in drinking, drugs, or addictive behaviors. It can also lead to deeper depression.

The process of restoring hope can take some time, and it may involve considerable learning about emotions and emotional modulation, all of which will help a depressed person. It is a significant movement when hope no longer triggers an automatic expectation of disappointment.

Scale Hope Back

Hope can be a scary thing to feel. If you let yourself hope that this time your son really is going to stay sober, for example, or that this time you really will get that prestigious fellowship, there's a part of you that also fears the devastation you will feel if those things don't come to pass. This may lead you to decide that it's safer not to hope at all.

One aspect of tolerating hope is not to get carried away with hoping for too much. "Hoping for too much" is, of course, not a problem for many depressed people, who may automatically assume the worst-case scenario! In fact, depressed people are sometimes *more* realistic about what could happen than "eternal optimists" are. They may be more willing to conceive of failure, disappointment, or loss, and this can lead to making better plans, being more prepared for trouble, or taking charge of life more effectively. For example, depressed people are often more realistic about their medical conditions and therefore tend to ask more questions and make more plans about coping with the failure of a medical treatment. However, realism is not the same as pessimism, and when it comes to hoping, the depression may make you balk at hoping for a positive outcome.

But changing that sense of futility doesn't mean embracing the other extreme of wildly high expectations. There are four steps you can follow to bring hopefulness to a manageable level so that it can be tolerated without triggering a network of negativity.

1. Identify small hopes.
2. Plan and carry out predictable and "doable" actions to make it a reality.
3. Observe when hope comes to fruition.
4. Learn to emotionally tolerate small successes.

How might this look in action? It is too much for a person in an ugly divorce, for instance, to hope for a happy family. It is more realistic—and less triggering—for him to hope for having a good dinner with the kids.

In being hopeful just for a good dinner, he can actually prepare for that one thing. For example, he could look forward to seeing his children and greet them with enthusiasm, which will make it more likely that he *will* have a good time. What he hopes for is more likely to happen.

One of my clients, Mike, was very depressed, feeling hopeless about his marriage and hopeless about his "miserable" job ever changing. He would not look for new work because he was afraid that at his age he could never find anything that paid as well, but he was also hopeless that he could ever feel good about the job he had. So we created the small hope that he might occasionally have good days at work. To his surprise, when he did not focus on hating his current job but rather allowed himself small hopes, he did have some good days. Those small hopes did not lead to disappointment, and he began to feel less scared of hoping his life could change. True, hoping for a good *life* was just too much for now, but as he got used to the idea that sometimes good things happened without "the other shoe dropping," and as he brought those small hopes to conscious awareness, he became less fearful of hope itself.

Another good way to scale back hope is to learn to set small enough goals for recovery from depression itself. Setting your sights too high will be inevitably disappointing, but not hoping for anything will cause you not to try. It is not unusual for people with depression to feel helpless about recovering and to hope for too little from therapy because the idea of feeling good again is too huge to imagine succeeding at. Similarly, people who have made progress in their recovery from depression may become distraught when symptoms reappear, and they may jump to the conclusion that they have "failed" in their efforts to get better and feel like giving up hope entirely.

How can you figure out what size hope is the right size? For people who feel helpless about ever feeling better, the key is the "just a *little bit* better" in this question: "If I felt just a *little bit* better, what would I expect of myself?" For example, if you hope to have a big, supportive circle of friends but you are at this moment isolated, that is an overwhelming hope. Ask yourself instead, "If I were just a little bit less depressed, would I call a friend for dinner?" That is more reasonable and achievable. If you were just a little less depressed, would you walk to work tomorrow instead of driving? If you were just a little bit less depressed, would you do the dishes tonight? Those might all be doable expectations, but you have not tried them because they did not seem like a big enough goal.

If you are feeling hopeless because your symptoms have returned when you thought you'd "beaten" your depression, again, adjust your expectations. How realistic is it to hope that you will *never again* feel low on energy or overreact to a disappointment? A better goal is to work toward having *longer* periods of recovery and build skills to more quickly and effectively deal with symptoms in case they do crop up. Hope depends on reasonable expectations of success.

Make Affirmations About What You Hope For

Affirmations are positive statements about what you want to be true about yourself or your situation. The affirmation is a way to create an image of reality in your mind—seeing and feeling the outcome you desire. Affirmations can be of great help when they are used productively. They are a way to embody both faith and hope for the depressed person, reminding him or her of the need to feel both of those in practical ways.

Affirmations are usually outcome-oriented: how you want things to be when you are no longer depressed, when you have grown into a more positive person, when you have achieved what you are striving for. Affirmations are more than wishful thinking. They are statements of the life you want, and a way to remind you of your goals. They should be related to those small, achievable goals that a person with depression can handle. In making an affirmation, you exercise the power of positive thinking on purpose. Many people believe that positive affirmations attract to them the positive circumstances they desire. Very possibly that has to do with the likelihood that you tend to take action toward your goals when you keep them in mind. But those affirmations will help even more if you share them with others to let them know of your goals and request their help or encouragement. People are more likely to help you if you ask for it, and you are more likely to meet your goals with help than alone. Additionally, when you are clear about a goal, you are engaging the prefrontal cortex to stimulate motor activity toward the goal whenever you visualize yourself achieving it.

Affirmations also help with the ruminative quality of depression. Think about the brain benefits of repeating positive thoughts. Every time those neurons fire down positive pathways, they strengthen the positive emotions and counterbalance the negative, depressed pathways. You therefore increase your resources for positive thinking. Seeing yourself and all the good feelings and thoughts you will have as you succeed is a way to establish positive neural networks. Because rumination on worry and negativity creates stress and damage from stress, interrupting negative thinking and substituting a positive thought makes for a healthier brain. Thought-stopping, and then substituting an affirmation for the negative thought, corrects the direction of all that ruminative neuronal activity. Every time you interrupt negative self-talk, you weaken the power of the negative to control your thoughts.

It was long assumed that affirmations were always good and that any kind of affirmation would make a person feel better. An interesting study in 2009, however, showed how affirmations sometimes make people feel worse (Crawford, 2010; Wood, 2009). When people who did not feel good about themselves recited affirmations like "I am good," they actually felt worse about themselves. But people who already had good self-esteem did feel better. This finding gets back to what is unbelievable versus what is believable and achievable. If a person believes "I am not good enough," it flies in the face of reason that saying "I *am* good enough" will help. Years ago on *Saturday Night Live*, Al Franken crystallized this problem with affirmations that were self-defeating when his character, Stuart Smalley, would affirm, "I'm good enough, I'm smart enough, and doggone it, people like me." It was a perfect satire of the way people misuse the concept of affirmations, trying to believe in a reality that is unlikely or impossible (especially if all they do is talk about it). Dejection and depression lie in wait if you affirm unrealistic goals.

A similar problem can occur in how parents praise children. If you praise a child for a good drawing when the child has put in effort, the child will feel proud. If you praise the child for a fabulous drawing when the child knows he or she was just scribbling, the child will not value the praise, recognizing it as false. Self-esteem only rises in the presence of deserved praise.

In applying that principle to affirmations, the key is to keep them related to small, achievable goals and to take action based on them. I would feel pretty bad about myself if I affirmed "I am an Olympic swimmer" when in fact I was taking my first swimming lesson. But I might be more able to jump in the pool if I affirmed, "I have learned other things and I can learn this too." How we select an affirmation and use it makes a difference in whether it is useful or not. Following are some simple guidelines for selecting the right words for the affirmation:

- Make a statement that is specific and an "I statement" or a statement about what condition will come to fruition. For example, "I remain calm whenever I speak to the boss" or "The job I need is opening up for me at the right time." Specificity will help remind you to keep the affirmation believable.
- Word the affirmation so that it is in the present tense. Say: "I am _____" as if it were happening at this moment. "I *am* cheerful and calm when seeing my ex-husband." "I *am* achieving my goal of completing the course with an A."
- Then repeat the affirmation aloud a few times in a row, and do that a few times every day. Or carry a reminder token, such as a smooth stone in your pocket, so that every time you see or touch the token you can say your affirmations to yourself.
- Make part of the affirmation a visualization of what actions you can take to make the affirmation become a reality.

What are some examples of useful affirmations? Although they are best when exactly worded for an individual's situation, some examples are:

- "I am increasingly ready to have a loving romantic relationship."
- "Love is all around me, and I see it more and more."
- "I am able to find good and positive moments in every day."
- "The home I need is becoming available and I am preparing to own it."
- "Every day, in every way, I am getting better and better." (This is a generic affirmation that gets to the issue of making progress even though perfection is never attainable.)

Dealing With Hope

1. Identify small hopes and set small, reasonable goals.
2. Identify small feelings and resolve them before they get big.
3. Make affirmations for what you hope for.
4. Plan and carry out doable actions.
5. Observe when hope comes to fruition.
6. Notice and tolerate the small successes.

BUILD POSITIVE BRAIN CIRCUITRY

Cultivating positive thoughts draws on the decision-making power of your left prefrontal cortex to modulate the negative input of the overactive amygdala and the hypersensitive right brain. Um, in English, please? You can *choose* to ignore negative thoughts and emphasize positive ones, even when your emotions are not in the mood. This isn't about becoming a naïve Pollyanna or reducing your thinking to the clichés found on inspirational posters picturing fluffy kittens wearing graduation caps. It is a powerful, research-based approach that rewires the brain to become more flexible.

In depression, negative neural networking rules the brain. And this negativity shuts down your options. If you feel as if others are judging you negatively, for example, you probably aren't on the phone calling those people to come over and party. If you are feeling unlovable, you aren't catching the eye of that good-looking colleague at a meeting to see if a mutual cup of coffee might be on the agenda. If you feel pessimistic about the possibility of getting a job, you aren't sending out resumes. You probably aren't doing much of anything at *all*. You're stuck. And the less you do, the worse your situation seems. Your lack of a date seems to *confirm* that you are unlovable. Your lack of a job makes you even more pessimistic about getting one. It's a self-fulfilling prophecy—a self-reinforcing cycle of negativity.

Neuronal firing (activity in your brain) causes brain growth: more blood supply, more cells that support neurons, and more synaptic connections. When neurons fire, they strengthen their connections, literally building up the circuit, not unlike building bigger muscles by using them. This means that when negativity rules, it just gets bigger and bigger. But you can interrupt this process by *intentionally* building positive circuitry instead. It works in the same way: The more you practice positive thinking, the more you make future positive thinking easier.

Barbara Frederickson's (2009) research reveals how positive emotions form circuitry for more positive experiences. This is because the feelings themselves prompt you to take action. As Frederickson explained, positive emotions help people find more creative solutions to problems and feel closer to friends and family. Those become personal resources that have ongoing benefits. Positive emotions open you to new experiences by sparking the interest, willingness, and action to do new things, which further enhances your possibilities for more positive experience. Frederickson (2001, 2009) described this as "broadening your repertoire."

Putting It in Practice

"Okay, this sounds good in theory," you may say, "but how on earth am I supposed to be positive when everything seems so horrible?" Interrupting negative brain circuitry isn't easy and takes practice. You may need a therapist to help you identify the brighter parts of your life and help you practice experiencing joy, positive thinking, and gratitude. But there are also things you can do on your own to become better able to savor the good parts of life and living:

Pay attention to your senses. A great way to begin building positive circuitry is to start noticing. Try taking sensory breaks several times a day for a moment or two. For example:

1. Look out the window and see the color of the sky, noticing how clouds and sky have depth and texture and vivid or soft coloration.
2. When you walk into a new space, sniff. Notice if the scents are pleasing. Aroma is fleeting because we habituate to it very quickly. Build your appreciation for scent.
3. When you sit to eat, take the first taste slowly. Feel it on your tongue, sense it with your teeth. Don't speak for just a moment while you feel that swallow go all the way down.
4. Listen. So often we have music or TV in the background without giving it our full attention. Try this: Turn it off. Now, depending on your circumstances and what would be most pleasing to you, do one of two things: (1) Pick a bit of music you know you like, put it on, and sit still for just a couple of minutes, only listening without doing anything else. (2) Step outside or open a window and listen to the world around you. How many things can you hear?
5. Feel your skin. One of the most pleasing things you might feel "on demand" is putting some lotion or cream on your hands. Try that and pay attention to the whole of the moment. Feel the coolness of the cream, sense its texture, spread it on and feel the comfort of your hands massaging each other and the softening and soothing of the skin.

Remember and repeat past joyful experiences. This exercise was introduced in Chapter 8 as part of balancing your life, but it bears repeating in the context of brain-based interventions. Refer to Chapter 8 for a full description; a short review is provided here to jog your memory:

1. Think of a positive event that happened in the past and re-member the details of it.
2. Describe it in detail, covering all of your senses.
3. Repeat this experience as soon as possible.
4. Make a commitment for when you will do it.
5. Decide how you will be accountable for doing it.

Develop your ability to see positives. This one is simple, but not easy. If you are a believer that building your capacity for joy, delight, interest, contentment, or love will defeat your depression and undo your knotty, negative thinking, committing to an action plan is something you will want to do. The best way to accomplish this is to have a "positive buddy"—someone to whom you will communicate positive thoughts and who will be waiting with bated breath to hear them! All it takes is this: Commit to reflect on positives during the week and bring that into discussion with your buddy. If you are shy about asking someone to listen to you, carry around an index card in your pocket or purse instead. Every time you notice something positive, make a tally mark; this will build your awareness of what is positive, and thinking about it long enough to tally it will help build that brain.

Here are some ways you might look for positives in some of the ma-jor positive emotion arenas:

- Look for joy—find a child and play. A few minutes with a child under the age of 5 or so will have you laughing in no time.
- Look for interest—this may be hard if you are depressed, but there are ways.
  - ○ Get on-line. If you are depressed and own a computer, you are probably surfing the Internet. What caught your inter-est? What did you click on? Watch your thoughts here. I am going to bet that you felt interest in something and then somehow squashed it. You might have looked at a new line of sports cars coming out and then said, "Yes, but

I could never own one." All this exercise takes is the willingness to notice you were interested.

○ Walk around your neighborhood. What do you take time to look at?

○ I never thought I would say it, but go shopping. Well, go window-shopping so you don't depress yourself with the bills. What do you see that you would be willing to save money for?

○ After you read the newspaper or listen to the morning news, pick one item of interest to comment on to a person you talk with during the day. Do not pick something you want to complain about! Your comment should start with something like this, "Hey, did you know _____?"

• Look for contentment—any experience in the week about which you could remark, "This is enough." Did you have enough to eat? Did you have enough sleep? Did you watch a movie or read a book that left you feeling glad you saw or read it?

• Look for love—this is too challenging if you think of it as wanting to feel love *from* others. You are only in charge of *you* feeling love for others. Contemplate whom in your life you love. What would you like to do for that person? You may even think about the love you feel for your pet. Sometimes getting a sense of love for a pet is less complicated to feel. If you cannot take action at this moment to behave in a loving way, just imagine you are doing it. It may not be as potent as taking the action, but it will still build your brain in positive ways.

Building brain circuitry for positive emotions will build your personal resources. Strong circuitry for joy will help you have more of it. You will have more options for how to think and behave. This will make you a better problem-solver and give you more capacity to calm yourself in troubling situations. In other words, you can be more flexible because you have a whole range of other emotions to use. If you have suffered depression for a while, you probably need to think about positive circuit-building like body-building: At first it will feel awkward and something of a strain, but the stronger you get, the more you can do.

As you practice building positive brain circuitry, try to interweave it with the techniques for other aspects of your type of depression. For example, if you have the lethargy of endogenous depression, you might combine the "Start the Train Rolling: Reward Yourself" method (explained in Chapter 6) with the "Remember and Repeat Past Joyful Experiences" method discussed in Chapter 8. If you are burned out, you will need sleep and change in your work habits before you can effectively change your thought habits. If you suffer plunges into despair, you will do well to emphasize positives as you plan for a different way to act. Gradually, as you habitually choose the way you think, it will diminish the negativity of depression.

Build Circuitry for Joy

1. *Pay attention to your senses.* Take breaks several times a day to look, sniff, taste, listen, and feel.
2. *Remember and repeat past joyful experiences.*
3. *Notice positives.* Talk about them with a "positive buddy" or tally them on an index card. Look for joy, interest, contentment, and love of others.

The challenge of depression is believing that the small changes will really matter. Having faith that it is possible to change your explanatory style, build your positive brain circuitry, and find a good balance between disappointment and hope can result in depression relief. And that is something we all hope for.

Increasing your flexibility is about making a decision to try something new in order to create a broader range of feelings and behaviors. You will develop more options by trying new ideas and seeing how they work. When you feel yourself getting immobile and thinking you have no choice in a situation or that you will be trapped in whatever decision you make, take a moment to remember that that is the depression talking. The beauty of life is that it is always changing—situations evolve, and if you can stay flexible in how you think about them and react to them, you'll stay one step ahead.

TWELVE

Technique #10:

Learn to Live Fully

Recovering from depression isn't just about getting rid of symptoms—it's also about focusing on how to live in a different way. If you have been depressed for years, you might not even have a vision of how you would feel if the depression were not there. You might not even believe that is a good idea to give up depressed ways of thinking and being. People with depression often see themselves as realistic rather than pessimistic. If you tell them to think optimistically, they roll their eyes and think you are a fool. "The world doesn't work that way," they may tell you, and they think it is safer to be on the lookout for bad things that could come their way so that they can be prepared.

Bad things *do* happen. Yes, they do. *And good things happen too.* Living fully means embracing all that happens. You can be not only safe but also much more resilient if you can fully appreciate all the wonderful, delightful experiences that come to you. Don't dismiss the value of focusing on positive thinking and positive outcomes just because there are also unfortunate experiences. Even though embracing positive attitudes might feel unfamiliar or even scary, once you start to live more fully, you will see that depression is only one of the vantage points from which to view your world. You might come to like the positive point of view.

BELIEVE IN POSITIVES AS USEFUL

Ironically, you are probably pessimistic about taking on an optimistic viewpoint. If you are going to employ positive thinking with enthusiasm instead of pessimism, knowing the statistics of happiness might help you take it seriously. Depressed people often think that changing their circumstances—their wealth, or health, or relationships, for example—will free them from the depression. But scientific studies show that happiness *precedes* a great deal of what of what people want (Lyubomisky, 2007). Frederickson's (2009) research indicates that positive emotions precede success—they even *create* conditions for success—in many arenas of life. Developing happiness can lead to:

- Better immune function
- More energy and creativity
- Better relationships
- More productivity at work
- A longer life

"Great," you say. "So if I'm depressed, I'll be sicker, in worse relationships, and die early. How depressing!" Don't despair! Research on the neurobiological basis of feeling joy suggests that about 50% of how likely you are to be joyful or depressed comes from your genetic predisposition to that stance (Coady et al., 2005). That means that you also have a 50% chance to affect your happiness. The same research looked at the relative happiness of various groups and found that even people whose circumstances might seem undesirable, such as paraplegics, could feel happy on a day-to-day basis depending on their focus. The overall life satisfaction was about the same among paraplegics as the general population. What made the difference, once they had adapted to their new circumstances, was that they focused on what they had—mealtimes with family, time with friends, daily activities they enjoyed—instead of on what they had lost. Sonya Lyubomirsky's (2007) research further supports that. Her team determined that about 10% of your unhappiness is what happens to you, and 40% is what you do about your circumstances.

Again, positive thinking is not Pollyanna thinking. In *Positivity*, Barbara Frederickson (2009) made the case for an approach to life that she called "positivity as a means to an end"—the end being a longer life, a healthier life, resourcefulness and resilience when facing difficulties, better social ties, and an overall higher quality of life. She has researched this topic for years and has presented the convincing case that positive emotions prepare us to take action on our own behalf and be resilient when difficulties occur. She described how all emotions prompt action sequences: Fear, for instance, prompts you to escape from the frightening situation, and your brain and body provide the physical and mental means to do just that. When you have positive emotions, you also are prompted to act. For example, if you feel interested in other people, you show curiosity about them. You inquire about who they are and what they do and generally get to know them. You may have a sense of energy or liveliness that communicates your interest. This positive emotion and its resulting actions pique the other person's interest in you and thus foster a good social exchange. Positive emotions prepare us to take action in support of good relationships, self-care, and fulfilling our potential. Frederickson identified ten positive emotions—joy, gratitude, serenity, interest, hope, pride, amusement, inspiration, awe, and love— and she convincing demonstrated that these emotions make for a high quality of life, even promoting our long-term wellbeing via their role in developing good relationships with others and prompting creative solutions to thorny problems.

Emphasizing positives in your life is a decision you make. It is a decision to use your rational left brain to override your pessimistic, overactive right brain. You will be more persistent in carrying out the following ideas if you believe they will benefit you. Once you emphasize positives— and see and feel the benefits for yourself—it will be easy to continue. For now, believe this: What you focus your attention on is your choice. Focusing on the positive will have lifelong benefits far beyond relief from depression. Wouldn't that be enough reason to try it?

BREATHE IN THE NOW

A simple place to start living fully is in breathing. You cannot feel yourself if you do not breathe. You might notice how often you hold your breath when you do not want to feel something. Holding still—a way not to feel—requires the holding of breath. Breathing helps you feel your body, feel your emotions, and even release your emotions. People who have been traumatized typically hold their breath, without even realizing they do it, whenever a situation triggers a fleeting thought of the traumatic experience. People who are tense from stress also tend to hold their breath. It is an endemic problem with depression, so releasing tension and feeling more fully starts with learning to breathe.

The goal of living fully is to become aware of the present moment and what is happening in it. Awareness is the first principle of mindfulness, and becoming aware means taking time to notice. Becoming able to notice starts with being able to feel your breath, which will allow you to sense how your body feels when you breathe. Go ahead and try it now. For many people it works best to lie down and rest a hand on your belly, but you can also do it seated. Find a posture that is as relaxed and supported as possible. Close your eyes if you are comfortable doing so, or find a focal point. If you are somewhere where you can light a candle, directing your gaze at the flame can be an excellent focal point. Inhaling through your nose and exhaling through your mouth is most comfortable. Then try the following exercise.

Awareness of Breath
1. Breathe in. Notice the sensation of the breath as it enters.
2. Breathe out. Follow the breath with your attention as it leaves.
3. As you continue to breathe in, notice how your body feels the breath entering.
4. As you continue to breathe out, notice how your body feels the breath leaving.
5. If you have thoughts that come into your mind, simply acknowledge them as if they were clouds scudding across the sky on a breezy day. They come and go and you do not need to hold onto them or be disturbed by them.
6. After a brief time of noticing your breath, stop the focused awareness of breath.
7. Notice what your body feels like at this time.
8. What else are you aware of?

You may want to extend this awareness of breath to a meditative experience of scanning your body. In that exercise, you "breathe into" each part of your body and simply notice that part of your body as you breathe into it and out of it. There are nice examples of this in *The Power of Focusing* (Cornell, 1996) and *The Mindful Way through Depression* (Williams et al., 2007). You may also want to extend this exercise to a practice of control of awareness, shifting between your breath and what you take in through your senses. There is an example of this in the Appendix titled "Mindful Awareness With Shifting Attention."

PAY ATTENTION TO YOUR SENSES

Paying attention to your senses, discussed in the previous chapter, is an ideal way to become more connected to the present moment. It can also be combined in creative ways with breathing exercises. Go ahead and try it—as you listen to the world around you or feel the sensation of your skin, notice your breath at the same time and see how it deepens your sensory awareness.

DO SOMETHING WITH FULL AWARENESS

Ah, multitasking! We are constantly encouraged to do this. In job interviews people are asked how well they multitask, as if it is a skill they picked up at technical school that will aid them in their work. Rarely are they asked how well they pay attention! Our culture creates the impression that if you are doing only one thing, you are somehow inadequate. What does this have to do with depression? Depression leaves you flat emotionally and physically. You may try to compensate by doing more than one thing at a time or try to avoid negative thoughts by getting too busy. This can lead to burnout and the fretful, irritable, anxiety-ridden symptoms of depression.

People also may pester themselves with thoughts while doing activities, and if you are depressed, you know those thoughts are rarely helpful.

They are typically not about the activity but rather full of criticism about *how* you are doing the activity. Or maybe your thoughts are full of fretting about the next thing you will do or what you need to be doing instead of what you *are* doing. You know how this goes: If you are painting a room, instead of feeling the brush in your hand and hearing the sound of it on the wall and observing the flow of the paint, you might be thinking, "Oh, there I go again, splattering. And why did I pick this color anyway? And what if I don't like it when it is done?" Or maybe you are full of thoughts about how you ought to be checking your email instead of painting.

By engaging more fully in the now you *feel* more sensations—so many of which are really good—and you spend less time in negative thinking. Doing something with full awareness can be an antidote to depression. You can learn to do one thing at a time with full attention. It will settle and restore your spirits. So how do you go about becoming aware of your actions in the moment? Here's one idea: The next time you find yourself reading a book or watching TV while eating, *stop* it. Just eat. Even if you only take a few mouthfuls, try to taste and chew and swallow while paying complete attention to the experience. How does this affect your experience of eating?

Life is full of activities that allow you to practice turning off your thoughts and staying aware of your action. Some ideas include:

- Washing dishes
- Drinking tea or coffee
- Brushing your teeth
- Taking a shower
- Putting lotion on your skin
- Pulling weeds in the garden
- Walking the dog

Marcia Linehan (1993) described one way to fit this kind of awareness into your everyday life as "taking a long cut." Everyone takes short cuts—cut across the grass to the porch, across the parking lot to the store—but what if you took a "long cut" and walked the long way around to where you are going, taking it all in and getting the sensation of a walk? What if you just drank your coffee without also reading the paper? A friend of mine who was advised to decrease her coffee consumption chose to have one *really good* cup of coffee per day and drink it with great awareness. She reported that this change did not feel like a loss, because she became aware of the pleasure of the smell and taste and warmth of the coffee in a new way. Thich Nhat Hanh (1999) wrote a miraculous little book called *The Miracle of Mindfulness* in which he articulately described the peace of being in the moment. You may want to read his book to if you want to learn more about how to take in your everyday moments with awareness.

LEARN TO SAVOR EXPERIENCE

Savoring is an interesting antidote to negative thinking. It is completely impossible to be negative while you are savoring something. Savoring means being in total awareness of the experience. It is different from mindfulness in that it is an intentional, appraising awareness. This means that you deliberately select an experience to notice and you contemplate its qualities while you are in the experience. If noticing a sunset, for example, you can assess the depth and range of the colors and the moments of change as it fades, and you can pay attention to how you are enjoying it. You may be noticing your happiness or awe or interest in the experience and what it is like to be alone or with others while viewing it.

You can savor many things. You could savor the process of baking a cake or taking a walk. You could savor an emotion you feel. You could savor the taste and texture of food you are eating. You could savor the look on a friend's face or the moment when you awaken in a cozy bed. You could savor the feeling of putting on dry clothes after you have been swimming. When you savor something, you will have a sense of immediacy about it. Not only are you mindfully aware, but you are also having an awareness of how you are sensing, feeling, and thinking at the moment of savoring. Bryant and Veroff (2007) wrote about savoring as the missing process of building resources that you can draw on to enrich your life. They saw it as the "positive counterpart of coping." Whereas coping may involve problem-solving, social support, prayer, cognitive reappraisal, wishful thinking, and avoidance, *savoring* is the capacity to attend to, appreciate, and enhance the positive experiences of our lives. Savoring builds the capacity to feel pleasure, which is something very different than the ability to cope with trouble when it comes.

You can learn to savor and practice savoring, but it will entail some planning on your part. You do not need a partner for this; it is an internal process. You might want to practice this using a memory of a positive experience until you feel prepared to savor life as it happens. Pick any part of an experience: the components of it, the outcome of it, or the actions you did or observed. Now, pay attention to what was going on. What were the accompanying environmental features? Then mindfully attend to the totality of your:

- *Sensations.* What came in through your senses? What did you feel in your body?
- *Perceptions.* What did you perceive to be happening?
- *Thoughts.* What were you thinking while this went on?
- *Behaviors.* What were you doing?
- *Emotions.* What were you feeling?

The following exercise is something you can do to practice savoring in the here and now. It involves eating an orange. (If you prefer, substitute a raisin or an almond or other food item.) Follow each process completely in thought, action, sensation, and emotion:

1. Look at the orange.
2. Hold and touch it, being aware of its texture.
3. Smell it as you peel it; feel it on your fingers.
4. Open a segment of the orange.
5. Place it on your lips; place it on your teeth.

6. Taste it.
7. Feel what it is like to chew it.
8. Swallow it.

Attention and *appreciation* are two vital components of savoring. You do not need to savor only joyful moments. You might want to savor a positive experience for its novelty or complexity, even if it is not joyful. A good example of this comes from a movie called *Ladies in Lavender*. In this film, actresses Judy Dench and Maggie Smith play two elderly sisters, Ursula and Janet, living on the coast of England in 1936 as World War II is threatening. A young man washes up on the beach, unconscious, and they carry him into their small cottage. As they care for him, Ursula, who has never been in love, falls in love with him. Ursula knows her love will be unrequited, and although this is agonizing for her, she still cherishes every aspect of the emotion of falling in love. She mindfully attends to her longing, her perceptions of the young man's appearance, her thoughts about what it would be like to have someone love her physically and be able to live with a lover, and her emotions, which are intense and unfamiliar. At the same time, she carefully monitors her own behavior so as not to betray her emotion and create a problem. The whole of the experience enriches her life.

Savoring can become a powerful means of emphasizing the positive and opening vistas of sensation that enrich your life. Absorbed in complexity, you might find the many levels of experiencing divert you from simple, black-and-white negative thinking. Becoming conscious of how many ways there are to delve into an experience, you can put negative appraisal behind you. Explore what *is* and savor it. What a change from the "blah" of depression!

PRACTICE GRATITUDE

Most of the things people hope for are things that will give them a better life: more love, better health, more money, and so on. They think they will be grateful when their circumstances change and they get what they want. However, researchers like Emmons (2007), Lyubomirsky (2007), and Frederickson (2009) have demonstrated that gratitude can be practiced at any time, and the condition of happiness exists without any discernable connection to status, money, or achievement. That means that you can achieve happiness without waiting to get that raise or that perfect husband first. You just have to start looking around. Practicing gratitude is demonstrated to be a powerful way to eliminate depression by creating an awareness of good feelings and happiness.

How does gratitude contribute to feeling less depressed? In the process of being grateful, individuals recognize, acknowledge, and appreciate a gift they have received. It may be a tangible gift or a gift of emotional or spiritual value, but in either case it comes to us as grace, something given rather than earned. Of course, your efforts may have had something to do with your getting what you are grateful for—your home or your good marriage or good job—but there is an element of grace that had a role as well. After all, it is possible that your efforts might have come to naught. Recognizing that gift is part of practicing gratitude.

When you feel gratitude, you acknowledge the role of being a recipient. That might feel uncomfortably dependent for some, but just think about the feeling that wells in you when you are spared from injury in an accident or have a moment when the beauty of nature engulfs you. You feel gratitude for those moments—and it is directed outward. When you take deliberate notice of things for which you are grateful, you enhance and enrich your life.

The benefits that accrue to people who practice gratitude are surprising and highly desirable (Emmons, 2007; Frederickson, 2009; Lyubomirsky, 2007). People who practice gratitude:

- Feel closer to others and feel loved
- Are more social and less isolated
- Are more likely to help others and to be seen as helpful by others

- Are perceived as happier and more pleasant by friends, family, and partners

The point here is that if you are in the habit of noticing what you are grateful for, it is going to have an impact on your emotions, your mood, and your behavior. You are going to be more focused on what is right and good, and you will be more likely to comment on those things if you are really *practicing* gratitude. Plus, if you are generally feeling better and behaving more pleasantly, other people will find you more pleasant to be around, and you will find yourself less isolated. Barbara Frederickson (2001, 2009) found that when you express gratitude, you create a situation in which the people around you reciprocate. She noted that gratitude has effects that ripple outward toward others. When you receive expressions of gratitude, it raises your self-esteem and good feelings about yourself and your relationships. When you have been treated kindly you immediately treat others around you more kindly. So you feel better and the person you spoke to about your gratitude feels better, too.

There are physical benefits for people who practice grateful thinking as well. These people tend to:

- Exercise more regularly
- Have fewer illness symptoms and recover more quickly
- Show less of the stress-induced DNA damage that ages cells
- Sleep better and fall asleep faster
- Feel better about their lives and feel more optimistic

So, how can a person learn to practice gratitude to begin to benefit from it right away? There are many ways to do this. Following are some good ones.

Get off the pity pot. Just stop thinking about and expressing self-pity. This will require you to recognize self-pitying when you are doing it. One sure way to tell if you are on the pity pot is to notice if you are having negative feelings like helplessness or resentment or believing that things are unfair. Self-pity usually involves expecting negative outcomes, whereas problem-solving involves seeing how action will result in positive change. So when you notice self-pity, stop! Refocus your attention on what is going right.

Amplify good memories. This means that as you discuss your past, distant or recent, you focus on things that were good, happy, or exciting. Discuss those things aloud. Literally start a conversation with "Hey, I was just remembering when _____" (fill in the blank with a recollection of a good time you had, preferably one that you shared with the person you are talking to). Also, look at pictures of happy times and think about what was good about the time. Do this often. Keep happy pictures in your workplace and home.

Practice a specific forgiveness model. Many times people who are depressed nurse resentment and feelings of being injured. It is as if they think they will feel better if they can blame someone for their woes. The problem is that you are the only who is injured by your resentment. The person you resent is not suffering—you are. Let go! Follow your religion or follow a model like the one in the 12-step self-help programs. The steps in a forgiveness model include: (1) acknowledging that the situation is in the past, (2) turning your attention to yourself and asking for guidance to see and correct your contribution to the situation, regardless of why the other person injured you, and (3) specifically forgiving the other person. You can do that all inside of yourself without the other person acknowledging his or her wrong. Newberg and Waldman (2009) described a similar approach to forgiveness for people of any (or no) religious affiliation. They demonstrated the great value to you if you forgive others for the wrongs they have done to you. As noted earlier, one particularly helpful tool to release your pain of resentment is to pray every day for 30 days for the person who has injured you—to pray for that person's wellbeing in all things. You will be relieved of your burden of resentment.

Keep a gratitude journal. Emmons (2007), Frederickson (2009), and Lyubomirsky (2007) have all discussed their research on the benefits of a gratitude journal. How do you keep one? There are several ways. You can write down three blessings every day, or, if you find it difficult to keep that commitment, just once a week, perhaps on Friday nights or on Sunday mornings as part of a religious practice. Another way is to end every day by writing down what went right in your day and why it did. When you not only think about *what* was right but also *why* it was right, you strengthen brain circuitry for positive emotions and positive thoughts. You also prepare yourself to see more positives in the world around you by strengthening the memory of the event. And when you write, you use more of your brain to make the thoughts real and strong.

Martin Seligman (2002) described the long-term antidepressant benefits of making a gratitude visit with a testimonial. He instructed the participants to write a short description, about 300 words, of how another person made a positive difference in their life. Then they visited the person and read their testimonial, sharing how they experienced the positive impact on their life. The outcome for the grateful individuals was long-lasting positive feelings.

Maureen was a client who was having a hard time complying with the suggestion to keep a gratitude journal. In discussing what thoughts went through her mind when she sat to write, she noticed this one: "I cannot be grateful because I am afraid I will lose what I have." She had a sort of superstitious view that if she acknowledged that she had something good, it would be taken away as a punishment. If you have such a view, you need some outside help to examine where that attitude came from and get rid of it as soon as possible. Just by bringing it to awareness, Maureen could laugh at the ridiculousness of such a thought, and she was able to talk about how she had come to think that way in her very rigid and somber family of origin. Her belief did not evaporate into thin air just by seeing it for what it was, but every time she thought that false belief, she deliberately dismissed it, and slowly it stopped interfering with her appreciation of what was good in her life. She could push the idea aside to look at things no one could take from her and gradually felt both safe and blessed.

Max was an older client who had trouble with the gratitude list because he swore he could only think of trivial things. He was upset that his future no longer held big, exciting events such as fantastic sales successes and exhilarating romantic ventures. In retirement, with a settled marriage, he felt as if the big moments of life were over, and that was depressing to him. He asked, "How can I practice gratitude when I have such silly things to be grateful for, like a bowl of popcorn while I watch the news and my puppy who sits on my lap?" Perhaps the right question was, "How could I *not* be grateful when I have these things?" However, his point was important. He believed one could only be grateful for huge things: perfect health or being saved from disaster. After all, he had sought therapy to get big solutions and help him find big things to be grateful for. But to his surprise, he liked making long lists of "trivial" things to be grateful for. After a while he saw that his life was made of small, delightful, and even joyous moments much more than it was made of big, startling events, and that it always had been so. He could be grateful that in retirement he had more time to appreciate each one of them.

Ways to Practice Gratitude
1. Get off the pity pot.
2. Amplify good memories.
3. Practice a specific forgiveness model.
4. Keep a gratitude journal.

Living life more fully often requires slowing down—a concept that is not too culturally acceptable here in the U.S. You will find that when you allow yourself moments of full awareness, of sensory appreciation of an experience, or of gratitude, you will automatically slow yourself down to notice and stay with the sensation. This is a very different kind of slowing down than what happens in depression. In depression, the slowing is due to immobility, withdrawal, and lack of interest. Living life fully is the opposite of that: It's about connecting to the world in a profound—and profoundly rewarding—way.

Appendix A

Worksheets and Information for Readers

FOCUS ON STRENGTHS: I DO WHAT I AM

What we do changes how we feel about ourselves, and opportunities to do our best give us self-esteem of the most important kind. People with depression may forget that they have strengths and positives.

- Make a list of your best strengths (e.g., hard worker, honest, kind, creative, disciplined).
- Make a list of opportunities to use your strengths.
- Every day, note: Did I use my strengths? How?

	Strength	Strength	Strength	Strength
Day_____ Used in:				
Day _____ Used in:				
Day_____ Used in:				
Day _____ Used in:				
Day _____ Used in:				

AN ACTION PLAN FOR YOUR STRENGTHS

Creating an action plan—and committing to it—is an important component of making the strength list effective. Find someone (such as your therapist) to hold you to the following "contract."

I, _____ , understand and agree with the principle that utilizing my strengths and talents is a natural and important part of living a vital life. I commit to increasing my pleasure and vitality by employing my strengths and talents in the following way:

I plan to use _____ (strength or talent) by _____ (name an activity). The actions steps necessary to achieve this are:

1.

2.

3.

4.

I will (do) _____

by the following date _____

Signed: _____

EXERCISE

This is the single most important thing you can do. Make a plan you will commit to. To figure out how to begin incorporating exercise into your life, answer the following questions:

1. What do you like to do?
2. What do you remember liking to do?
3. What are your opportunities to do it?
4. Who would do it with you?
5. What is the largest possible step you can take in the direction of exercise?
6. What will you commit to this week?
7. How will you be accountable?

START THE TRAIN ROLLING

1. Make a list of rewards. What do you like to do, even though you are depressed? If the answer is "nothing," ask yourself, "What am I *doing with my time* even though I am depressed?" Are you playing video games? solitaire? watching TV? listening to music? soaking in the tub? talking on the phone? Make a list.

Reward #1: _____
Reward #2: _____
Reward #3: _____
Reward #4: _____
Reward #5: _____

2. What *should* you be doing with your time? Make a list of things that are being left partially done or undone (e.g., returning phone calls, doing homework, finishing projects for work, doing home tasks such as cleaning, gardening, car care, and so on). Break the activity down into the individual steps it takes.

Activity: _____

Step #1: _____
Step #2: _____
Step #3: _____
Step #4: _____
Step #5: _____

3. What is the largest step you believe you can do for one of the tasks? It doesn't matter how small the step is; just commit to doing it at a certain time or on a certain day.

Step: _____ When I will do it: _____

4. Which reward will you choose for when you do it?

5. Call someone to report in on your success.

DISCOVERING YOUR BALANCE
THROUGH YOUR VALUES

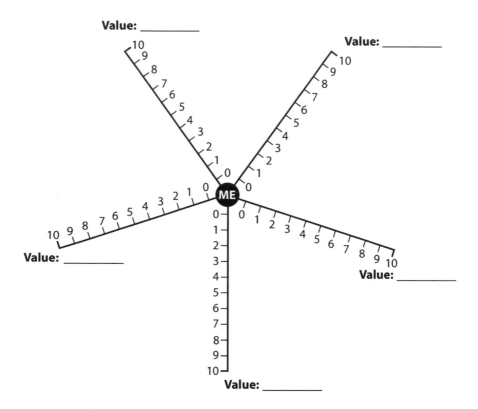

MINDFULNESS AWARENESS
WITH SHIFTING ATTENTION

This exercise is to teach awareness and control of attention. It is a simple meditative moment expanded. This method is a nonverbal experience of self-direction of attention.

1. Breathe.
   - Follow the breath into your body.
   - Notice each sensation as breath flows in. Notice coolness of air, pressure of airflow, and how it feels through your nose, throat, trachea, and lungs. Feel your heart beating and the blood flowing through your arteries and veins.
   - Follow the breath out of your body. Note the sensations of pressure, warmth, and how it feels exhaling through your mouth.
2. Without opening your eyes, breathe your awareness into the room around you.
   - Note with awareness every sound in the environment, paying special attention to location, intensity, and any movement that you can detect.
3. Shift your awareness back to your breath in your body, and then back to the external world. Repeat this several times.

Notes:

CLEAR THE MIND, CENTER THE BODY

This method is used to clear the mind to rest, relax, or be less ruminative.

1. Sit comfortably, and breathe evenly.
2. Notice any part of you that is tense, painful, or stiff.
3. Breathe into whatever part feels most uncomfortable to you.
4. Imagine there is a container in front of you—one that can be closed tightly but is now open and waiting for all the things that are pressing on your awareness at this time.
5. Now ask yourself, "How is it for me right at this moment?"
6. Notice each thing as it comes up, whether it's a physical feeling, a thought, a situation, a worry, a problem, and so on. See it, name it, and set it inside the container.
7. When no more life things come to mind, ask if there is anything else.
8. When no more things present themselves, put the lid on the container and imagine it being placed somewhere away from you and secure, where you can, if desired, gain access to it later.

Are there special things you want to remember that makes this work best for you? Do you want to do it on paper? Use worry dolls? Make it your own way to really clear your mind.

Notes:

DEVELOP AN ATTITUDE OF GRATITUDE

Practicing gratitude enhances positive feelings as nothing else can. The "attitude of gratitude" involves spending a few minutes each evening before bedtime recounting the pleasant things that happened during the day or the things you have to be grateful for. Here are some ways to do this:

- List five things for which you feel grateful (blessings) daily for 2 weeks.
- Make a written list each day of three things that went well and why they did.
- Create a weekly journal of all the things in a week that were very positive and for which you might feel grateful.

DEVELOP AN ATTITUDE OF APPRECIATION

Find five situations in which you notice a positive thing about someone and say it out loud to that person. The appreciation must be genuine, but it may be just a small thing. This exercise will help you notice good things and make you feel good every day. When you notice what is good and helpful in others—a behavior that is in your control—you also get some genuine self-esteem for being kind and observant. You will feel:

- More grateful
- More in control of your life
- More valuable (doing something nice that pleases others)
- More likeable (your nice comment elicits a happy reaction from others)

Write the recipient of the comment on a card like this and review the list each evening to see if you can remember the five comments you made that day.

	Mon	Tues	Wed	Thurs	Fri	Sat	Sun
Recipient 1							
Recipient 2							
Recipient 3							
Recipient 4							
Recipient 5							

Appendix B

Worksheets and Scales for Therapists

EXPANDING ASSESSMENT QUESTIONS TO ADDRESS BURNOUT

by Margaret Wehrenberg and Laurel Coppersmith

DON'T JUST ASK THIS:	BUT ALSO ASK THIS:
PRESENTING PROBLEM What is the presenting problem?	How does work present problems in your life?
HEALTH/MENTAL-HEALTH HISTORY Have you ever been treated for depression, anxiety, or a related disorder?	Does work stress affect you? How?
Do you have any other medical conditions?	Are your medical conditions affected by stress?
Are you having difficulty with your spouse/partner?	Are you having difficulty with your supervisor or coworkers?
Have you experienced any trauma, past or recent?	Have there been any critical incidents in your workplace?
SELF-ESTEEM Have you experienced any losses, either past or recent, that you are still struggling with?	Has your job changed recently? Is your job in jeopardy? If so, do you know what is required to keep it?
What coping mechanisms have you used in the past to deal with difficult times?	What have been your most effective tools for dealing with work stress?
Do you feel that your threshold for dealing with adversity has been adequate in the past?	Do you feel there has been a change in your ability to rebound from work stress?

LIFESTYLE Do you smoke?	How many hours/days do you work? How many of those are at home, on personal or uncompensated time?
Have you gained or lost weight recently?	Do you travel for work? How much?
Do you use any drugs, prescribed or otherwise, to cope with mood or energy problems?	Do you telecommute
Have you noticed any changes in your behavior lately?	What is your history with this workplace (length of service, changes in position, duties)?
Do you have difficulty sleeping?	How does your workplace handle conflict, mistakes, and disseminating or receiving information (feedback loops)?
What role has work played in your life?	Does your family complain about your work and its effect on you?

COMPARISON OF COGNITIVE, EMOTIONAL, BEHAVIORAL, AND PHYSICAL
SIGNS OF BURNOUT, ANXIETY, AND DEPRESSION AND THEIR STAGES
AND PROGRESSION

	Burnout	Anxiety	Depression
Cognitive	Focused tenacious attention	Inconsistent inattentiveness due to preoccupation caused by anxiety; may be focused when not anxious	Mild and moderate depression: Short bursts of focus followed by loss of concentration
	Then: Mental fatigue; may seem inattentive	More persistent inattentiveness with intensity of anxiety	Persistent inability to concentrate, which worsens with length of depression and its severity
	Later: Poor concentration and lack of attention; depression	Negativity and rumination	Hopelessness, apathy
	End stage: Depression, hopelessness, and negativity		
Emotional	Compulsivity ("I must"); disappearance of joy; feelings of personal "obligation"; labile emotions	General anxiety disorder: Worry and solemnity	Mild but persistent negativity and hopeless or helpless feelings that intensify
	Persistent anxiety	Rigidity or even rituals to protect from anxiety; good, positive feelings may exist between bouts of anxiety	Feelings of obligation to perform, irritability, and little sense of joy (but not despair)
	Depressed moods alternate with resolving to do more.		
	Feelings of victimization or criticism, which evolve into clinical depression	Panic or social anxiety: Possible feelings of discouragement, helplessness to change	Disengaged and empty feelings that interfere with motivation to recover

(continued)

	Burnout	Anxiety	Depression
Behavioral	Excessive work and longer hours to feel one "deserves" a break Good activities feeling like "requirements," which leads to isolation; weight increase Increased distraction and accident-proneness Eventually all signs of anxiety/depression are seen in nonlinear sequence	Possible excessive work patterns to relieve anxiety Impulse-driven activities (shopping sprees, sex, alcohol use, eating, etc.) Distraction both mentally and physically Immobilization	Loss of interest in work; decreased hours or ineffective work Social withdrawal; decrease in weight (20% show increase) Increase in zone-out activities (TV, computer, etc.) Lethargy
Physical	Frantic bursts of energy in response to identifiable stressor or demand Depletion of physical resources, including neurotransmitter deficiency, persistent fatigue, and immunosuppression Musculoskeletal injury or ergonomic injury Gastrointestinal and cardiovascular problems; disrupted but restorative sleep	Hyperactivity Tension-induced musculoskeletal distress (headache, TMJ, high blood pressure, or irritated gastrointestinal symptoms) Heart palpitations, racing heart, flushing, sweating, shakiness (all transient and reversible) Exhaustion due to chronic hyperactivation of stress response (similar to burnout); persistently disrupted nonrestorative sleep	Decreasing energy; undereating; sleep diminishment such as early morning awakening (20% have hypersomnia) Muscular pain similar to fibromyalgia; inactivity and lethargy (interferes with recuperation from illness or surgery) Persistent listlessness; sleep nonrestorative of mental or emotional energy

	Burnout	Anxiety	Depression
Stages	Stress is perceived as exhilarating and promoting growth. *No stress* is seen as akin to "death." When perceived demands exceed resources (stress overload), discomfort ensues. Failure to manage stress progresses to burnout, causing clinical symptomatology in physical, emotional, or mental arenas.	Mild: Intensity and severity of symptoms is minimally intrusive on intra- and interpersonal function or daily responsibilities. Moderate: Symptoms begin to interfere with cognition and behavior. Reassurance-seeking and self-medication increase, as does physical, mental, and emotional discomfort. Increases in nondirected motor activity occur. Severe: Sleep becomes impaired, as does ability to solve problems or complete tasks. Helpless or frantic feelings increase. Dependency marks relationships.	Mild: Intensity and severity of symptoms is minimally intrusive on intra- and interpersonal function or daily responsibilities. Blue mood, low energy, and pessimism are present. Moderate: Cognition becomes distorted and negative. Efforts at self-medication may be taken. Lethargy increases and sleep is impaired. Severe: Vegetative markers worsen. Tasks cannot be completed. Social and emotional isolation worsen. Suicidal ideation may occur.
Course progression	Burnout begins with erratic anxiety or negativity. Then steadily decreasing energy, dark moods, increased anxiety, and failure in interpersonal relations. Finally, isolation, depression, and anxiety culminate.	Anxiety can be present for years with some good and some not-good days until the person eventually realizes the personal costs of being anxious, panicky, or socially phobic. Usually a specific event intensifies the desire to seek treatment.	Depression or dysthymia may be tolerated in mild form, but without periods of good days (unlike in burnout or anxiety). As depression worsens, the inability to self-motivate prompts others to seek treatment for the depressed person.

SHIROM-MELAMED BURNOUT MEASURE (SMBM)*

Following are a number of statements that describe different feelings you may have at work. The letters before each item represent the three subscales of physical fatigue (P), emotional exhaustion (E), and cognitive weariness (C). Please indicate how often, in the past 30 workdays, you have felt each of the following feelings.

How often have you felt this way at work?

		Never or almost quently	Very infre- quently	Quite infre- quently	Some- times	Quite frequently	Very frequently	Always or almost always
P	1. I feel tired	1	2	3	4	5	6	7
P	2. I have no energy for going to work in the morning							
		1	2	3	4	5	6	7
P	3. I feel physically drained							
		1	2	3	4	5	6	7
P	4. I feel fed up	1	2	3	4	5	6	7
P	5. I feel like my "batteries" are "dead"							
		1	2	3	4	5	6	7
P	6. I feel burned out	1	2	3	4	5	6	7
C	7. My thinking process is slow							
		1	2	3	4	5	6	7
C	8. I have difficulty concentrating							
		1	2	3	4	5	6	7
C	9. I feel I'm not thinking clearly							
		1	2	3	4	5	6	7
C	10. I feel I'm not focused in my thinking							
		1	2	3	4	5	6	7
C	11. I have difficulty thinking about complex things							
		1	2	3	4	5	6	7
E	12. I feel I am unable to be sensitive to the needs of coworkers and customers							
		1	2	3	4	5	6	7
E	13. I feel I am not capable of investing emotionally in coworkers and customers							
		1	2	3	4	5	6	7
E	14. I feel I am not capable of being sympathetic to coworkers and customers							
	1	2	3	4	5	6	7	

* Used with permission of Dr. Arie Shirom. Norms for the SMBM and its facets can be found on Shirom's Web site at http://www.shirom.org/arie/research.htm.

SHIROM-MELAMED VIGOR MEASURE (SMVM)*

Following are a number of statements that describe different feelings you may have at work. The letters before each item represent the three subscales of physical strength (P), emotional energy (E), and cognitive liveliness (C). Please indicate how often, in the past 30 workdays, you have felt each of the following feelings.

How often have you felt this way at work?

	Never or almost quently	Very infre- quently	Quite infre- quently	Some- times	Quite frequently	Very frequently	Always or almost always
P 1. I feel full of pep	1	2	3	4	5	6	7
P 2. I feel I have physical strength	1	2	3	4	5	6	7
P 3. I feel vigorous	1	2	3	4	5	6	7
P 4. I feel energetic	1	2	3	4	5	6	7
P 5. I have a feeling of vitality	1	2	3	4	5	6	7
C 6. I feel I can think rapidly	1	2	3	4	5	6	7
C 7. I feel I am able to contribute new ideas	1	2	3	4	5	6	7
C 8. I feel able to be creative	1	2	3	4	5	6	7
E 9. I feel able to show warmth to others	1	2	3	4	5	6	7
E 10. I feel able to be sensitive to the needs of coworkers and customers	1	2	3	4	5	6	7
E 11. I feel I am capable of investing emotionally in coworkers and customers	1	2	3	4	5	6	7
E 12. I feel capable of being sympathetic to coworkers and customers	1	2	3	4	5	6	7

* Used with permission of Dr. Arie Shirom. Norms for the SMVM and its facets can be found on Shirom's Web site at http://www.shirom.org/arie/research.htm.

PROGRESSIVE MUSCLE RELAXATION VISUALIZATION FOR RELEASE OF TENSION

The following relaxation visualization will take 10 to 15 minutes.

1. Make sure your client is in a relaxed position (e.g., sitting upright or lying flat).
2. Have the client close his eyes if he is comfortable doing so and then instruct him to allow his focus to rest entirely on the sensations of each muscle group as you name them.
3. Begin at the head or feet, and name each muscle group, instructing the client to tense, hold, then relax. Your script for this should be something like, "Tense your toes, curl them tight, tight, tight. Now release. Feel the warmth flood into them. Feel the energy and warmth suffuse those muscles. With each exhalation, the warmth flows into the . . . [arm, leg, etc.]." Repeat the tense, hold, release three times for each muscle group.
4. The order of group could be: scalp, forehead, face, neck (don't move the head in circles; instead, lean it forward and then back, and then side to side, letting its weight stretch the neck), shoulders, upper arms, forearms and wrists, fingers, chest, back, buttocks, thighs, shins, calves, ankles, and feet.
5. If going top-down, keep adding the sense of energy flowing down through the relaxed muscles, and end with the awareness of the soles of the feet feeling connected to the earth through the floor.
6. If going bottom-up, end with the energy flowing in with each breath and now coursing down through the body with each exhalation.

This classic visualization is drawn from yoga techniques:

1. Imagine that above your head there is a sphere of light/energy.
2. The light is the color you most associate with [peace, calm, healing, energy, etc.].
3. As you inhale, you draw it into your body through your breath or through the crown chakra.
4. As you exhale, the flow of energy streams through your body. The physical experience of warmth and vibrant energy relaxes each part of your body as the breath is exhaled downward from the top of the head through each part of the body, one breath at a time.
5. It may connect through your spine as roots into the earth.
6. It may connect through the soles of your feet.
7. As your body fills with energy, that energy exudes through every pore, forming an envelope of energy around your body.
8. Find a word that you associate with the sensation of total relaxation, such as "calm," or even a sound such as "ah" or "mmm."
9. As the envelope of energy fades through the day it can be renewed with deep breath, imaging light, and saying or hearing the sound you chose.
10. This energy provides a barrier to negativity for the day.

Recommended Reading and Resources

THE BRAIN AND METHODS TO WORK WITH IT

Amen, D., & Routh, L. (2004). *Healing anxiety and depression*. New York: Penguin.
Walsh, D., & Bennett, N. (2004). *Why do they act that way? A survival guide to the adolescent brain for you and your teen*. New York: Free Press.
Wehrenberg, M., & Prinz, S. (2007). *The anxious brain*. New York: Norton.

LISTENING TO YOUR BODY

Childre, D., & Martin, H. (1999). *The heartmath solution*. San Francisco: Harper Collins.
Cornell, A. W. (1996). *The power of focusing*. Oakland, CA: New Harbinger.
Gendlin, E. (1998). *Focusing-oriented psychotherapy*. New York: Guilford.

Various technological devices exist to assess, monitor, and alter aspects of autonomic nervous-system functioning in order to train the body to diminish and release stress. Check out the options at the following websites. They offer devices for biofeedback of various types and hand-held or computer-based devices to improve physical and psychological wellbeing.
www.heartmath.com
www.stresseraser.com
www.wilddivine.com

WORKSHEETS AND ACTIVITIES FOR SOCIAL SKILLS, ASSERTIVENESS, AND ANGER MANAGEMENT

Carter, L., & Minirth, F. (1993). *The anger workbook*. Nashville, TN: Thomas Nelson.
Eifert, G., McKay, M., & Forsyth, J. (2005). *Acceptance and commitment therapy for anxiety disorders*. Oakland, CA: New Harbinger.

Eifert, G., McKay, M., & Forsyth, J. (2006). *ACT on life not on anger: The new acceptance & commitment therapy guide to problem anger*. Oakland, CA: New Harbinger.

Khalsa, S. (1996). *Group exercise for enhancing social skills and self-esteem*. Sarasota, FL: Professional Resource Press.

Madson, P. R. (2005). *Improv wisdom*. New York: Crown.

Novotni, M. (1999). *What does everybody else know that I don't know?* Plantation, FL: Specialty Press.

O'Hanlon, B. (1999). *Do one thing different*. New York: William Morrow.

Robbins, J. M. (2002). *Acting techniques in everyday life*. New York: Marlowe.

Seigel, D., & Hartzell, M. (2003). *Parenting from the inside out*. New York: Putnam.

Wilson, B., & DeMaria, R. (2009). *He's just no good for you: A guide to getting out of a destructive relationship*. Guilford, CT: GPP Life.

Zeff, T., & Aron, E. (2004). *The highly sensitive person's survival guide: Essential skills for living well in an overstimulating world (step-by-step guides)*. Oakland, CA: New Harbinger.

RELAXATION, MEDITATION

Brantley, J., Millstine, W., & Matik, W. (2007). *Five good minutes: 100 mindful practices to help you relieve stress and bring your best to work*. Oakland, CA: New Harbinger.

Davis, M., McKay, M., & Eshelman, E. (2007). *The relaxation and stress reduction workbook*. Oakland, CA: New Harbinger.

Ensley, E. (2007). *Prayer that relieves stress and worry*. Fortson, GA: Contemplative Press.

Newberg, A., & Waldman, M. (2009). *How god changes your brain*. New York: Ballantine.

Nhat Hanh, T. (1999). *The miracle of mindfulness*. Boston: Beacon.

Siegel, D. (2007). *The mindful brain: Reflection and attunement in the cultivation of well-being*. New York: Norton.

NUTRITION AND SUPPLEMENTS

Amen, D. & Routh, L. (2003). *Healing anxiety and depression*. New York: Penguin.

Brown, R., Gerberg, P., & Muskin, P. (2009). *How to use herbs, nutrients, and yoga in mental health care*. New York: Norton.

DesMaisons, K. (1998). *Potatoes, not Prozac*. New York: Simon & Schuster.

Hendler, S., & Rovik, M. S. (Eds.). (2001). *Physicians desk reference: PDR for nutritional supplements*. Des Moines, IA: Thompson Healthcare.

Henslin, E. (2008). *This is your brain on joy*. Nashville, TN: Thomas Nelson.

Northrup, C. (2006). *The wisdom of menopause: Creating physical and emotional health and healing during the change* (2nd ed.). New York: Bantam.

Northrup, C. (2006). *Women's bodies, women's wisdom: Creating physical and emotional health and healing*. New York: Bantam.

Weil, A. (2000). *Eating well for optimal health*. New York: Knopf.

THERAPY

Baker, D. (2004). *What happy people know*. New York: St. Martin's Griffin.

Burns, D. (1999). *The feeling good handbook*. New York: Plume.

Ecker, B., & Hully, L. (2007). *Coherence therapy manual*. [Available on their Web site at www.coherencetherapy.org.]

Gallo, F., & Vincenzi, H. (2000). *Energy tapping*. Oakland, CA: New Harbinger.

McMullin, R. (2005). *Taking out your mental trash*. New York: Norton.

Pratt, G., & Lambrou, P. (2000). *Instant emotional healing: Acupressure for the emotions*. New York: Broadway Books.

Shapiro, F. (2001). *Eye movement desensitization and reprocessing: Basic principles, protocols, and procedures* (2nd ed.). New York: Guilford.

Wehrenberg, M. (2008). *The 10 best-ever anxiety management techniques*. New York: Norton.

DEPRESSION SUPPORT RESOURCES

The Depression and Bipolar Support Alliance (DBSA) is the leading patient-directed national organization focusing on the most prevalent mental illnesses. The organization fosters an environment of understanding about the impact and management of these life-threatening illnesses by providing up-to-date, scientifically based tools and information written in language the general public can understand. DBSA supports research to promote more timely diagnosis, develop more effective and tolerable treatments, and discover a cure. The organization works to ensure that people living with mood disorders are treated equitably.

www.dbsalliance.org

MENTAL HEALTH ORGANIZATIONS FOR MORE RESOURCES

National Institute of Mental Health
www.nimh.nih.gov

American Psychological Association
750 First Street NE
Washington, D.C. 20002
(800) 374-2721
www.apa.org

American Psychiatric Association
1000 Wilson Boulevard, Suite 1825
Arlington, VA 22209
(703) 907-7300
www.psych.org
apa@psych.org

Anxiety Disorder Association of America
8730 Georgia Avenue, Suite 600
Silver Spring, MD 20910
(240) 485-1001
www.adaa.org

Obsessive-Compulsive Foundation
676 State Street
New Haven, CT 06511
(203) 401-2070
www.ocfoundation.org

OTHER THERAPIES

To learn more about EMDR and how to be trained or find a therapist who practices
    EMDR, contact:
EMDR International Association
5806 Mesa Drive, Suite 360
Austin, TX 78731
(512) 451-5200 or toll-free in the U.S (866) 451-5200
www.emdria.org
info@emdria.org

To learn more about energy therapies, contact:
Fred Gallo and Harry Vincenzi energy-tapping information at:
www.energypsych.com

George Pratt and Peter Lambrou and instant emotional-healing information at:
www.instantemotionalhealing.com

HELP WITH ADDICTIONS

National Institute of Drug Addiction
www.nida.nih.gov

National Clearinghouse on Drug and Alcohol Addiction
(800) 729-6686

Addiction self-help:
www.alcoholics-anonymous.org
www.rational.org
www.smartrecovery.org
www.ca.org (Cocaine Anonymous)

Family help with addiction:
www.al-anon.alateen.org
www.familiesanonymous.org

TRAUMA

For resources, pamphlets, and education on trauma for professionals and the general
    public, contact:
International Society for Traumatic Stress Studies (ISTSS)
60 Revere Drive, Suite 500
Northbrook, IL 60062
(847) 480-9028
www.istss.org
istss@istss.org

Other good resources include:
Sidran Traumatic Stress Foundation
200 E. Joppa Road, Suite 207
Baltimore, MD 21286
(410) 825-8888
www.sidran.org

International Critical Incident Stress Foundation
10176 Baltimore National Pike, Unit 201
Ellicott City, MD 21042
(410) 750-9600
www.icisf.org

MEDICATION ASSISTANCE

The National Alliance on Mental Illness provides a list of resources for people who can-
    not afford medication or who do not have insurance. They also have information
    and resources for other mental illnesses.
NAMI
Colonial Place Three
2107 Wilson Boulevard, Suite 300
Arlington, VA 22201
(800) 950-NAMI (6264)
www.nami.org/Template.cfm?section=about_medications&Template=/ContentMan-
    agement/contentDisplay.cfm&ContentID=19169

HERBAL MEDICINE AND SUPPLEMENTS

This section of the University of Pittsburgh website offers an impressive list of resources, websites, and groups who study and promote herbal remedies.
www.pitt.edu/~cbw/herb.html

The National Library of Medicine and the National Institutes of Health sponsor Medline, which has a variety of options for nutritional and alternative-medicine treatments.
medlineplus.gov

The American Botanical Council is an independent, nonprofit research and education organization dedicated to providing accurate and reliable information for consumers, healthcare practitioners, researchers, educators, industry, and the media.
abc.herbalgram.org

GUIDED IMAGERY AND RELAXATION AUDIO CDS

Some of the best available guided imagery for anxiety, depression, and trauma recovery can be ordered from:
Belleruth Naparstak
891 Moe Drive, Suite C
Akron, OH 44310
(800) 800-8661
www.healthjourneys.com

Audio CD with breathing and relaxation techniques as described in this book, from:
Margaret Wehrenberg
1555 Naperville/Wheaton Road
Naperville, IL 60563
(630) 961-2854
www.margaretwehrenberg.com

SLEEP HYGIENE

Sponsored by the American Academy of Sleep Medicine, this terrific education site will give you all the ideas you need to make sleep work for reducing depression.
www.sleepeducation.com

You can find a sleep specialist through the American Academy of Sleep Medicine (AASM), which accredits centers and labs that treat people who have sleep problems. AASM accreditation is the "gold standard" for the field.
www.aasmnet.org

RESOURCES FOR WORK, ABILITIES, AND CAREER

Buckingham, M., & Clifton, D. (2001). *Now, discover your strengths.* New York: Free Press.
Seligman, M. (2002). *Authentic happiness.* New York: Free Press.

For assessment of your work abilities and career options, visit the website of Mary Jane Murphy:
www.murphycounseling.com

Popular websites with descriptions of all professions and assessment tools for strength, ability, and style:
www.bls.gov/oco
www.dol.state.ga.us/js/assessment_link.htm#personality_profiles (This website has many assessments regarding personality, work values, skills, and interests.)
www.onetcenter.org/tools.html (These assessments may have associated fees.)

References

A. A. World Services. (2001). *The big book* (4th ed.). New York: A. A. World Services.

Addis, M., & Martell, C. (2004). *Overcoming depression one step at a time*. Oakland, CA: New Harbinger.

Alspaugh, L. (2009). *Depression and insomnia linked*. Retrieved Aug 31, 2009, from http://www.livestrong.com/article/14211-depression-and-insomnia-linked/

Amen, D., & Routh, L. (2003). *Healing anxiety and depression*. New York: Penguin.

American Psychiatric Association. (2000). *Diagnostic and statistical manual of mental disorders* (4th ed., text rev.). Washington, DC: Author.

Bajwa, S., Bermpohl, F., Rigonatti, S., Pascual-Leone, A., Boggio, P., & Fregni, F. (2008). Impaired interhemispheric interactions in patients with major depression. *Journal of Nervous and Mental Disease, 196*(9), 671–677.

Bartholomew, J. B. (2005). Brief aerobic exercise may improve mood, well-being in major depression. *Medicine and Science in Sports and Exercise, 37*, 2032–2037.

Benson, H. (1996). *Timeless healing: The power and biology of belief*. New York: Fireside.

Benson, H., & Proctor, W. (2003). *The breakout principle*. New York: Scribner.

Bergmann, U. (1998). Speculations on the neurobiology of EMDR. *Traumatology, 4*(1), 4–16. Retrieved April 20, 2010, from http://www.fsu.edu/~trauma/art1v4i1.html

Blackburn, I. M., & Moore, R. G. (1997). Controlled acute and follow-up trial of cognitive therapy and pharmacotherapy in out-patients with recurrent depression. *The British Journal of Psychiatry, 171*, 328–334.

Brown, R., Gerbarg, P., & Muskin, P. (2009). *How to use herbs, nutrients, and yoga in mental health care*. New York: Norton.

Bryant, F., & Veroff, J. (2007). *Savoring: A new model of positive experience*. Mahwah, NJ: Lawrence Erlbaum.

Buckingham, M., & Clifton, D. (2001). *Now, discover your strengths*. New York: Free Press.

Burns, S. (2009). Faith and hope. Private Communication.

Cameron, O., Huang, G., Nichols, T., Koeppe, R., Minoshima, S., Rose, D., et al. (2007). Reduced gamma-aminobutyric acid-sub(a)-benzodiazepine binding sites in insular cortex of individuals with panic disorder. *Archives of General Psychiatry, 64*(7), 793–800.

Childre, D., & Martin, H. (1999). *The heartmath solution.* San Francisco: Harper Collins.

Clark, D., Ehlers, A., & McManus, F. (2003). Cognitive therapy versus fluoxetine in generalized social phobia: A randomized placebo-controlled trial. *Journal of Consulting and Clinical Psychology, 71,* 1058–1067.

Coady, E., Cray, D., & Park, A. (2005, January 17). The new science of happiness. *Time Magazine, 165*(3), A1–A68.

Cornell, A. (1996). *The power of focusing: A practical guide to emotional self-healing.* Oakland, CA: New Harbinger.

Craft, L. (2005). Exercise and clinical depression: Examining two psychological mechanisms. *Psychology of Sport and Exercise, 6*(2), 151–171.

Crawford, T. (2009, July 2). Sorry Oprah: Self-help books seldom helpful. *Canwest News Service.* Retrieved April 12, 2010, from http://www.canada.com/health/Sorry+Oprah+Self+help+books+seldom+helpful/1756585/story.html

Csikszentmihalyi, M. (1990). *Flow: The psychology of optimal experience.* New York: HarperCollins.

Cynkar, A. (2007, June). A prescription for exercise. *Monitor on Psychology, 38,* 42–43.

Delgado, P. L., Price, L. H., Miller, H. L., Salomon, R. M., Aghajanian, G. K., Heninger, G. R., et al. (1994). Serotonin and the neurobiology of depression: Effects of tryptophan depletion in drug-free depressed patients. *Archives of General Psychiatry, 51,* 865–874.

DesMaisons, K. (1998). *Potatoes not Prozac.* New York: Simon & Schuster.

Diener, E., & Biswas-Diener, R. (2008). *Happiness: Unlocking the mysteries of psychological wealth.* New York: Wiley-Blackwell.

Diener, E., Emmons, R., Larsen, R., & Griffin, S. (1985). The satisfaction with life scale. *Journal of Personality Assessment, 49,* 71–75.

Emmons, R. (2007). *Thanks! How practicing gratitude can make you happier.* New York: Houghton-Mifflin.

Fava, G., Rafanelli, C., & Grandi, S. (1998). Prevention of recurrent depression with cognitive behavioral therapy. *Archives of General Psychiatry, 55,* 816.

Felitti, V., Anda, R., Nordenberg, D., Williamson, D., Spitz, A., Edwards, V., et al. (1998). The relationship of adult health status to childhood abuse and household dysfunction. *American Journal of Preventive Medicine, 14,* 245–258.

Frank, E. (1991). Interpersonal psychotherapy as a maintenance treatment for patients with recurrent depression. *Psychotherapy, 28,* 259–266.

Fredrickson, B. L. (2001). The role of positive emotions in positive psychology: The broaden-and-build theory of positive emotions. *American Psychologist, 56,* 218–226.

Fredrickson, B. L. (2009). *Positivity: Groundbreaking research reveals how to embrace the hidden strength of positive emotions, overcome negativity, and thrive.* New York: Crown.

Freudenberger, H., & North, G. (1985). *Women's burnout.* New York: Doubleday.

Gendlin, E. T. (1981). *Focusing.* New York: Bantam.

Gendlin, E. T. (1998). *Focusing-oriented psychotherapy.* New York: Guilford.

Glasser, W. (1976). *Positive addiction.* New York: Harper and Row.

Goodyer, I. M. (2008). Emanuel Miller lecture: Early onset depressions—meanings, mechanisms and processes. *Journal of Child Psychology and Psychiatry, 49*(12), 1239–1256.

Gould, R., Otto, M. W., & Pollack, M. H. (1995). A meta-analysis of treatment outcome for panic disorder. *Clinical Psychology Review, 15,* 819–844.

Hardy, G. E., Cahill, J., Shapiro, D. A., Barkham, M., Rees, A., & Macaskill, N. (2001). Personality style a factor in response. *Journal of Consulting and Clinical Psychology, 69*(5), 841–845.

Hart, A. (2007). *Thrilled to death: How the endless pursuit of pleasure is leaving us numb.* Nashville, TN: Thomas Nelson.

Haskell, W. L., Lee, I. M., Pate, R. R., Powell, K. E., Blair, S. N., Franklin, B. A., et al. (2007). Physical activity and public health. Updated recommendation for adults from the American College of Sports Medicine and the American Heart Association. *Circulation, 116*(9), 1081.

Jetten, J., Haslam, C., Haslam, A., & Branscombe, N. (2009, September). Groups as therapy? Socializing and mental health. *Scientific American.* Retrieved April 20, 2010, from http://www.scientificamerican.com/article.cfm?id=the-social-cure

Johnstone, T., van Reekum, C., Urry, H., Kalin, N., & Davidson, R. (2007). Failure to regulate: Counterproductive recruitment of top-down prefrontal-subcortical circuitry in major depression. *Journal of Neuroscience, 27*(33), 8877–8884.

Kendler, K., Thornton, L., & Gardner, C. (2001). Genetic risk, number of previous depressive episodes, and stressful life events in predicting onset of major depression. *American Journal of Psychiatry, 158*(4), 582–586.

Kiive, E., Maaroos, J., Shlik, J., Toru, I., & Harro, J. (2004). Growth hormone, cortisol and prolactin responses to physical exercise: Higher prolactin response in depressed patients. *Progress in Neuro-Psychopharmacology & Biological Psychiatry, 28*(6), 1007–1013.

Kroenke, K. (2007). Anxiety disorders in primary care: Prevalence, impairment, comorbidity, and detection. *Annals of Internal Medicine, 146,* 317–325.

Lambert, K. (2008, August). Depressingly easy. *Scientific American Mind, 19,* 30–37.

Lavretsky, H., Ballmaier, M., Pham, D., Toga, A., & Kumar, A. (2007). Neuroanatomical characteristics of geriatric apathy and depression: A magnetic resonance imaging study. *American Journal of Geriatric Psychiatry, 15*(5), 386–394.

Lindbergh, A. (1955). *Gift from the sea.* New York: Pantheon.

Linehan, M. (1993). *Cognitive-behavioral therapy of borderline personality disorder.* New York: Guilford.

Lyubomirsky, S. (2007). *The how of happiness.* New York: Penguin.

Maier, S. (2001). Exposure to the stressor environment prevents the temporal dissipation of behavioral depression/learned helplessness. *Biological Psychiatry, 49*(9), 763–773.

Manger, T. A., & Motta, R. W. (2005). The impact of an exercise program on posttraumatic stress disorder, anxiety, and depression. *International Journal of Emergency Mental Health, 7*(1), 49–57.

Melamed, S., & Shirom, A. (2005). *Shirom-Melamed vigor measure.* Retrieved October 6, 2009, from http://www.tau.ac.il/~ashirom/pdf/ShiromMelamedVigorMeasure-English.doc

Melamed, S., Shirom, A., Toker, S., Berliner, S., & Shapira, I. (2006). Burnout and risk of cardiovascular disease: Evidence, possible causal paths, and promising research directions. *Psychological Bulletin, 132*(3), 327–353.

Menahem, S. (2005). The power of prayer revisited. Retrieved March 18, 2010, from http://www.drmenahem.com/articles.htm

National Institute of Mental Health. (2006). *Questions and answers about the NIMH sequenced treatment alternatives to relieve depression (STAR*D) study: Background.* Retrieved April 20, 2010, from http://www.nimh.nih.gov/trials/practical/stard/backgroundstudy.shtml

National Institute of Mental Health. (2006). *Questions and answers about the NIMH sequenced treatment alternatives to relieve depression (STAR*D) study: Background.* Retrieved April 20, 2010, from http://www.nimh.nih.gov/trials/practical/stard/backgroundStudy.shtml

National Institute of Mental Health. (2008). *The numbers count: Mental disorders in America.* Retrieved Aug 31, 2009, from http://www.nimh.nih.gov/health/publications/the-numbers-count-mental-disorders-in-america/index.shtml#MajorDepressive

Nemeroff, C. (2004). Neurobiological consequences of childhood trauma. *Journal of Clinical Psychiatry, 65*(Supp 11),18–28.

Newberg, A., & Waldman, M. (2009). *How god changes your brain.* New York: Ballantine.

Nhat Hanh, T. (1999). *The miracle of mindfulness.* Boston: Beacon.

Nikonenko, I., Boda, B., Steen, S., Knott, G., Welker, E., & Muller, D. (2008). PSD-95 promotes synaptogenesis and multiinervated spine formation through nitric oxide signaling [Electronic version]. *Journal of Cell Biology, 183*(6), 1115–1127.

Novotney, A. (2009, October). Resilient kids learn better. *Monitor on Psychology, 40,* 32–33.

O'Hanlon, B. (1999). *Do one thing different.* New York: William Morrow.

O'Riordan, M. (2007). ACSM/AHA updates physical activity recommendations, including guidelines for older adults CME/CE. Retrieved August 25, 2007, from http://www.medscape.com/viewarticle/561102

Penedo, F. J., & Dahn, J. R. (2005). Exercise and well-being: A review of mental and physical health benefits associated with physical activity. *Current Opinion in Psychiatry, 18*(2), 189–193.

Perlis, R. H., Nierenberg, A. A., Alpert, J. E., Pava, J., Matthews, J. D., Buchin, J., et al. (2002). Effects of adding cognitive therapy to fluoxetine dose increase on risk of relapse and residual depressive symptoms in continuation treatment of major depressive disorder. *Journal of Clinical Psychopharmacology, 22*(5), 474–480.

Perlis, M., Smith, M., & Jungquist, C. (2005). *Cognitive behavioral treatment of insomnia.* New York: Springer-Verlag.

Ratey, J., & Hagerman, E. (2008). *Spark: The revolutionary new science of exercise and the brain.* New York: Little, Brown.

Real, T. (1997). *I don't want to talk about it.* New York: Fireside.

Rothschild, B. (2000). *The body remembers.* New York: Norton.

Schore, A. (2003). *Affect dysregulation and repair of the self.* New York: Norton.

Seligman, M. (2002). *Authentic happiness.* New York: Free Press.

Shelton, R. (2007). The molecular neurobiology of depression. *Psychiatric Clinics of North America, 30*(1), 1–11.

Siegel, D. (2007). *The mindful brain: Reflection and attunement in the cultivation of wellbeing.* New York: Norton.

Siegel, D., & Hartzell, M. (2003). *Parenting from the inside out.* New York: Putnam.

Talbott, S. (2002). *The cortisol connection: Why stress makes you fat and ruins your health—and what you can do about it.* Alameda, CA: Hunter House.

Taylor, S. (2002). *The tending instinct.* New York: Henry Holt.

Toker, S., Shirom, A., Shapira, I., Berliner, S., & Melamed, S. (2005). The association between burnout, depression, anxiety, and inflammation biomarkers: C-reactive protein and fibrinogen, in men and women. *Journal of Occupational Health Psychology, 10*(4), 344–362.

Wallace, B. A., & Shapiro, S. L. (2006). Mental balance and well-being: Building bridges between Buddhism and western psychology. *American Psychologist, 61,* 690–701.

Wehrenberg, M. (2008). The 10 best-ever anxiety management techniques. New York: Norton.

Weil, A. (1998). *Natural health, natural medicine: A comprehensive manual for wellness and self-care.* New York: Houghton-Mifflin.

Williams, M., Teasdale, J., Segal, Z., & Kabat-Zinn, J. (2007). *The mindful way through depression.* New York: Guilford.

Wolfersdorf, M., Maier, V., Froscher, W., Laage, M., & Straub, R. (1993). Folic acid deficiency in patients hospitalized with depression? A pilot study of clinical relevance. *Nervenharzt, 64*(4), 269–272.

Wood, J. V. (2009, March 20). Should we re-think positive thinking? *Psychology Today.* Retrieved April 12, 2010, from http://www.psychologytoday.com/blog/regarding-self-regard/200903/should-we-re-think-positive-thinking

Yapko, M. (2009). *Depression is contagious.* New York: Free Press.

Yehuda, R. (1997, March 14). Stress and glucocorticoid. *Science, 275,* 1662–1663.

Yehuda, R., Bierer, L., Schmeidler, J., Aferiat, D., Breslau, I., & Dolan, S. (2000). Low cortisol and risk for PTSD in adult offspring of holocaust survivors. *American Journal of Psychiatry, 157*(8), 1252–1259.

Yehuda, R., Golier, J., Halligan, S., Meaney, M., & Bierer, L. (2004). The ACTH response to dexamethasone in PTSD. *American Journal of Psychiatry, 161*(8), 1397–1403.

Yehuda, R., Harvey, P., Buschbaum, M., Tischler, L., & Schmeidler, J. (2007). Hippocampal volume in aging combat veterans with and without post-traumatic stress disorder: Relation to risk and resilience factors. *Journal of Psychiatric Research, 41*(5), 435–445.

Yehuda, R., & McFarlane, A. (Eds.). (1997). The psychobiology of posttraumatic stress disorder. *Annals of the New York Academy of Sciences, 821.*

Zeiss, A., Lewinsohn, P., & Muñoz, R. (1979). Nonspecific improvement effects in depression using interpersonal skills training, pleasant activity schedules, or cognitive training. *Journal of Consulting and Clinical Psychology, 47*(3), 427–439.

Index
